365 Meditations for Women by Women

Sally D. Sharpe, Editor

Kelly Clem, Hilda Davis, Sallie Dye, Cynthia Gadsden,

Monica Johnson, Ellen Mohney, Nell W. Mohney,

Nancy Nikolai, HiRho Park, Marie Schockey,

Lillian C. Smith, Anne Hagerman Wilcox

DIMENSIONS
FOR LIVING
NASHVILLE

365 MEDITATIONS FOR WOMEN BY WOMEN

Copyright © 2004 by Dimensions for Living

This book is printed on recycled, acid-free, elemental-chlorine–free paper.

Library of Congress Cataloging-in-Publication Data
365 meditations for women by women / Sally D. Sharpe, editor.
   p. cm.
  ISBN 0-687-06547-X (pbk. : alk. paper)
   1. Christian women—Prayer-books and devotions—English.   2. Devotional calendars.   I. Title: Three hundred sixty-five meditations for women by women.   II. Sharpe, Sally D., 1964-
  BV4844.A143 2004
  242′.643—dc22

2003025374

Scripture quotations labeled NRSV are from the New Revised Standard Version of the Bible, copyright © 1989 by the Division of Christian Education of the National Council of the Churches of Christ in the United States of America and are used by permission.

Scripture quotations labeled NIV are taken from the *Holy Bible: New International Version*. Copyright © 1973, 1978, 1984 by the International Bible Society. Used by permission of Zondervan Bible Publishers.

Scripture quotations labeled KJV are from the King James Version of the Bible.

Scripture quotations labeled NKJV are from The New King James Version. Copyright © 1979, 1980, 1982, Thomas Nelson Inc., Publishers.

Scripture quotations labeled CEV are from the Contemporary English Version, © 1991, 1992, 1995 by American Bible Society. Used by permission.

Scripture quotations labeled TLB are from *The Living Bible,* copyright © 1971 by Tyndale House Publishers, Inc., Wheaton, IL 60189. Used by permission. All rights reserved.

Scripture quotations labeled *The Message* are from *The Message: The Bible in Contemporary English*. Copyright © 1993, 1994, 1995, 1996, 2000, 2001, 2002. Used by permission of NavPress Publishing Group.

Scripture quotations labeled NLT are from the Holy Bible, New Living Translation, copyright © 1996. Used by permission of Tyndale House Publishers, Inc., Wheaton, IL 60189. Used by permission. All rights reserved.

Scripture quotations labeled NASB are from the New American Standard Bible, © The Lockman Foundation 1960, 1962, 1963, 1968, 1971, 1972, 1973, 1975, 1977. Used by permission.

04 05 06 07 08 09 10 11 12 13 — 10 9 8 7 6 5 4 3 2 1
MANUFACTURED IN THE UNITED STATES OF AMERICA

Contents

Introduction

Nurturing Our Relationship with God

s women, we have many roles and responsibilities. We are daughters, sisters, wives, mothers, stepmothers, grandmothers, caregivers, working women, leaders, teachers, pastors and pastors' wives, neighbors, friends—and on and on the list goes. Yet in *all* of these roles, we bring a special gift that God has given us: the gift of nurturing. Nurturing is helping others feel loved, appreciated, and capable of achieving all they are meant to be. It is helping others grow and mature—whether that growth be physical, mental, emotional, or spiritual. Every woman, whether she realizes it or not, is a nurturer. God made us that way.

We, too, however, need nurturing. Often we forget or ignore this fact, finding ourselves overextended and "drained" after giving all we have without taking time for our own needs. The myth of the superwoman is just that: a myth. We know this intellectually, and yet it seems we still strive—sometimes unconsciously—to "do it all." Our lives tend to be busy, hectic, and sometimes even frenzied, leaving little time for ourselves or for God.

"Be still, and know that I am God!" (Psalm 46:10 NRSV). I like the punctuation of the New Revised Standard Version because it uses an exclamation point. I don't know about you, but sometimes God has to shout at me to get my attention, especially when it comes to slowing down. Yet that's exactly what we must do if we are to receive the nurturing we so desperately need. God longs to wrap loving arms around us and give us rest, encouragement, hope, strength, peace, and joy if only we will be still and seek God. God is the only One who can "fill" us and make us whole. Psalm 63 expresses our need for God so beautifully.

> O God, you are my God, I seek you,
>   my soul thirsts for you;
> my flesh faints for you,
>   as in a dry and weary land where there is no water.
> So I have looked upon you in the sanctuary,

7

beholding your power and glory.
Because your steadfast love is better than life,
   my lips will praise you.
So I will bless you as long as I live;
   I will lift up my hands and call on your name.

My soul is satisfied as with a rich feast,
   and my mouth praises you with joyful lips
when I think of you on my bed,
   and meditate on you in the watches of the night;
for you have been my help,
   and in the shadow of your wings I sing for joy.
My soul clings to you;
   your right hand upholds me.

                        (Psalm 63:1-8 NRSV)

We were made to be in relationship with God; and when we make that relationship our number one priority, miraculously, we have the time and energy and resources we need for everything else.

365 Meditations for Women by Women is written to help you focus on your relationship with God. Twelve different Christian women share their reflections on what it means to be a woman of faith, walking with God day by day. As you make your way through the year (whether you start in January or June), encountering a different writer each month, you will find spiritual refreshment and a sense of camaraderie for the challenge of giving your relationship with God the time and attention it deserves. Though these women have diverse backgrounds, personalities, and ways of relating to God, there is a common theme among them: God loves you and longs to be in relationship with you.

Begin today to nurture your relationship with God. It's the most important nurturing of all!

Sally D. Sharpe
Editor

About the Writers

Kelly Clem (APRIL) is a United Methodist pastor who currently is serving as a missionary to Lithuania with her pastor husband, Dale. She has written articles for various periodicals, including one in *Guideposts* magazine about the tragic loss of her daughter, Hannah, and many friends in a tornado that struck her church in Goshen, Alabama, in 1994. Since then, Kelly and Dale have been featured in many major newspaper articles, journals, and network news specials, sharing their faith as it has helped them heal from their losses. She also has been privileged to participate in numerous speaking engagements in various gatherings in Alabama, Virginia, New York, Utah, and other places. She and Dale have two daughters, Sarah and Laurel Hope.

Hilda Davis (SEPTEMBER) is a breast cancer researcher whose specialty is the relationship between spirituality and cancer in African American women. She also teaches adjunct at both Tennessee State University and Vanderbilt Divinity School in Nashville. She leads women's retreats on health and spirituality, which was the topic of her doctoral dissertation. Her daughter, Erin, is an honor student at Dillard University in New Orleans.

Sallie Dye (OCTOBER) is a part-time bookkeeper for a family business and a former elementary school teacher who still enjoys working with children in her church and her children's school. She also enjoys leading women's Bible studies and seeing God work through women of diverse backgrounds and experiences. Sallie lives in Old Hickory, Tennessee, with her husband, James, and their daughters, Elizabeth, age eight, and Julianna, age five.

Cynthia Gadsden (MARCH) recently embarked on a new path by returning to school to study art, her lifelong passion. A writer since childhood, she plans to combine her two loves by writing and illustrating books for children and adults. She lives in Nashville, Tennessee, where she enjoys spending time with her godsons, C. J. and Hayward, and her niece, Andrea.

Monica Johnson (NOVEMBER), a native of Annapolis, Maryland, is a full-time mother of three: Walter, age sixteen; Isaac, age three; and Lisa-Nicole, age one. She enjoys ministering through sign language and is the founder of Signs and Wonders sign language ministry, a ministry devoted to bridging the gap between the hearing and deaf culture. Monica is also the founder of Women of Destiny Ministry, which empowers women to achieve their God-given destiny. She resides with her family in Hermitage, Tennessee, where her husband, Daon, serves as an associate pastor and founder of the Warehouse Enterprises, a ministry devoted to the spirit, soul, and body.

Ellen Mohney (DECEMBER) is a recent graduate of Samford University in Birmingham, Alabama, where she majored in religion. Her college summers were spent ministering to youth—twice as a backpacking guide for The Rock at Ute Trail Ranch, a Christian camp in Colorado, and once as a youth intern for Signal Mountain Presbyterian Church in Chattanooga, Tennessee. She plans to enter full-time youth ministry.

Nell W. Mohney (JANUARY) is a motivational author and speaker who leads seminars for business and professional groups, spiritual-life retreats, and church gatherings nationwide. She is the author of nine books, including her latest release, *You Can Soar Like an Eagle*. In addition to being a regular contributor for the magazine *Chattanooga on the Move,* she writes a weekly feature in two regional newspapers. In 1999, she was listed in *Who's Who in America* and named to Tennessee Women of Distinction. Of all her roles, the ones she most enjoys are wife, mother, and grandmother.

Nancy Nikolai (JUNE) resides in Mount Juliet, Tennessee, with her husband, four children, and new puppy. She is a freelance television producer/reporter, freelance writer, Christian public speaker, soloist, and educator. Nancy is very active in her local church and leads a prayer group for her children's school. She also enjoys hiking, singing, reading, sewing, traveling to interesting places, and spending quality time with her family.

HiRho Park (FEBRUARY), a native of South Korea, has been involved in diversity issues and leadership development in various multicultural settings as a pastor, a seminary teacher, and committee chair within The United Methodist Church. She lives with her husband, JongWoo, who also is a pastor, and their daughter, Felicia, in Germantown, Maryland. In addition to her professional and pastoral endeavors, HiRho enjoys oil painting, playing the piano, reading, and swimming.

Marie Schockey (AUGUST) has been involved in youth work for twenty-six years. She and her husband, Nolan, opened their home to abused teenage girls for more than ten years. Then, after their five-and-a-half-year-old son, Caleb, died of a blood disease, she served as president of Candlelighters and attended more than ten funerals of children and teens that year alone. Marie and Nolan have worked with the youth of their church for many years and now serve as codirectors of a ministry in Juarez, Mexico, living out of a suitcase most of the year. Marie's son, Curtis, is married and lives in Durango, Colorado, with his wife, Chelly, and their brand new baby, Ava. Her other son, Colin, is in naval school at Fort Leonardwood, Missouri.

Lillian C. Smith (MAY) currently serves as Director of Ministries with Women and Persons of Color for The United Methodist Church. She is a graduate of Hampton University and Wesley Theological Seminary and an elder in the Baltimore-Washington Annual Conference. She and her husband, the Reverend David Cassidy, reside in Nashville, Tennessee, with their two sons.

Anne Hagerman Wilcox (JULY) is a teacher and freelance writer who lives in Boise, Idaho. Previously, Anne served as Bible study columnist for *Today's Christian Woman,* and has written several books including *A Woman's Workshop on Ruth.* She has one grown daughter, Jaime.

JANUARY

Past, Present, and Future

Nell W. Mohney

January 1   **A New Beginning**

"See, I am doing a new thing! Now it springs up; do you not perceive it?" (Isaiah 43:19 NIV)

When January first arrives each year, I think of the words of Louise Fletcher Tarkington: "I wish there were some wonderful place, called the land of beginning again." In a very real sense, there is such a place—the gift of a brand new year. It is a gift from God. What we do with it will be our gift to God.

As I enter this new beginning, there are three things I will do—one thing to cover each of the three "time zones" of my life. First, I will rid myself of some old things—things from the past. For example, I will clear my closet of things that have been hurriedly placed there in preparation for the holiday celebration, and, with God's help, I will clear my soul of any unresolved resentments or anxieties so that I may be open to receive God's message of love and direction. Second, I will live joyfully in the present day, remembering that each day is a precious gift from God. And third, I will walk confidently into the future, knowing that my trust is in Christ Jesus.

There are three "time zones" in each of our lives: past, present, and future—or, if you prefer, yesterday, today, and tomorrow. This month we will explore how we should learn from the past, but not live there; live fully in the present; and trust that the future is in God's hands.

Eternal God, thank you for the blessings of the past year and the possibilities of the new one. Help me walk confidently in faith. Amen.

13

January 2   Rejoice in the Day

This is the day the LORD has made; let us rejoice and be glad in it. (Psalm 118:24 NIV)

It was three days before Christmas, and the store was packed with last-minute shoppers. It sounded as if we had had a simultaneous drop in blood sugar. People were impatient, irritable, and pushy. Then it happened! A fatigued saleslady handed a package to the young shopper ahead of me and said woodenly, "Merry Christmas and happy new year."

"Oh, it is going to be!" replied the cheery customer.

"How do you know that?" asked the surprised salesperson.

"Well, there will be 365 days in the new year. If we live each of them in the spirit of the One whose birthday we are celebrating, it will be a happy new year," declared the young shopper as she jauntily walked away.

"She's right, you know," I said as I walked to the counter.

"I know," the saleslady replied. "Now, if I can only remember that for two more days!"

Loving and merciful God, thank you for your faithfulness in the past, and for your love made most evident through the life, death, and resurrection of Jesus Christ. Enable me to live each day through his power, rejoicing in your gift. Amen.

January 3   Live Fully Today

Then the LORD said to Moses, "I will rain down bread from heaven for you. The people are to go out each day and gather enough for that day." (Exodus 16:4a NIV)

The young woman in the department store at Christmas was right! Our time to live fully is today—not in worry about yesterday or in anxiety about tomorrow. I like the popular quotation attributed to African musician Babatunde Olatunji that says: "Yesterday is history. Tomorrow is a mystery. And today? Today is a gift. That's why we call it the present" *(African Music Encyclopedia)*.

God really taught us this lesson through the children of Israel during their days in the wilderness. Exodus 16:19-20 tells us that each morning manna was provided for their food. They couldn't save it for the following day or week because it would spoil. In a similar manner, we are given the gift of time in twenty-four-hour segments. Our supply for the day must be used by midnight tonight. We can't hold over a few hours until next week. How imperative it is for us to see each day as an incredible gift from God and to use it for God's glory.

Eternal God, thank you for the fresh mercies that come from your hand each day. Help me live fully in your Presence this day. Amen.

January 4   Look in Both Directions

Thomas said to him, "Lord, we don't know where you are going, so how can we know the way?" Jesus answered, "I am the way and the truth and the life." (John 14:5-6a NIV)

"Stop and look in both directions before you cross the street." These were the clear directions my mother gave me each morning before I left for elementary school. They are good directions for all of us as we begin a new year. After all, the month of January is named for Janus, who, according to the *Encyclopedia of Mythology, Religion, and the Unknown,* was a two-faced Roman god of gateways and passageways who was able to look in both directions. He was also the supposed protector of new beginnings.

Of course, as Christians, we serve the true God of new beginnings. As the apostle Paul reminds us, "If anyone is in Christ, there is a new creation" (2 Corinthians 5:17 NRSV). So, early in this month, let us look in both directions, leaving behind the old tired thoughts and actions and walking buoyantly into newness of life through the power of the One who said, "I am the way and the truth and the life."

O God, who renews and refreshes our world with sunshine and rain, renew my wilted spirit. Amen.

January 5   Leaving Nonessentials Behind

Let us throw off everything that hinders and the sin that so easily entangles, and let us run with perseverance the race marked out for us. (Hebrews 12:1 NIV)

The year was 1980, and I was packing for a month away from home. My husband, Ralph, and I were taking two groups to see the Passion Play in

15

Oberammergau, Germany. Realizing that we likely would encounter all kinds of weather, I was packing for every emergency. My suitcase was bulging! Even when I sat on it, it wouldn't fasten. Suddenly, I knew that the overstuffed suitcase was analogous to my overstuffed life. It was full of "stuff" and hectic activities. I was leaving little room for the spirit of Christ to cleanse, forgive, and empower me.

In the quietness of my bedroom, I stilled my spirit and prayed that as I removed the physical items from my suitcase, God would show me what needed to be removed and replaced in my spiritual life. In the next few days, I will discuss some of my confrontations. Perhaps they will trigger a response in your own life. Let's not be weighted down, so that we can "run with perseverance the race marked out for us."

May the Christ who has set me free through his death and resurrection enable me to remain free through his grace and forgiveness. Amen.

January 6   Throw Out Fear

For God hath not given us the spirit of fear; but of power, and of love, and of a sound mind. (2 Timothy 1:7 KJV)

Just as we remove items from an overstuffed suitcase, let us be willing to remove some harmful habits from our lives as we enter this new year.

In 1980, I knew that I needed to confront my fear of flying. I flew when necessary, but always fearfully, and often holding up my seat as if that small gesture would ensure safety. When I finally confronted my fear, I decided to do two things: (1) to follow Ralph Waldo Emerson's advice to "do the thing you fear, and the death of fear is certain," and (2) to increase my faith. Just as I trusted water to hold me up while swimming, more and more I began to trust Christ to be with me in life's difficult places. He stilled the troubled waters of my mind as he called to my remembrance this verse: "For God hath not given us the spirit of fear; but of power, and of love, and of a sound mind."

Since fear can block the power and presence of God in our lives, I challenge you to confront your fears. In the stillness of your quiet time, make a plan of action, and with the help of Christ, follow it.

Loving and most merciful God, thank you for being ever present in my life, bringing comfort and assurance. Amen.

January 7   Eliminate Worry

Do not be anxious about anything, but in everything, by prayer and petition, with thanksgiving, present your requests to God. (Philippians 4:6 NIV)

The Anglo-Saxon root word for worry means "to strangle." If you've ever been really worried about something, you know how right on target that description truly is! You feel as if you can't breathe. Worry is a misuse of the imagination.

When I was a small child, my family had a wonderful woman who worked as a housekeeper and cook. As far as I could tell, she had only one fault—she worried about everything. One day, my mother said to her, "Willie Mae, you shouldn't worry so much. You should trust God more." Her reply: "Mrs. Webb, Jesus told us that we would have tribulation in this world. When mine comes, I think He expects me to tribulate." And tribulate she did!

Rather than have my own mind go like a broken record in the same groove, I try to look at a problem or concern objectively, making a list of things I can do. Then, I follow the apostle Paul's suggestion to make my requests known to God, with thanksgiving. You see, when we pray with thanksgiving, we begin to trust God with our future, and there is no room for worry.

Eternal God, I'm so thankful that you are in charge of the universe! Enable me to trust you with the details. Amen.

January 8   Don't Linger in the Past

In all your ways acknowledge Him, And He shall direct your paths. (Proverbs 3:6 NKJV)

Do you remember the story of Lot's wife in the book of Genesis (chapter 19)? Once when I told the story to some inner-city children, I ended by saying, "Lot's wife looked back and turned into a pillar of salt." An eight-year-old boy raised his hand and said, "My mama looked back to the backseat to see what we were doing, and she turned into a telephone pole." Though we won't turn into salt or a telephone pole if we linger too long in the past, we will miss out on becoming all that God created us to be.

This week we will continue to look at some destructive habits we need to leave in the past. What is keeping you from being the new creation that Christ is calling you to be?

In my experience, when I acknowledge God in all my ways, I see God's faithfulness. Then I don't have to live in the past for security. I can walk confidently into today and trust God for tomorrow.

Merciful God, enable me to see the masterful plan you have in mind for me, and empower me to fulfill it. Amen.

January 9   Negate Negativism

Whatever is true, whatever is honorable, whatever is just, whatever is pure, whatever is pleasing, whatever is commendable ... think about these things. (Philippians 4:8 NRSV)

Do you know anyone you hope you don't see until after you've had a strong cup of coffee? Do others hope they won't see you until they've been fortified with caffeine? Actually, we produce climates wherever we go—in our homes, careers, churches, and social groups. Is the climate you create positive or negative?

Negativism begins with a thought that, left unchecked, becomes an attitude and then a habit. Most people don't plan to be negative. They simply don't stand guard over their thoughts, and soon their thoughts control them. This must be why Paul warned the Christians in Philippi, and us through them, to stay focused on things that are true, honest, pure, just, pleasing, and commendable.

In 1991, when I was recovering from cancer surgery, a woman I barely knew came to see me in the hospital. Her conversation was almost totally negative, including a recounting of the number of people with my kind of cancer who had died. Every ounce of strength I needed for recovery was sapped by negativism.

During the half hour after the woman's visit, I deliberately gave thanks for all my blessings. Seeing God's faithfulness changed my climate from negative to positive.

Is your climate positive or negative?

O Christ, keep us pure, loving, truthful, and obedient in our thoughts and in our actions. Amen.

January 10   Alter Anger

One who is slow to anger is better than the mighty, and one whose temper is controlled than one who captures a city. (Proverbs 16:32 NRSV)

The maître d' in a local restaurant was leading my husband, Ralph, and me to our table when Ralph stopped to ask a friend about his recent surgery. I followed the young maître d' to the table, where he whispered to me, "Will you call me at home and suggest some books on anger management? I am having problems!" I nodded as he walked stiffly away. I realized that his request was prompted by my newspaper column "Anger Management," carried that morning in our local paper.

Months later, when we returned to the restaurant, the young man looked much more relaxed. He told us that he had read the books, had attended an anger management clinic, and had kept a journal to alert him to the causes of his anger.

When Jesus became angry and drove the money changers out of the Temple (Luke 19:45-46), he was not acting out of personal hurt but out of a righteous desire to change an evil system. When our anger is out of control, it hurts and destroys. When it is Christ controlled, then it can make a difference for good in our world.

Eternal God, endow me with your wisdom and love so that I may constructively channel my anger to enlarge your purposes rather than destroy them. Amen.

January 11   Resist Resentments

"And when you stand praying, if you hold anything against anyone, forgive him, so that your Father in heaven may forgive you your sins." (Mark 11:25 NIV)

Resentment, a feeling of indignation over perceived hurts and offenses, is like a splinter that gets under your skin. If it isn't removed, it produces infection.

Several years ago, I was presenting some seminars at a bank when an employee came to talk with me. Basically, she was complaining about being left out of the office camaraderie. As I probed a little deeper, I discovered a long-held resentment that was infecting her physical health and her relationships.

Her sister had received a bit more of the family inheritance than she, and she hadn't spoken to her sister in the twenty years since. She wasn't hurting her sister, but she was destroying herself. The only way out was to forgive her sister and close the door on the past. She resisted the idea and probably is still clutching the grudge while spending far more each year on medical bills than her sister inherited.

As you enter this new year, do you need to seek forgiveness and reconciliation? Freedom is yours for the choosing!

Loving God, you have provided an escape for my hurts and traumas. Enable me to forgive others as you have forgiven me. Amen.

January 12   Banish Bad Attitudes

Your attitude should be the same as that of Christ Jesus. (Philippians 2:5 NIV)

"Boy, you need an attitude adjustment!" Those words from a woman's strident voice seemed to fill the gate area of a large airport where two hundred people had been waiting for more than an hour for a delayed flight. I knew they were coming from the exasperated mother of a teenage son, because I had heard his complaints about making the trip with his mother and little sister. Suddenly, I thought that God often must have felt like saying to me, "Woman, you need an attitude adjustment!"

An attitude is a thought that is consistently held so that it shapes our actions. The late William James wrote: "The greatest discovery of my generation is that human beings can alter their lives by altering their attitude of mind." I agree. I'm convinced that attitudes can make or break a marriage, friendship, business, church, or community.

This week we will look at bad attitudes in light of Paul's admonition, "Your attitude should be the same as that of Christ Jesus."

Forgive me, O God, for allowing my attitude to be shaped by my feelings rather than by your purposes. Give me the attitude of Christ Jesus. Amen.

January 13   Don't Play the Blame Game

Then the LORD God said to the woman, "What is this you have done?" The woman said, "The serpent deceived me, and I ate." (Genesis 3:13 NIV)

Since the Garden of Eden, when God confronted Adam and Eve about their disobedience, and Adam blamed Eve, and she blamed the serpent, we have been tempted to blame others when we have done wrong. We blame our genes, our environment, our spouses, our bosses, our rebellious teenagers, and on and on. A big step toward spiritual maturity is to take full responsibility for our lives. We must admit our mistakes.

I once heard a psychologist say there is one type of person who is hopeless in counseling: the one who blames others for his or her problems. Such a person chooses to be a victim. We must admit our mistakes, seek forgiveness, and, through Christ, return to the One who created us.

The book of 1 John reminds us, "If we confess our sins, he who is faithful and just will forgive us our sins and cleanse us from all unrighteousness. If we say that we have not sinned, we make him a liar, and his word is not in us" (1:9-10 NRSV). Let's never play the blame game!

Merciful God, help me be honest with myself, seek forgiveness for my sins, and forgive others so that I may grow spiritually. Amen.

January 14   Shun Self-Pity

We are hard pressed on every side, but not crushed; perplexed, but not in despair. (2 Corinthians 4:8 NIV)

It was a late Saturday afternoon in April 1986 when I sat in the Akron, Ohio, airport. We were in the midst of a spring thunderstorm, and I would have to fly on a small commuter plane—a perfect time to indulge in self-pity. I knew that self-pity puts us in a downward cycle of discouragement, despair, and depression. I also knew that I could stop the cycle, but I was enjoying my self-pity tremendously!

When I arrived home, I greeted Ralph with, "I'm too old to be doing this." His reply stunned me: "You haven't been reading the Bible much lately." With hands on my hips, I replied, "Excuse me?"

"Oh," he said, "remember the really old people in the Bible whom God used for service—Abraham was seventy-five; Moses was eighty; and Sarah ..."

I replied, "Don't mention Sarah to me." The thought of a woman having a baby at ninety gave me the hives! Both of us burst out laughing, and the cycle of self-pity was broken.

Self-pity needs to be "nipped in the bud" because it spawns a downward spiral of self-pity, discouragement, despair, and depression. Don't allow self-pity to block the power of the Holy Spirit in your life.

Loving God, help me focus on my blessings rather than on my difficulties so that I may serve you joyously. Amen.

January 15   Destroy Doubt and Distrust

And he did not do many deeds of power there, because of their unbelief. (Matthew 13:58 NRSV)

Once, while we were in Florida, Ralph and I passed a beautiful and totally deserted part of the beach. We put on our walking shoes and headed toward the sand. To get there we had to walk through what looked like a marsh, but what turned out to be quicksand. It was a horrible feeling of having nothing solid on which to stand. Only the sheer strength of Ralph's six-foot-two frame pulled us out.

I had experienced the same sensation in my first religion class in college. My encounter with classical biblical studies made me feel as if I were on a slippery slope. It was the strong faith of my professor that held me steady while my view of the greatness of God and Jesus grew.

Honest doubt is good if we are seeking the truth, but bad if it stems from basic distrust of people, institutions, or God, because it separates us from the resources we need. As today's verse reminds us, Jesus couldn't do many deeds of power in Nazareth "because of their unbelief."

Let's build our faith daily so that the "quicksand" of life cannot destroy our foundations.

Loving Lord, keep me from limiting you to my finite mind. Enable my unbelief to become trusting faith. Amen.

January 16   "Put Your Hand into the Hand of God"

The LORD is my light and my salvation; whom shall I fear? (Psalm 27:1 NRSV)

For the rest of the month, we will look at what we need for our journey through this new year. For example, we need to be sure that we are walking closely with God through Christ in every endeavor.

During the dark days of 1940, World War II was going badly for the Allies. England was bracing for a Nazi invasion. King George VI made a

Christmas broadcast that never has been forgotten by people around the world. In it he quoted some words from the poem "God Knows" by Minnie Louise Haskins:

> I said to the man
> Who stood at the gate of the year,
> "Give me a light
> That I may tread safely into the unknown."
> And he replied,
> "Go out into the darkness
> And put your hand into the hand of God.
> That shall be to you
> Better than light and safer than a known way."

This is a timeless reminder that our real security is not in our external circumstances, but in a loving God and in his Son, Jesus Christ.

O God of light and love, help me walk confidently into the new year knowing that you are my Light and my Salvation. Amen.

January 17   Our Ultimate Security

"A new command I give you: Love one another." (John 13:34a NIV)

Recently I received an e-mail message that tugged at my heartstrings and caused me to define anew our ultimate security. The message told of a young girl who had come to a Catholic orphanage. She always clutched a can whether she was in the dining room, on the playground, or asleep in her bed. When she was lonely or afraid, she would hold the can closely and rock back and forth.

Finally, the sisters learned that when the child was born, her mother had thrown her on a garbage heap. She had been rescued and placed in a foster home, growing up with an obsession about finding her mother. A social worker located the mother, who was dying of AIDS in a local hospital.

During an arranged visit, the mother held the child, asked for her forgiveness, and told her that she loved her. Then the mother died quietly. In the can were the mother's ashes, and in the child's heart was the assurance that she was loved.

Loving and merciful Lord, thank you for the human love that blesses me, and for the love of Christ, my Ultimate Security. Amen.

January 18   God Is the Initiator

God is love. (1 John 4:16b NIV)

In Francis Thompson's poem "The Hound of Heaven," he tells of trying to flee from God. Ralph and I were talking about the poem when he told me a beautiful story, reportedly told by a professor at Loyola University.

One day a young man named Larry walked into the professor's religion class combing his flaxen hair, which fell six inches below his shoulders. Long hair for boys was just coming into fashion at the time. Father John had never seen it before. He filed Larry under "S" for strange. Larry turned out to be the "atheist in residence" who smirked at the possibility of an unconditionally loving God.

When Larry had taken his final exam, he asked the professor, "Do you think I'll ever find God?" Trying a little shock therapy, Father John replied with a curt no. Then, when Larry neared the door, he added, "But I am absolutely sure that God will find you."

To be continued ...

Loving God, you seek us down every pathway of our hearts, but we must be the ones to stop running. Teach us to love as Christ loved us. Amen.

January 19   God Will Find Us

Everyone who loves has been born of God and knows God. (1 John 4:7b NIV)

Continued from yesterday ...

Several years after Larry's graduation, the professor was surprised to see him standing in the classroom doorway. He was emaciated, and his flaxen hair had fallen out from chemotherapy. As they talked, Larry told how he had tried to find God after the diagnosis of his cancer. Then he had remembered that the professor had said that sadness is going through life without telling those you love that you love them.

Larry said that he had started with the hardest, his dad. Upon hearing Larry say, "I love you, Dad," his father did two things Larry had never seen him do before. He cried, and he hugged Larry. Then they talked all night. As Larry talked to his mother and brother, he continued to feel God's overwhelming presence and the grace of Christ.

Larry agreed to share his story with the class. Before the scheduled date, however, Larry had another appointment. He made the great step from faith into the eternal dimension of life. The professor now tells this story for Larry.

Eternal God, help us remember that you constantly pursue us and that Jesus knocks at the door of our hearts; only we can open the door. Grant that it may be so. Amen.

January 20   A Sacrificial Kind of Love

"For God so loved the world that he gave his only Son." (John 3:16a NRSV)

It was two weeks before the senior prom, and because of my mother's illness, this was the first day we could look for my prom dress. I tried on dresses for hours, but the ones I liked were too expensive. Discouraged, I suggested that we shop again later.

After dinner, I went directly to my room ostensibly to study, but really to "lick my wounds" in private. At 2:00 A.M., I awakened with light coming from the nearby family room. I went to investigate. My mother was bent over a cutting table on which lay her most treasured material possession: a beautiful beige chiffon dress with Venetian lace inserts. Yet she was cutting it down to fit me.

"You can't do that, Mom," I declared. Holding it up, she exclaimed, "You'll be the prettiest girl at the prom." I wasn't the prettiest girl there, but I did have the prettiest dress because of the sacrificial love of my mother.

Loving God, may my life be shaped each day by your sacrificial love and the gift of your Son, Jesus Christ, my Savior. Amen.

January 21   The Power of Unconditional Love

"Greater love has no one than this, that he lay down his life for his friends." (John 15:13 NIV)

As a high school student, eager to find adventure, I couldn't understand why our neighbor Dorothy had brought her ill mother-in-law, Myra, to live with her. One day she told me the story.

Myra, who had lived in a loveless marriage, was unhappy when her son, Jim, had proposed to Dorothy. Myra had chosen someone else for her son, and she had done all she could to stop the wedding. When that hadn't worked, she had continued her sabotage after the marriage. Jim had always let it be known that his number one priority relationship was with Dorothy.

Myra's control had alienated her only "daughter." Since her son, Jim, was the love of her life, she didn't want to lose him; so she had decided, "If you can't beat them, join them." By that time, Dorothy had built up much resentment, but the logjam had been broken when she had seen Myra as a lonely, frightened, and emotionally needy woman. In their long talks, the two women had become friends.

Dorothy had brought Myra, now a widow, into her home so that Myra could experience God's unconditional love and see the love of Jesus.

Eternal God, thank you for loving me even when I wasn't aware of it, and certainly when I didn't deserve it. Help me share this love. Amen.

January 22   She Went Around Causing Sunrises!

But the fruit of the Spirit is love, joy, peace, patience, kindness, goodness, faithfulness, gentleness and self-control. (Galatians 5:22-23a NIV)

"She went around causing sunrises." These were the words Ralph and I found on a tombstone in England several years ago. We didn't know the woman buried there, but both of us thought immediately of a woman in our church back home.

Ruth must have been in her seventies at the time—petite, loving, attractive looking, and the most joyous Christian either of us knew. She created a climate of joy wherever she went. Her enveloping smile made you feel accepted. Her acts of thoughtfulness made you feel special. You soon knew that she was authentic and trustworthy. As a result, people constantly were sharing their joys and problems with her. She created a climate of joy.

Paul says that when the Spirit of Christ dwells within us, the fruit of the spirit will be evident in our lives: love, joy, peace, patience, kindness, goodness, faithfulness, gentleness, and self-control. Let us walk into this year with the flag of Christ's Spirit flying in our lives.

O Christ of all hope and joy, fill me with your Spirit so that I may cause sunrises instead of sunsets for others. Amen.

January 23   Choose to Be Joyful

"These things have I spoken unto you, that my joy might remain in you, and that your joy might be full." (John 15:11 KJV)

You can choose to be joyful! In her delightful book *Splashes of Joy in the Cesspool of Life* (Thomas Nelson, 1992), Barbara Johnson makes this profound observation: "Pain is inevitable but misery is a choice." We can choose to be joyful, or we can choose to be miserable.

There is a legend about Lucifer, the fallen angel. When asked what he missed most about heaven, he replied: "The sound of trumpets in the morning." Think of the countless people who get up, go to work, come home, eat, watch television, and go to bed. The next day, they repeat the same routine. They never hear the sound of trumpets.

The glorious truth is that despite our circumstances, joy can bubble up inside us if we choose to have Christ live in every area of our lives; if we read and internalize God's Word; if we associate with joyful people; and if we stay close to Jesus, the Master of joy. I've learned that whereas joy is a gift from God, we have to choose to accept it.

Eternal God, when life seems painful and heavy, help me choose to accept your gift of joy. Amen.

January 24   Live in "Day-tight Compartments"

"Sufficient unto the day is the evil thereof." (Matthew 6:34b KJV)

It was one of those days when bad news invaded my personal airways relentlessly. First, there was a call from a young woman telling me that she had lung cancer; then I learned of the sudden death of a good friend in another city. It was difficult to process all this along with the threat of an impending flood in our area.

How do we react when stressful days come? Recently, I read about a time during World War II when Dr. William Ousler was lecturing to medical students at Yale University. Many of their friends were dying in battle. They, themselves, would likely be called into military service. Dr. Ousler gave those students some excellent advice: Learn to live in day-tight compartments. He reminded them of this petition in the Lord's Prayer: "Give us this day our daily bread." He knew that day-tight living gives us the ability to find God's peace, to focus on what needs to be done, and to receive the power to do it.

Gracious God, help me remember that I live only one day at a time, and help me live today in your power and peace. Amen.

January 25   "More Things Are Wrought by Prayer Than This World Dreams Of"
(Alfred, Lord Tennyson, *"Idylls of the King: The Passing of Arthur"*)

"Lord, teach us to pray." (Luke 11:1 NRSV)

Seeing the power of Jesus' life after he spent hours in prayer, the disciples asked, "Lord, teach us to pray." Have we discovered prayer's power?

My friend Joe told me about a minister who was working late at his office one night. At ten o'clock, he telephoned his wife, but there was no answer. Thinking that was unusual, he telephoned again as he was leaving. She answered right away. "Why didn't you answer when I telephoned earlier?" he asked. Her reply: "Our telephone has not rung all evening."

On Monday morning, he received a strange telephone call from a man who asked, "Why did you call me at 10:00 P.M. on Saturday?" Before the minister could answer, the man said, "When I was at the end of my rope and held a gun to my head, I prayed, 'God, if you are there, send me a sign.'" At that moment the telephone rang, and the caller ID read, "Almighty God." The pastor's church was named Almighty God Tabernacle.

My Father in heaven, enable me to remember anew that "more things are wrought by prayer than this world dreams of." Amen.

January 26   You Are Accepted

[Be] confident of this, that he who began a good work in you will carry it on to completion until the day of Christ Jesus. (Philippians 1:6 NIV)

On the eve of Ralph's forty-first birthday, he was notified of his election as president of a church-related college. He and our sons, ages eight and six, were celebrating excitedly around the dinner table. After dinner I saw our six-year-old seated on the back steps with his head in his hands.

Quickly I joined him and asked, "Is something wrong?" Then he blurted out, "If Daddy is elected president of a college, will I have to know everything?" I gave him a big hug and assured him that he would be accepted just as he was. He didn't have to be any different.

Later, as Ralph and I laughed about the incident, I commented that in new situations we all feel insecure and need to know we are accepted as we are. That is what Christ does for us. He accepts us as we are—"warts and all." Then, with our commitment to him, he helps us become all that we were created to be.

Eternal God, help me remember who I am and whose I am—created by God, redeemed by Christ, and empowered by the Holy Spirit. Amen.

January 27   Take Laughter on Your Journey

A merry heart doeth good like a medicine. (Proverbs 17:22a KJV)

Mamie McCullough is one of my favorite Christian motivational speakers. She is interesting, informative, and funny; and she makes you feel that you can conquer the world. One of my favorite stories she tells is about her experience one morning after a grueling speaking tour.

It seems Mamie had slept late that morning, trying to recover from the tour. After awakening, she put on an old slate-gray robe with only one button left and scuffs that made her walk with a shuffle. Her hair was in pink curlers. Realizing that her husband had forgotten to take out the garbage, she grabbed the garbage in one hand, clutched the robe with the other, and, with curlers flying and scuffs shuffling, she ran as fast as she could to the street. The collectors were approaching before she would arrive, so she called out, "Is it too late?"

"They took one look at me," she reports, "and replied, 'No. Hop on!'"

Mamie McCullough always lifts my spirits! How often do we lift the spirits of others? Laughter helps us keep our perspective. It's like internal jogging. It lifts our spirit as well as the spirits of others. Let's remember to take laughter on our journey!

Creative and loving God, keep me so attuned to the joy of your presence that I can see humor in life and keep my perspective. Amen.

January 28   Let the Peace of Christ Envelop You

"Peace I leave with you; my peace I give you. I do not give to you as the world gives." (John 14:27a, b NIV)

The year was 1873 when a Chicago businessman, Horatio Spafford, was stunned to learn from the newspaper that the ship carrying his family to Europe had sunk in the Atlantic. Two weeks later, a cablegram from his wife, Anna, read: "Saved. Alone."

In their ship's collision with another vessel, Anna was stunned by a falling mast. Gaining consciousness, she learned that all four of their children had gone down with 474 other passengers. She was one of 22 survivors, who were plucked from icy waters by a small sailing vessel, which headed for Cardiff, Wales.

Horatio sailed immediately to join his wife. When the ship reached the spot where his children were drowned, he wrote a hymn that has inspired millions:

> When peace like a river, attendeth my way;
> When sorrows like sea billows roll;
> Whatever my lot, Thou hast taught me to say,
> "It is well, it is well, with my soul."

Peace is a fruit of the Spirit of Christ dwelling within us. It anchors and blesses us in the midst of life's difficulties. Look at where your life is fragmented, overcommitted, and cluttered. Then pray specifically for the "peace that passes understanding."

Lord of all life, thank you that the presence of Christ within me blesses me with a peace that passes understanding. Amen.

January 29   The Power of Hope

But if we hope for what we do not yet have, we wait for it patiently. (Romans 8:25 NIV)

We all need hope, for when we lose hope, we stop trying.

In 1950, Florence Chadwick set a new women's speed record for swimming the English Channel. She learned determination in an earlier race from Catalina Island to Los Angeles, which she lost. In that race, the weather was cold, the smog was thick, and her fear about a killer whale depleted her supply of hope.

In the rescue boat that traveled alongside her, Chadwick's mother and trainer offered words of encouragement and a warm drink when she grew discouraged. Even this didn't persuade her to continue. She gave up less than one-fourth of a mile from the Los Angeles shoreline!

The following year, Chadwick completed the race in record time. As she commented to reporters, she kept her hope by seeing the shoreline in her mind.

Marriages, jobs, and friendships can be saved if we don't quit but keep our focus "on the shoreline." As the apostle Paul says, "For in this hope we were saved" (Romans 8:24 NIV).

God of faith, hope, and love, may I claim the power of hope by remembering my resources available in Jesus Christ. Amen.

January 30   God Is Our Best Hope

Hope thou in God: for I shall yet praise him, who is the health of my countenance, and my God. (Psalm 42:11b KJV)

A statue stands on the lawn of the Metropolitan United Methodist Church on Woodward Avenue in Detroit, Michigan. The statue is the result of a sermon preached by Dr. Merton S. Rice during the height of the Great Depression, when the attitude of hope for the future was at a premium.

You see, one day there was in the congregation of discouraged people a notable artist. He was so impressed by the sensible message of undefeated faith and hope that he hurried to his studio and created the statue that stands on the church lawn. The statue depicts a man struggling in adversity with his muscles straining to overcome. On the base of the statue are the words from Psalm 42:11: "Hope thou in God: for I shall praise him."

May we always remember that when we are in despair, God is our best hope. God holds us steady in temptation and difficulties, strengthens our spirits when our bodies are weak, and enables us to walk confidently into the future—even into the next dimension of life.

Eternal God, help me hold tightly to the eternal hope found in you and your son, Jesus, the Christ. Amen.

January 31   We Are the Children of God

So God created man in his own image, in the image of God he created him; male and female he created them. (Genesis 1:27 NIV)

An interesting story from Tennessee history is that of Ben Hooper. At the end of the nineteenth century, an out-of-wedlock child, Ben Hooper, lived in a small town with his mother. Such circumstances of birth were not accepted in that day. Parents would not allow their children to play with Ben, not even in school. He usually read during recess and sat with his teacher at lunch. Saturdays, when he went to the community store with his mother, were worse. The men, in loud voices, would say, "Wonder who that boy's father is. Bet his mother doesn't even know."

One day a new young pastor came to town, and everybody liked him. Ben started slipping into the back pew late and leaving early. One Sunday the pastor went to the back of the church to announce the closing hymn, and there was no escape for Ben. Following the benediction, the minister put a hand on Ben's shoulder and in a loud voice asked, "Son, who is your father?" There was silence throughout the church. Then the minister said, "I know who he is. God is your father! I want you to go out with your head erect and never let anyone put you down again. You are a child of the King!"

Ben Hooper said, "That day I became governor of Tennessee," which, in reality, he did in 1912. Let us, like Ben Hooper, receive our feeling of self-worth from the One who created us and not from the opinions of others. Only then can we learn from the past, live fully today, and trust God for tomorrow.

Help me remember that I am created by you, God, and redeemed by Jesus Christ. May I live like a child of the King! Amen.

FEBRUARY

Celebrating Our Differences

HiRho Park

February 1   **I Do Choose**

Jesus stretched out his hand and touched him, and said to him [the leper], "I do choose. Be made clean!" (Mark 1:41 NRSV)

A leper said, "If you choose, you can make me clean." Jesus did not hesitate and said, "I do choose. Be made clean!" Jesus publicly welcomed the man back into community.

Jesus already has chosen us and welcomed us to God's world. It's our turn to choose. Will we stand up for love of all people, for peace, for harmony, and for reconciliation in our communities?

We are accepted by God, not because our spirits are unblemished; but because Jesus has entered our human condition and has claimed, "I do choose you." Jesus touches us, making us clean and acceptable to God, restoring us by healing relationships with one another. Just as Jesus determined to terminate the condition of leprosy that separated the man from the community, our choice has power to reconcile those conditions that create separations among us.

This month, which is Black History Month, we will explore the healing of all who have been separated because of the "leprosy" we have created in our society: racism. It's our choice whether or not to terminate this illness among us.

God, help me embrace all people in our human community. Amen.

February 2   Being Intentional

We must grow up in every way into him who is the head, into Christ. (Ephesians 4:15b NRSV)

I was the first ethnic minority pastor for a predominantly Caucasian congregation. One day my senior pastor and I went to visit an elderly lady who was in her nineties. When he introduced me to her, she said, "Oh ... I'm going to love her."

I still remember that statement because she was intentionally reaching out to someone who was very different from the people she had been associated with all her life. She was eager to establish the relationship between us, regardless of our differences. Of course, I intentionally visited her many times afterward until she died. I know she accepted me as I am, and I loved her.

Being intentional about reaching out to others facilitates reconciliation. It is a positive and hope-filled activity that speaks to the readiness of an open heart, changing our perspective from passive to active.

In today's scripture, the "must" conveys an intentional spirit. To understand and respect differences, we must intentionally listen to and learn from one another. After all, God was intentional about loving us through the saving act of Jesus Christ.

How can you intentionally reach out to someone who is different from you today?

God, help me be intentional about respecting differences with my actions and my words. Amen.

February 3   In the Image of God

"Let us make humankind in our image, according to our likeness." (Genesis 1:26a NRSV)

I was listening to an Asian woman who owned an ice-cream shop. She said that at first she had hired Chinese and Korean young people because she had wanted to provide them work. Then she had realized that she was not getting many Caucasian customers, which was the majority of that community. So she had hired more Caucasians, especially young blonds, and the profit had increased.

We express our prejudice even without words. Does God also show favoritism? We read in Genesis that God created human beings in God's image (1:26-31). Here *image* means "likeness," which has to do with representation. It means we are the imitators of God's character: the character of not showing favoritism. As a sovereign Creator, God did not show favor to one group over another (Acts 17:24, 26). God was pleased with all.

This is why we should denounce favoritism according to racial and cultural backgrounds. It is our responsibility to honor God's creation by affirming the absolute value, authority, and dignity of every individual.

In what ways do you express the Christian belief that all are equal and made in the likeness of God?

Creator God, thank you for the gift of your image in us. May this precious image of yours be radiant through us. Amen.

February 4   We Are Interrelated

"Since we are God's offspring . . ." (Acts 17:29a NRSV)

As offspring of the Creator, we all are interrelated. This interdependence is a character of creation (Acts 17:24-31). Latino theologian José Comlin has said that the authentic person exists only in community. In other words, we become who we are meant to be only as we relate to others.

As Christians, then, we need to be a fellowship of people who make God visible through our service to others, regardless of our differences. Jesus reminded us: "Just as I have loved you, you also should love one another. By this everyone will know that you are my disciples" (John 13:34-35).

Loving one another also results in equality. Paul said, "If one member suffers, all suffer together with it; if one member is honored, all rejoice together with it" (1 Corinthians 12:26 NRSV). When we recognize our differences and also realize that we each offer something the other needs, we create equality in our relationships.

Recognizing and embracing our interdependence compels us to seek freedom and justice for all, and urges us to initiate relationships with people who are different from us. Accepting our interrelatedness is the first step in loving our neighbors as ourselves.

Have you prayed for the people of your community today?

God of community, we are grateful that we are your offspring. Amen.

February 5   Diversity

For just as the body is one and has many members, and all the members of the body, though many, are one body, so it is with Christ. (1 Corinthians 12:12 NRSV)

Diversity is not a new concept. For centuries human beings understood and lived in the reality of diversity without ever using the word. Stephen A. Rhodes said that diversity assumes we hold a common truth but express it in different ways. Though we may not always agree, we are committed to working on the underlying unity amid our differences.

How, then, can we be unified in a diverse community and world? The scripture teaches us that we need to "clothe [ourselves] with love, which binds everything together in perfect harmony" (Colossians 3:14 NRSV). When we practice love, we do not "domesticate" the Lord in the name of tradition or culture; instead, we free Christ from our own boxes of "isms." We let all people experience the love of Christ that promotes harmony and wholeness.

How can you help others experience the love of Christ today?

God, let your love bind your people together this day. Amen.

February 6   Expectation

"You will receive power when the Holy Spirit has come upon you; and you will be my witnesses in Jerusalem, in all Judea and Samaria, and to the ends of the earth." (Acts 1:8 NRSV)

Michelangelo's *Creation* is an expression of expectation—God and a human being reaching out to each other in the expectation of being in a loving relationship, being united as one, and coming to the day when there is no sorrow or tears.

Reaching out to someone is an expression of expectation, which is a choice. It is a choice to live with a yearning to understand someone who is different. It is an expression of being honest, of taking a risk, of being vulnerable.

Reaching out is *agape* (love) in action—reaching out in the expectation of loving others just as they are, as God loves them. Jesus Christ calls us to be witnesses to the ends of the earth. Do we truly understand what it means to reach out to someone who does not understand life or see the world as we do?

Reaching out starts with a deep respect of the dignity of another person. It is the commitment to reach out to one another in the expectation of uniting as God's people.

Look around you. Where can you begin to reach out in expectation?

God of expectation, thank you for reaching out to us first in expectation of loving relationship. Oh, what a willing God! Help us reach out to others in expectation. Amen.

February 7   Patience

But if we hope for what we do not see, we wait for it with patience. (Romans 8:25 NRSV)

There was an African bird named Kang. It was the plain color of wood, while all the other birds were very colorful. One day Kang complained to the Creator and said, "How come you left me unpainted when you painted everyone else with beautiful colors?" The Creator said, "I wanted you to have beautiful colors, too, but you could not stand still."

This short African bird story teaches us the importance of patience. I have learned that building a multicultural ministry takes time. Much effort and energy go into developing cross-cultural relationships. Churches that are multicultural and multiracial grow slowly but surely. Often we get anxious because we cannot see the mystery of God, which has not been revealed fully yet in our midst. Yet Jesus taught us that ministry is about building relationships among people and understanding who we are as we become naked before God.

Building multicultural relationships demands patience. God has endured with much patience stubborn people like you and me, yet how impatient are we with people whose ways of thinking and appearances are different from us?

How can you practice patience with others today?

Patient God, help us clothe ourselves with patience as we deal with differences. Amen.

February 8   Privilege

"A bruised reed he will not break, and a dimly burning wick he will not quench; he will faithfully bring forth justice." (Isaiah 42:3 NRSV)

Many Americans are concerned about building a balanced multicultural society, and there is hope. Affirmative Action, for example, has given opportunities to minority communities to be part of different sectors of the American social structure. Still, it's true that Affirmative Action has been highly controversial ever since the term was used by John F. Kennedy in 1961.

You've heard the political debates, and perhaps you have strong feelings yourself. Take a moment to distance yourself from the uproar and listen for the still, small voice of God. Could the argument essentially be about human greediness and the capacity of compassion? Could it be that sharing is difficult for us because of our greed and selfish craving for power? Could it be that a balanced society will be realized only when those who are privileged are willing to release the power and share opportunities with those who are less privileged and much exploited?

God regards the lowly of society (Psalm 138:6). May we always remember that privilege is a result of our choices, both political and personal.

When have you quenched others' flame of hope and motivation by abusing your privilege?

God of compassion, reveal any greed or jealousy against my sisters and brothers that may be hidden in my heart, and free me from it. Amen.

February 9   The Lord's Song

How could we sing the LORD's song in a foreign land? (Psalm 137:4 NRSV)

The Lord's song is a song of hope, a song of life, and a song of liberation. When we experience oppression, this song in our hearts dies. The Israelites could not sing the Lord's song when they were in exile in Babylon because they were slaves and were treated as second-class citizens. Yet prophets such as Isaiah and Jeremiah did not stop reminding them that God loved them and cared for them enough to give them freedom one day.

It's easy for newcomers to America to be discouraged from singing the Lord's song because of hardships due to language barriers and discrimination in the workplace. We can help them sing the Lord's song continually, just as the prophets of the Old Testament did for the Israelites in exile, by speaking for their human rights, advocating integrity of life for their families, and extending the hand of friendship. We are all sojourners in this journey of life, and the Lord's song we sing should be contagious.

How can you promote hope and share the grace of God with those who are new to your community?

Author of the song in our hearts, help us sing the melody of love and grace with those who recently have immigrated to this country. Amen.

February 10   Partiality

"Who was I that I could hinder God?" (Acts 11:17b NRSV)

Peter was a faithful Jew who never had eaten anything that was profane and unclean. But God showed him a vision with all kinds of four-footed creatures and reptiles and birds in a large sheet, and God asked him to kill them and eat (Acts 10:9-16). Peter refused to eat since they were profane, according to his learning. God told him that what God has made clean, nobody should call profane or unclean. After that vision, Peter realized that God shows no partiality against the Gentile. He confessed, "In every nation anyone who fears [God] and does what is right is acceptable to [God].... [God] is Lord of all" (Acts 10:34, 36 NRSV).

Partiality is like a pebble that hits the windshield, creating a little crack. If you do not fix it right away, the crack will get bigger and bigger, and, eventually, the window will be shattered.

Having partiality against certain kinds of people distorts the picture of God's creation. It destroys the unity in society and creates fissures among people.

Do you have any partiality in your heart in a secret place?

God of no partiality, may I accept others as you accept me. Amen.

February 11   Resurrection

I want to know Christ and the power of his resurrection and the sharing of his sufferings by becoming like him in his death, if somehow I may attain the resurrection from the dead. (Philippians 3:10-11 NRSV)

S. H. Payer wrote, "Live each day to the fullest. / Then you can look forward with confidence and back without regret" (Cleveland: American

Greetings, 1970). I think this poet understood the true meaning of resurrection—the sanctification of life.

To live life to the fullest means to live a life of resurrection each day and every moment. As Jesus died, he died with the handful of hate in my heart, the fist of my bitterness, and the armful of my sorrow in being unappreciated. As I remind myself of these negative feelings, I lose sight of the beauty of the present moment. Resurrection means that I choose to die with the dark force of my life so that I will be empowered to live life again to the fullest, to see the world with fresh eyes, to appreciate people around me, and to smell the sweet aroma of resurrection.

Resurrection means knowing what true equality means in this life: respect and love. Resurrection means living life with acceptance and appreciation so that death becomes life.

Will you live a life of resurrection today?

God of resurrection, grant me the power of resurrection so that I may live this day to the fullest. Amen.

February 12   Sharing Facilities

Awe came upon everyone.... All who believed were together and had all things in common. (Acts 2:43-44 NRSV)

"Could you share your building with us?"

The church leaders said, "Yes, we can share."

One of the issues of multicultural ministry is sharing facilities. Sharing facilities often offers a blessing to each congregation involved, yet it also can become a source of conflict because of failure to understand cultural differences about food, children, and time-related issues. Conflict breaks out when we expect those who are using our facilities to conform to our way of life.

The first Christian community in the book of Acts had to learn to share their resources. This sharing was only possible because of their spiritual life together—they prayed for one another and studied the Word of God together. As a result, they were able to accept one another as equally dispossessed rather than treat one another unfairly because of their own fullness and plenty.

Sharing facilities is not only sharing a building but also celebrating our spirituality in Christ as God's people. When we share facilities, we participate in the lifestyle of Jesus, who was dispossessed, and step out on a new path of partnership in ministry.

Don't you want to take this awesome experience to your church?

Sharing God, grant us courage to share. Amen.

February 13   Sacrifice

"No one has greater love than this, to lay down one's life for one's friends." (John 15:13 NRSV)

What is sacrifice? It involves relinquishing power and position to empower the less powerful. It's something we do not have to do yet are compelled to do so. It's releasing my fist of greed. It's sharing life—the life of Christ and the life of abundance. It teaches us that life can be different—can be shaped by you and me.

Self-confidence is necessary for sacrifice. Persons who are insecure about themselves are busy trying to hold on to what they have. All their energy is used to protect their images. If Jesus had not been confident in who he was and what his life was about, he would not have been able to lay his life down for his friends.

The words *privilege* and *sacrifice* go hand in hand, for they remind us of lessons we learned in childhood: share and take turns. Why, then, is sacrifice such a foreign word to us? Sacrifice becomes a familiar word to us when we learn to accept others as God's children, and when we are confident in being children of God ourselves. Sacrifice helps us see the extension of our lives in others.

What sacrifice do you need to make today?

God of sacrifice, Christ showed us an example of sacrifice by emptying himself to the point of death so that we may have life. Teach us to sacrifice. Amen.

February 14   God's Requirement

All this is from God, who reconciled us to himself through Christ, and has given us the ministry of reconciliation. (2 Corinthians 5:18 NRSV)

In his book *Parting the Waters,* Taylor Branch witnesses to the boldness of African American children. He writes that even the children were bold on May 2, 1963, in Birmingham—children who marched for freedom and equality for all people. There were 958 children who had signed up for jail on that day. Martin Luther King Jr. said, "Now, finally, your children, your daughters and sons, are in jail, many of them." King continued to the parents of children, "Don't worry about them.... They are suffering for what they believe, and they are suffering to make this nation a better nation" (*Parting the Waters,* New York: Simon & Schuster, 1988).

God is seeking those who are willing to suffer for what they believe. Are we ready to suffer and sacrifice as Jesus did to make this world a better place? We can lamely follow behind society's efforts, or we can accept Christ's call to be ambassadors of reconciliation. After all, what message do we have if we don't have the message of reconciliation to God and to one another through Jesus Christ?

We cannot keep silent about what we believe is true. God calls us to be "ambassadors for Christ."

How will you respond to this call of God today?

God, use us to break down the dividing walls among us. Amen.

February 15   Reconciliation

In Christ God was reconciling the world to himself, not counting their trespasses against them, and entrusting the message of reconciliation to us. (2 Corinthians 5:19 NRSV)

Reconciliation has twofold reality: It has already happened by God, and yet it still is in process through us. Biblically, reconciliation is a gift of salvation through the redeeming grace of Christ. We have been reconciled to God through Jesus Christ. This is an accomplished fact. But this reconciliation must continue to work through us, crossing racial, ethnic, social, and gender barriers. Personal and social transformation must be in progress in order for real spiritual growth to take place.

Reconciliation is the bridging of fractures between individuals and groups regardless of their differences. Reconciliation condemns our tendency to strive for power over one another, which is the core of racism, conflicts, and war. Reconciliation denounces the ranking of individuals and nations into levels that share unequal power in communities and societies. Reconciliation is peacemaking. Reconciliation is overcoming fear, alienation, estrangement, hostility, and enmity through the Spirit of Christ, who was not afraid to be wounded by human frailty.

How can you be involved in reconciliation today?

Reconciling God, may we be "the repairer of the breach, the restorer of streets to live in" (Isaiah 58:12b). Amen.

February 16   Possibility

"Let the little children come to me, and do not stop them; for it is to such as these that the kingdom of heaven belongs." (Matthew 19:14 NRSV)

God beholds the unique gifts within us and gives us the possibility to develop them further. A child represents growth with potential—unlimited possibility. As members of the kingdom of God, we become like children who believe that all things are possible in God. We grow together and fully participate in every level of community life with confidence.

How often do we ignore the gifts of others? Accepting the gifts of others means affirming the touch of the Creator within them. It means cultivating the possibilities of being a human community as God has visualized it for us.

We encourage our children to be what they want to be. Do we really mean it? Do we truly believe that an ethnic minority child can be all he or she can be in this social system? Do we really mean that a little girl does not have to try harder than a little boy in order to receive equal opportunities when she grows up?

We say there is endless possibility for everyone. Why, then, is there such a term as "glass ceiling"? God calls us to dismantle our society's oppressive characteristics and to energize one another by daring to live out our belief that all things are possible in God.

What can you do to affirm the gifts of an ethnic minority child in your community?

God of unlimited possibility, help me cultivate the possibility within me and others. Amen.

February 17   A New Creation in Christ

If anyone is in Christ, there is a new creation: everything old has passed away; see, everything has become new! (2 Corinthians 5:17 NRSV)

Hermann Hesse, the author of *Demian,* said, "A bird should hatch from the shell," which means that a bird is not fully a bird unless it breaks the shell that transforms its life from a fetus to an independent life.

What kind of shell does the church, the Body of Christ, need to hatch from in order to reform its life? Issues of gender, race, and status offer evidence of the church's crimes against humanity. Christ is weeping behind the bar of isolation and exclusion.

What kind of shell do we as individual Christians need to break through in order to live transformed lives? If we see ourselves within a solid shell of exclusion, there is neither transformation nor new creation in Christ.

What kind of "shell" is keeping you from being the new creation you are meant to be in Christ?

Ever renewing God, grant me eyes to see the shell that is surrounding me. Give me the courage to hatch from that shell so that I may live a transformed life as an individual and a member of the Body of Christ. Amen.

February 18   Listening

To draw near to listen is better than the sacrifice offered by fools. (Ecclesiastes 5:1b NRSV)

I love to "listen" in an art museum. I "hear" the life of van Gogh as I stand in front of his masterpieces. His art whispers to me about his struggles as a brilliant and creative person who strived to survive in a society where he didn't fit in. He tried different careers before deciding to be an artist at age twenty-seven. Finally, he listened to the spiritual inner voice, and his soul was at ease with his decision.

Are we good listeners? Are you listening to the loving and grace-filled voice of God, who guides your life like the quiet sound of the ocean in the summer night? What does God want you to do? How does God want you to live your life?

Wouldn't it be a better world if we listened to one another better—listening to one another's stories rather than judging them because of our individual preferences and backgrounds?

Who needs your uncritical listening ear today?

Listening God, you listen to me—my joys and sorrows, my ambitions and despair, my love and hate, and my preferences and prejudice. Help me listen before I judge. Amen.

February 19   The Fresh Breath of God

In the beginning when God created the heavens and the earth, the earth was a form-less void and darkness covered the face of the deep, while a wind from God swept over the face of the waters. (Genesis 1:1-2 NRSV)

This morning I was in Yoga class with my daughter, Felicia. The instruc-tor kept emphasizing one thing throughout the class: breathing. The key ele-ment of Yoga is to breathe air into the body parts where you feel tension. Different postures help open up the body parts so that we can breathe into them. I felt very spiritual and meditative when I was breathing into the deep-est parts of my body.

After the class, I realized that I've been taking the importance of breath-ing for granted. God breathed into our being so that we could have life. Where do we have tension in our lives? Are there any parts that we need to open up and allow God to breathe into so that our lives will be renewed and transformed?

Just as we rarely pay attention to the relationship between breathing and our body parts, so also we may not realize that our lives are suffocating because we lack the fresh breath of God.

Where is there tension in your life? What area of your life do you need to open up to God's breath?

God, breathe your fresh breath into my being so that I may be alive spiritu-ally today. Amen.

February 20   The Vision of the Church

After this I looked, and there was a great multitude that no one could count, from every nation, from all tribes and peoples and languages, standing before the throne and before the Lamb, robed in white, with palm branches in their hands. They cried out in a loud voice, saying, "Salvation belongs to our God who is seated on the throne, and to the Lamb!" (Revelation 7:9-10 NRSV)

This picture of the multitude from every nation depicts the vision of being a church. It is the desire of God to be praised by every nation—by all tribes and people and languages. Think about your church. How inclusive is it? Are you striving to include different groups of people in your congregation? Does your church have a mission statement that clearly states the openness of your church? Or is your church an expression of ethnocentrism (judging other cultures and people in terms of our own cultural norms, causing us to feel superior)?

Don't we sometimes pretend that differences don't exist, which includes confining differences to broad categories? Let us center the vision of the church around the ministry of Jesus Christ, who lived within an exclusive cultural and ethnic community yet whose ministry was inclusive beyond any limitations or boundaries. God's vision for the church insists on unity, not conformity.

How can you encourage or help your church to be an inclusive community?

God, I pray that your church may reflect your vision for human community. Help me play a part. Amen.

February 21   Racism

How very good and pleasant it is when kindred live together in unity! (Psalm 133:1 NRSV)

Have you ever thought that the kind of words we use make a difference in our lives? Eric Law, author of *The Wolf Shall Dwell with the Lamb,* says that racism has stages. Stereotypes are distorted pictures about certain ethnic groups that are learned from people around us. Prejudice is the result of stereotyping a certain group of people. Prejudice develops into discrimination, which is acting upon prejudiced feeling, whether individually or cooperatively. Racism is discrimination against a certain race or ethnic group, which eventually results in social exclusion and robs persons of opportunities for full participation.

The antidote for racism in our society is family education. It starts with what we say about people at home. It starts with the eyes and ears of our children as they observe an attitude that appreciates the unique dignity of other persons. Racism is learned; therefore, it can be unlearned.

What stereotypes have you learned and perhaps passed on? Are you aware of any prejudice, discrimination, or racism in your own heart or in your family? What kind of attitude toward people of other races do others see in you?

God, I confess that prejudice—my own and others'—has bred years of pain and suffering. Forgive us and grant us new eyes to see the beauty of others. Amen.

February 22   Freedom

"If you continue in my word, you are truly my disciples; and you will know the truth, and the truth will make you free." (John 8:31b-32 NRSV)

I dream someday we will look at the ocean sitting side by side, loving each other's soul.

I dream someday we will stand side by side in a vast open space, facing the warm breeze as we free each other's burdens.

I dream someday we will look in each other's eyes, calming down the frightfulness of our past and celebrating the simplicity of the moment.

I dream someday we will confess that God has journeyed in us and with us, acknowledging that we are called to strive for a new world of loving acceptance.

I dream someday our conscious recognition of our own limitations will be the witness of Christ's humility and suffering.

I dream someday we will testify that God, who reads our minds, has reformulated the questions of our confusion and set us on an unexpected path, which is love.

What do you dream?

God of freedom, free me from the bondage of hate and bitterness. Amen.

February 23   Love

Let us love, not in word or speech, but in truth and action. (1 John 3:18 NRSV)

As Christians, we often say that we love one another, yet do we really know what love means?

Love awakens all the senses within us, making us very sensitive to one another's feelings and emotions. My nephew Noah, who is ten, wrote, "Love is knowing that you hurt someone." How often do we hurt others with words and actions, not even realizing what we have done? According to a child, we don't even know what love is.

God must have a sore soul since God is love. God, who is full of love, must be aching since God senses our hurts and sorrows. Yet, this allows Christ to be the "wounded healer," as Henri Nouwen once said, for Christ brought the everlasting love of God into our reality.

If we say we love one another and yet we hurt someone, we are not practicing love. Let us love one another by lifting up one another's lives with grace, and let us walk toward the dawn of hope.

How can you show genuine love to someone who is hurting today?

Loving God, help me love others with truth and action. Grant me a sensitive soul. Amen.

February 24   The Challenge to Change

What does the LORD require of you but to do justice, and to love kindness, and to walk humbly with your God? (Micah 6:8b NRSV)

God's challenge to us is to change—from where we are now to where we can be.

It's a challenge to leave our comfort zones. Gregory of Nyssa said, "To be a human being, one has to change." He said that true perfection was "never to stop growing towards what is better and never placing any limit on perfection." Changing means making a conscious decision to be different than we are now; it means acknowledging the open-ended hope for humanity.

During a conversation about inclusiveness, one of my colleagues said, "The world resists it, but Jesus demands it." Jesus demands the change of present injustice for the cause of justice. It's sad that we cannot disagree without demonizing one another. If we can disagree with one another in love, that will be a change.

How is God calling you to change in your attitude and/or your interaction with those who are different?

God, may I celebrate your infinite creative revelation today. Amen.

February 25   The Soul of the Church

"Truly I tell you, just as you did it to one of the least of these who are members of my family, you did it to me." (Matthew 25:40 NRSV)

If we say that the church is the Body of Christ, where is the soul of the church? Jesus demonstrated that the soul of the church lies in identifying itself with the marginalized—those who are rejected by organized religion and neglected in society, including "persons with disabilities."

Nancy L. Eiesland, author of *The Disabled God* (Abingdon Press, 1994), explains the distinctions among different terms for "persons with disabilities." Impairment is an abnormality or loss of physiological form or function. Disability describes the consequences of the impairment that produce an inability to perform some task or activity considered necessary. Handicap denotes a social disadvantage resulting from an impairment or disability. These terms show us the progressive impact they have upon the lives of "persons with disabilities," from personal struggle and pain to social exclusion.

Just as Jesus ministered to "the least of these," so also we are called to minister to those who have been forgotten by society, remembering that salvation is experienced in the margin of society. Caring for the soul of the church means caring for the poor, the meek, and the disadvantaged.

How is the soul of your church?

God, heal and renew the soul of your church. Amen.

February 26   Hope

In former generations this mystery was not made known to humankind, as it has now been revealed to his holy apostles and prophets by the Spirit: that is, the Gentiles have become fellow heirs, members of the same body, and sharers in the promise in Christ Jesus through the gospel. (Ephesians 3:5-6 NRSV)

Jürgen Moltmann once said, "Hope today is reality tomorrow." As morning comes with the dawn without exception, our hope in God is ever present in our lives. Hope for a truly inclusive community is about making room for God's creativity in the midst of our conventional understandings of life. It's about the promises of God and the potential of bringing needed changes. This hope extends God's creative power to all people by offering a future amid the ambiguous and even hopeless discords that threaten our lives. This hope is a genuine commitment to openness. It is confronting social reality with spiritual commitment built upon the foundation of the inclusive love of God.

The Resurrection is an expression of God's hope for humanity. God's hope bestows abundance against the poverty of our cross-cultural experience, for in Christ we have the assurance that hope today truly will be reality tomorrow.

In what ways do you need to make room for God's creativity in your thinking and in your life? How can you be a messenger of God's hope in Christ?

God of hope, may I and my brothers and sisters in Christ declare the distinctive message of hope for humanity through Jesus Christ. Amen.

February 27   Social Inequality

There is no longer Jew or Greek, there is no longer slave or free, there is no longer male and female; for all of you are one in Christ Jesus. (Galatians 3:28 NRSV)

Sociologist Claude S. Fisher has said that inequality results when we choose policies that exploit the marginalized—women and ethnic minority and lower-class people. Social inequality is about gender, race, and economic power. Surprisingly, one of the institutions of society that generates social inequality is the church.

According to one study, nearly one-third of clergywomen in my denomination were not serving local churches during a given year (The United Methodist Clergywomen Retention Study, 2000). Why? Discrimination, lack of acceptance, and stereotypes limiting them to certain gender roles are some of the main reasons.

This presents a challenge. Even though an institution may have an egalitarian policy, if it is not put into practice, the institution and its people will suffer the dysfunctions of social inequality—which not only maintains the status quo (the traditional roles of women and men) but also limits the discovery and creative use of available human resources and talents.

A truly inclusive community is formed only when we learn and teach mutual respect, seeking a shared vision of a harmonious life together as women and men of God.

Are you living according to Galatians 3:28 as you interact with others?

God of many images, help each of us practice what we believe. Amen.

February 28   Boldness

If God is for us, who is against us? (Romans 8:31b NRSV)

Henry G. Apenzeller was the first American missionary to Korea from the Methodist Church in 1885. He might have felt insecure about his ministry in Korea since he did not fully know the language or culture. But with conviction in his heart that God had called him to proclaim the good news of salvation in Jesus Christ to the Korean people, he could be bold in preaching and teaching the gospel. His faithful commitment to God's calling became a seed to the development of Christianity in Korea. Today Korea has one of the fastest-growing Christian communities in the world.

Because one person responded to the calling of God, despite fear of uncertainty and cultural, racial, and language differences, more than one hundred years later, I, a Korean woman, can stand before the people of God boldly proclaiming God's free grace to all people. God has mysterious ways of connecting people. God is continually calling people who are bold enough to say, "Here I am, Lord. Send me."

Are you ready to answer the call of God with boldness?

God, grant me the boldness to respond to your call to reach out to the world beyond what I know. Amen.

February 29   Justice

Let justice roll down like waters, and righteousness like an ever-flowing stream. (Amos 5:24 NRSV)

What is justice? We generally think of the word in light of social and political circumstances. Yet, we also are "justified" by God's grace through the redemptive grace of Jesus Christ. Therefore, we should understand the concept of justice on a personal level as well as a community level. Individual and social salvation should go hand in hand.

How can we live a life of justice? Those who want to live a life of justice are those who seek righteousness. This involves showing mercy to our fellow human beings, for they, too, have experienced God's mercy. Mercy includes both compassion and forgiveness. In Hebrew, the concept of mercy is an action rather than an attitude.

Being a peacemaker is another way of living a life of justice. Peacemakers are those who devote themselves to the hard work of reconciling hostile individuals, families, groups, and nations.

Most of all, the one who lives a life of justice has a spirit that is "in tune" with God all the time through prayer, giving thanks to God in all circumstances.

Justice and peace start with me and you—not with politicians or the courts, but with the faithful lives of Christians who live by the spirit of God.

Are you living a life of justice?

God, bless our lives as we seek to live a life of justice. Amen.

MARCH

My Legacy

Cynthia Gadsden

March 1   **Trunks, Roots, and Branches**

The waters nourished it, deep springs made it grow tall; their streams flowed all around its base and sent their channels to all the trees of the field. So it towered higher than all the trees of the field; its boughs increased and its branches grew long, spreading because of abundant waters. (Ezekiel 31:4-5 NIV)

Trees are one of nature's most magnificent gifts. They symbolize strength and beauty, and are intriguing and mysterious with their unique shapes, unusual twists, and unexpected bends. Their strength allows them to survive and stand tall even in the harshest conditions, while their beauty presents itself to the world with bold, outstretched, welcoming arms.

Picture yourself as a tree. Like people, a tree can only stand and grow tall from a solid foundation. Each one has a complex root structure, offering support and constant nourishment. We, too, have a root system, except that ours is made up of all the people we've known to this point. Think of the people who form your roots (that is, parents, siblings, extended family, teachers, mentors, colleagues, bosses, church members, friends, and so on).

Your trunk or base is created from your life experience, with all its knots, worn places, new growth, and strong bark. Each represents a part of your life journey.

Who makes up your branches and limbs? It might be your children or those of friends and family, students, people you've mentored, colleagues, and others you care about and love.

Like the tree described in Ezekiel, we grow strong and tall through the nourishing waters of God's abundant, loving grace in the form of people who touch our lives. Likewise, others are touched by our lives.

53

This month we will consider our lives, our legacy, and our heritage. Part of who we are as individuals is the result of what we received (heritage), and what we will leave behind (legacy). Like trees, each of us is a unique vessel of the past and portal for the future.

Thank you, God, for blessing me with people and experiences that have helped me grow tall, strong, and full. Amen.

March 2   Enough

"My grace is sufficient for you, for my power is made perfect in weakness." (2 Corinthians 12:9 NIV)

Would that there were an award for people who come to understand the concept of enough. Good enough.... When you have self-respect you have enough, and when you have enough, you have self-respect. (Gail Sheehy in Quotable Women of the Twentieth Century, *Tracey Quinn, ed. [New York: William Morrow, 1999], p. 197)*

Too often we view ourselves through others' eyes, and more often than not we come up short. Suddenly, it's as if everything connected with us is preceded by the word *too*. Too short, too tall, too fat, too thin, too pushy, too loud, too quiet. In a world obsessed with image, it's easy to shape our perception of ourselves to fit someone else's version of us.

Books, magazines, and television are eager to tell and show us what's important and how we should live, feel, and think. But when we turn to an electronic box or sheets of paper to define who we are and our values, isn't it time to stop, evaluate, and rethink what we're doing and how we're living?

Living according to someone else's image shortchanges us, those who love and care about us, and the world in which we live. Only when we are willing to be *truly* who we are can we receive all that God has in store for us.

Today I have all that I need. Today I have enough. Today I am enough. Amen.

March 3   Accepting the God in Me

God gave Stephen the power to work great miracles and wonders among the people. (Acts 6:8 CEV)

"I'm a fat girl!" declares Laure Redmond in *Feel Good Naked*. Although no longer outwardly true, years of wrestling with extra pounds, comments from well-intentioned family members, and verbal and emotional abuse from schoolmates and others have left their mark.

Raised in New Orleans, Redmond learned to love food and hate her body early. Coming from a family of gourmet cooks and women who wore their weight well wasn't easy for Redmond. A friend's example in high school, though, helped Redmond begin to see her inner and outer self in a new light. Through physical activity and movement she began a new relationship with her body. No longer a prison, Redmond's body became the physical manifestation of the beauty within her. Redmond now looks at herself in the mirror and can feel good naked.

Like Redmond, many of us secretly despise our physical selves. We dread really looking at ourselves for fear of what we might see; but by boxing ourselves into unrealistic molds of beauty and acceptability, we limit our ability to be all that we can be as sparks of God's divine light. What if, like Redmond, we were to shift our focus from others' opinions to the quiet voice within that says we are marvelous just as we are?

Lord, help me recognize the excellence of you in me. Amen.

March 4   A Comfort Prayer

The LORD is my shepherd, I shall not want. He makes me lie down in green pastures; he leads me beside still waters; he restores my soul. (Psalm 23:1-3a NRSV)

Some children had a comfort toy or blanket; I had a comfort prayer. At around age ten, I started experiencing periods when waves of sadness and fear would engulf me, and I would dissolve into tears. Sometimes I would cry for fifteen minutes, other times for hours.

One night my mother called my grandmother—the prayer warrior. My grandmother could make anything better with prayer. During visits to my grandmother's house, I often slept in her bed. Each morning before daylight she would get up, kneel, clasp her hands, place her elbows on the bed, and begin to pray. Most times these were quiet, whispered conversations with God. Once, though, I was shaken awake by her urgent entreaties for help. I had no idea whom she was praying for, but I wondered what kind of trouble they were in. I'm convinced God was listening and ready to respond.

The night my mother called, my grandmother prayed for me. After she finished, for the first time since the sadness and fear had started, I felt a sense of peace that relieved the frightening gnawing in the pit of my belly. Then she told me to memorize the Twenty-third Psalm and recite it whenever I was afraid. Although I had more periods of fear, they were never again as intense or as frequent after that night.

Even now the words of this psalm are like a calming balm, especially when the world seems a little too dim. God's presence in our lives can take many forms—an unexpected word or event, or even a praying grandmother with a comforting scripture.

God, I give thanks for your healing words that help hurting hearts. Amen.

March 5   Be Careful What You Wish For

"And how does a man benefit if he gains the whole world and loses his soul in the process? For is anything worth more than his soul?" (Mark 8:36-37 TLB)

Several music television programs chronicle the life stories of rock stars, divas, and musical geniuses as they climb the road to fame and stardom. These shows showcase wannabe stars' relentless drive to be number one, and the reality of life once they reach that coveted spot. Too often they find that the thing they have single-mindedly pursued for years ends up consuming and controlling them.

Unfortunately, this doesn't happen only to megastars. In a society that celebrates more, bigger, and better, too many of us end up chasing our tails only to find ourselves controlled by the chase. We end up with lives controlled by overprogrammed day schedulers in a quest for higher salaries, bigger houses and cars, and fancier vacations.

We find ourselves living a *structured chaos*. We get up earlier and earlier so we can squeeze in more and more activities before our workday even starts. Then we run errands, exercise, or schedule personal appointments during lunch. After work it's off to church, the grocery, after-school sports or activities, more chores, and maybe even a little more work before falling exhausted into bed to do it all again tomorrow.

Is this really the legacy we want to leave of ourselves?

God, help me find a better way of living that nourishes my spirit, renews my soul, and keeps me centered in you. Amen.

March 6   The Creative Spirit

Faith is the substance of things hoped for, the evidence of things not seen. (Hebrews 11:1 KJV)

In *Freeing the Creative Spirit: Drawing on the Power of Art to Tap the Magic and Wisdom Within* (HarperSanFrancisco, 1992), Adriana Diaz writes, "I was taught that prayer, like good manners, consisted of 'Please' and 'Thank you.' My religious education had no connection to the many hours I spent coloring, drawing, and painting" (p. 1).

Diaz goes on to share that one of her earliest spiritual experiences came when she was in college learning to draw. "That experience made me realize that there is more to the world than what seems apparent.... The drawing class was teaching me to develop my eyes to see the things I normally took for granted" (p. 1).

Like many of us, Diaz was raised to believe that the creative spark, of which we are all a part, has no connection to the God we seek in prayer for guidance and comfort. Yet, how can that be, when we ourselves are created beings? Did creativity somehow stop with our own creation? Certainly not. As Diaz says, "Creativity is . . . a manifestation of the divine. While the human concept of God has taken many forms, one aspect of divinity connects creeds and practices around the world: that of God as supreme creator" (p. 2).

Each of us was created out of divine love. Like faith, creativity is unseen, but present nonetheless.

Lord, help me see the world anew through creative eyes. Amen.

March 7   Something of Socially Redeeming Value

And now these three remain: faith, hope and love. But the greatest of these is love. (1 Corinthians 13:13 NIV)

A co-worker once said he wanted to do something of socially redeeming value. Unfortunately, he didn't see that living each day and lovingly relating to people could do just that. Instead, he dreamed of doing big things, things that changed society, that changed the world. He didn't recognize that his interactions with others and his relationships with friends, families, and co-workers were the avenue to fulfilling his dream.

He paid little attention to relationships, often leaving pain and hurt feelings in his wake. He, like many people, believed that his mark on the world had to affect hundreds, thousands, or millions. Or, that if it didn't involve a lot of money, it didn't really count.

Perhaps we need to update our thinking. Small acts do count. Small acts can indeed change the world. For instance, if every person helped one person, and that person did the same, and the process continued, the world would change. What could be more socially redeeming than a community, society, or world that has learned to love itself and one another?

God, help me change the world every day by sharing love. Help me make my love count. Amen.

March 8   Bread and Table

"Give us this day our daily bread." (Matthew 6:11 NRSV)

Millions of people will gather with friends or family, give thanks, and participate in the ritual of sharing a meal today. Although our lifestyles, customs, rituals, and histories may differ, in many ways we are alike. We give thanks for the bread on our tables and ask God's blessings on those who share it. The God who hears and answers our prayers is the same God who hears and answers prayers the world over.

Unfortunately, clothing, language, and skin color keep us at a distance from one another. But a child's shy grace before family dinner is recognizable in any language. A shout of laughter at a good joke isn't limited to a specific culture or race.

Picture women gathered around a television to hear the latest local news, or to talk about world conflicts or the economy. Or imagine men listening to music or conversing over a midday meal. These snapshots of life transcend the borders of race, religion, status, and money. They provide the daily thread that binds us together in the human village. In the end, we really are one big family, eating different bread at different tables but loving the same God.

Bless my home and table Lord, and bless everyone else's as well. Amen.

March 9   Teach Me

Let the words of my mouth and the meditation of my heart be acceptable to you, O LORD, my rock and my redeemer. (Psalm 19:14 NRSV)

This verse forms the first three lines of a song that was sung after the pastoral prayer in the church where I grew up. The song ends: "Will thou teach me how to serve thee? Will thou teach me how to pray?"

Although I sung these words many times, I never really thought about them. As a child, I assumed they were being asked of God. Now I realize they could be from a child to a parent. Whatever the age, the questioner is someone wanting to learn about the Christian faith.

How *does* one learn about faith? How and where did I learn to serve and pray? The answer to these questions is *by example.* In my case, I learned through the examples of my father as a pastor; my grandmothers' prayer lives and devotion to their churches; my mother and aunts' work in their communities; and my teachers, friends, church family, and other concerned adults. Each provided important lessons about faith and life, and all are a part of my spiritual heritage.

The best way to teach or learn the Christian faith is by example. Jesus, the greatest teacher, knew this instinctively. Will we follow his lead?

Thank you, God, for providing examples that showed me your way. Help me follow their example as I now teach and lead others. Amen.

March 10   Passing It Down

"For what is man's lot from God above, his heritage from the Almighty on high?" (Job 31:2 NIV)

Who's in *your* family tree? What are the traits and assets you see in them? A grandmother whose loving faith and leadership holds a family together? A father whose independent spirit enables him to follow his own path? A mother whose ingenuity and business sense manage the household budget?

These are your family's jewels. They are also your touchstones—places to revisit throughout your lifetime during difficulties and challenges for reassurance and guidance. We live in a connected cosmos. Part of our being resides in our bloodline, in our heritage, in what has been passed from one generation to the next.

My strength and faith come from my grandmothers. Both raised their children as single mothers, struggling to provide for them while keeping their families intact. Each had a strong faith and relied heavily on God. Both worked to instill the value of faith in their children and grandchildren. My paternal grandmother was like a solid oak. She exuded quiet character and radiated a warm, nurturing love. My maternal grandmother was a prayer warrior—a loving but strong disciplinarian who brooked no argument when she laid down the law.

The present often has roots in the past. What have you received from those who have gone before?

God of grace and love, thank you for all I have received through family and faith. Amen.

March 11   Living Creatively

Jesus looked at them and said, "With man this is impossible, but with God all things are possible." (Matthew 19:26 NIV)

Susan L. Taylor, editorial director of *Essence* magazine, writes, "Life itself is a work of art, and those who live it well do so creatively, artfully.... Creativity is ... placed in us by God so we can see clearly how to turn any situation to our advantage and shape the life we want at every level. We are the heirs of people who have used the gift of creativity well—the make-a-way women in our families, the can-do men in our history" (*Essence,* April 2003, p. 9).

Who are or have been the make-a-way women in your life? What about the can-do men? Whether part of your biological or adopted family, these individuals can serve as ancestral or present-day role models. Their lives can be like roadmaps that show how to live creatively and fully, using all our God-given talents, skills, and gifts to be fully engaged in the world.

Living creatively means not being limited by present circumstances but finding a way to create a life that is meaningful to you. What is God calling you to do in your life? Following God's whispers, calls, and sometimes shouts is living creatively. This is the path that make-a-way women and can-do men choose to follow. What about you?

Lord, help me use the gift of creative living to create the best life that I can. Amen.

March 12   Somebody Prayed for Me

We pray that you'll live well for the Master, making him proud of you as you work hard in his orchard. As you learn more and more how God works, you will learn how to do your work. We pray that you'll have the strength to stick it out over the long haul—not the grim strength of gritting your teeth but the glory-strength God gives. (Colossians 1:10-12 The Message)

In the song "Testimony," a singer recounts the story of her solid religious upbringing and her emotional, spiritual, and physical spiral downward after being enticed into the high life of the music business. Her story is woven together with the melodic thread, "But I had a praying grandmother. . . ." As she talks about this grandmother, who by the sheer force of prayer kept her from toppling over the edge into the dark pit of self-destruction, you get a clear picture of the power of a loving but fierce prayer warrior.

Many of us can look back and see places where *somebody prayed for me.* In many instances, it was a mother, grandmother, aunt—someone who knew the power of prayer. These women are our spiritual role models. They have traveled the path before us, and in some cases, have posted signs that can show us the way.

Without even knowing it, many of our spiritual mothers have followed in the footsteps of women from the ancient church such as Julian of Norwich, Teresa of Avila, Hildegard of Bingen, and Catherine of Siena. These were the first-known women leaders, preachers, writers, and teachers. They persisted in the face of unbelievable opposition and obstacles and, in the end, have influenced millions. Our grandmothers, great-grandmothers, mothers, sisters, aunts, cousins—biological or adopted, well known or little known—are our link to these early women who first discovered the power of prayer.

Prayer is our spiritual birthright. Somebody prayed for us, and we are richer for it.

Lord, today I celebrate those who prayed for me, and I pray for those yet to come. Amen.

March 13   A Generous Spirit

But Elijah said to her, "Don't be afraid! Go ahead and cook that 'last meal,' but bake me a little loaf of bread first; and afterwards there will still be enough food for you and your son. For the Lord God of Israel says that there will always be plenty of flour and oil left in your containers until the time when the Lord sends rain, and the crops grow again!" (1 Kings 17:13-14 TLB)

What was the attitude in your household toward money when you were growing up? The answer to this question can provide powerful insights into your current attitude toward money and generosity. Although often tied to money, generosity really has little to do with the number of dollars in your bank account. Generosity is an expression of who you are and how you truly feel about yourself and others. Moreover, it's an attitude that is more important than any amount of money you may ever receive or accumulate in your lifetime. Sometimes people with generous spirits are hard to come by.

A quick scan of our consumer-driven, greed-producing society often leads us to believe that without access to vast stashes of cash, credit, and cars, we have little in the way of real wealth or worth. To learn this lesson too well, though, is to miss the one provided in the story of the widow of Zarephath. Here we learn that simply offering the best of what we have and who we are can bring the greatest blessing—God's abundant and loving grace.

Cultivate in me a richness, Lord—a richness of spirit that overflows and spreads to everyone I meet. Amen.

March 14   Out of the Dark

Now faith is the assurance of things hoped for, the conviction of things not seen. (Hebrews 11:1 NRSV)

"Most of us link the dark to negative feelings of fear, terror, death, and uncertainty, associations that have been imposed on the dark by we humans, who have learned to love the light and repel the dark," says Beverly J. Shamana in *Seeing in the Dark: A Vision of Creativity and Spirituality*. Moreover, Shamana says that a knowledge of "myth, culture, and the Spirit reveals meanings of darkness that hold it sacred and vital to our spiritual journey" (Nashville: Abingdon Press, 2001, p. 97).

Creating, like faith, is about meeting God in the dark. When we sit down to draw, write, or transform our life in a new way, we are creating while moving forward in faith. The darkness keeps us from seeing what's up ahead, so our only option is to step out in faith.

Many people see faith as a silent, passive activity. Edith Hamilton disagrees: "Faith is not belief. Belief is passive. Faith is active" (*Quotable Women of the Twentieth Century*, p. 85).

Faith is manifested vision, our belief becoming reality. Faith, like creating, requires not only an image of what is yet to be, but also intentional work to bring that image to reality and openness to mystery. It requires a walk in darkness.

Lord, help me grow comfortable in the still, sacred mystery of darkness in order to better know you and me. Amen.

March 15 — Tying Up Lions

"Yes, be bold and strong! Banish fear and doubt! For remember, the Lord your God is with you wherever you go." (Joshua 1:9 TLB)

An Ethiopian proverb says, "When spiderwebs unite they can tie up a lion" (Adrienne Betz, *Scholastic Treasury of Quotations for Children* [Scholastic Books, 1988], p. 53). That's a great image, but imagine how one spider might feel facing a lion.

One summer I, along with my dad, my cousin, and a few hundred other folk, marched to protest a proposal to change the South Carolina state flag. The march took place in downtown Columbia past the capitol building where supporters of the flag were both visible and vocal. Ours was a silent march; organizers had instructed us to remain quiet regardless of what was said or shouted. As we walked, accompanied by the police, I realized that I was following in the footsteps of the student-led demonstrations for civil rights. As we listened to the opposition's shouts and chants, I recognized that those who had marched before me must have felt the same way—protected yet vulnerable. The majority of protestors, like me, were just ordinary people who supported change and ended up making history.

God calls ordinary people to do extraordinary things, things they never imagined they could do. And when God calls hundreds, thousands, or millions of people, lions get tied up and societies change.

Lord, give me the courage to do my part when it's lion-tying time. Amen.

March 16 — A Servant's Prayer

And he told them many things in parables, saying: "Listen! A sower went out to sow. . . . Other seeds fell on good soil and brought forth grain, some a hundred-fold, some sixty, some thirty. Let anyone with ears listen!" (Matthew 13:3, 8-9 NRSV)

Saint Francis of Assisi's well-known prayer reads:

Lord, make me an instrument of Thy peace. Where there is hatred, let me sow love; where there is injury, pardon; where there is doubt, faith; where there is despair, hope; where there is sadness, joy; where there is darkness, light.

O Divine Master, grant that I may not so much seek to be consoled, as to console; not so much to be understood, as to understand; not so much to be loved, as to love. For it is in giving that we receive, it is in pardoning that we are pardoned, it is in dying that we are born to eternal life.

This is an intriguing talk with God, as if by someone who is ready to start down a new path. This is the prayer of someone who isn't satisfied with himself or herself and has decided to participate more fully with others. This is a prayer for shifting focus, for moving from self-involvement to involving self. This is the prayer of someone who seeks an expanded vision of what it is to live as God asks, and to be about God's business.

Perhaps we could all use a little focus shifting today.

Lord, I, too, am ready for a focus shift. Help me sow new seeds that will take root and bear great fruit for your work. Amen.

March 17   My Legacy

God blesses everyone who has wisdom and common sense.... In her right hand Wisdom holds a long life, and in her left hand are wealth and honor. Wisdom makes life pleasant and leads us safely along. Wisdom is a life-giving tree, the source of happiness for all who hold on to her. (Proverbs 3:13, 16-18 CEV)

Mary McLeod Bethune, founder of Bethune-Cookman College and a presidential advisor, had her last will and testament published upon her death. In it she left a legacy of her philosophy of living and service.

Most parents work, struggle, and sacrifice, hoping to provide better opportunities for their children. This, they hope, will be their legacy to their children and grandchildren. Unfortunately, often what they intend to leave and what they actually leave don't match. Instead of love and opportunity, they leave loneliness, frustration, and anger at a parent or parents who were not around. Adults without children can get just as trapped in the quest for a better life, failing to provide the thing their loved ones crave most—*their time*. Often we spend more time thinking about, establishing, and reviewing our long- and short-term professional and personal goals than we do our goals for our families.

Bethune's legacy begins with "I leave you love," and goes on to talk about hope, confidence, education, power, and faith. What about your legacy? What would it say if written down? Would your intended legacy match reality?

God, help me be intentional and attentive every day to the legacy I'm leaving. Amen.

March 18   I'm Not Ready

But Moses said to God, "Who am I, that I should go to Pharaoh and bring the Israelites out of Egypt?" (Exodus 3:11 NIV)

"I'm not ready." This was a young preacher's response to being asked, right before worship, to preach the Sunday morning message.

Gulp. "Uh, I'd rather not." This is the way many of us would likely respond to an unexpected request or challenge or opportunity. Like the young preacher, we feel unsure of ourselves, unprepared, and frightened of failure. We believe our abilities aren't up to the challenge, particularly if we haven't had time to prepare.

Often we fail to seize opportunities out of fear. We feel like Moses when God said, "You will be my spokesman. You will be my mouthpiece."

Instead of saying, "Right! I'm your go-to girl," we say, like Moses, "Ah, excuse me, but you can't mean me. I'm not the right person. I'm not qualified. I don't speak eloquently. I have no experience. My clothes are all wrong."

We can find many excuses and reasons not to, when the only reason we need is that God chose us. If we are God's chosen, then how can we fail?

I'm not ready! Who *is* when God calls? That's what faith is all about—stepping out, moving ahead, committing before you're ready or fully prepared.

I'm ready, Lord, to do all that you ask. With your help, I know anything is possible. Amen.

March 19   Anger Management

Make your words good—you will be glad you did. Words can bring death or life! Talk too much, and you will eat everything you say. (Proverbs 18:20-21 CEV)

Billye Avery writes in *An Altar of Words* that unexpressed anger is dangerous, destructive, and nonproductive (pp. 10-11). If you've ever been on the receiving end of an unwarranted angry outburst, you're familiar with unexpressed anger. Someone unloads on you for no reason. Afterward, you feel frustrated, hurt, and angry.

Unexpressed anger has a basis in fear—fear of how it would be received if expressed, or of the underlying feelings causing the anger. Whatever the reasons, it wreaks havoc on personal relationships. As women, we are taught to care for others but to offer little of that same nurturing care to ourselves. Instead, we allow feelings to bubble and build below the surface until, eventually, we erupt. Then, we lash out in anger in relationships with friends, children, spouses, siblings, or coworkers—anyone who happens to be in our path. Unfortunately, rather than clearing the air, this behavior creates chaos and lingering emotional wounds.

Each day of our lives we are building word by word, action by action, our future legacy. Is this the type of legacy you want to leave?

Lord, help me avoid the buildup of anger by expressing my hurt in ways that lead to healing. Amen.

March 20   Value and Worth

The price of wisdom is above rubies. (Job 28:18b KJV)

In *A Price Above Rubies,* Rene Zellweger plays a young Jewish woman suffocated by her life as a wife and mother. While her husband, a kind, self-absorbed intellectual, spends his time studying and talking about religious matters, Zellweger feels stifled in their closed religious community. Quietly, she slips into a dark depression.

Her brother-in-law, the head of the family, agrees to let her work in his fine-gems store. She thrives, but suffers consequences outside of her protected cocoon. She is repeatedly raped by her brother-in-law at work, and incurs the disapproval of the other mothers in her community.

Her worldview expands when she meets a young artist who is Hispanic, values women, and embraces life. When their affair is discovered, her brother-in-law casts her out of her home, family, and community.

Alone and scared, Zellweger heads out into the cold night. Her life journey to that point had included joys, disappointments, and even missteps. However, along the way she gained the courage, strength, and wisdom that come through experience and faith—often at a high price. Battered but not defeated, she walks into her new life with a new sense of value and worth.

Hard-won wisdom is more valuable than gold or rubies; and once you've gained it, no one can take it away.

God of wonder and power, give me the courage to live a life of wisdom, a wisdom that is more precious than any gem. Amen.

March 21   Finding My Voice

Then the LORD spoke to you out of the fire. You heard the sound of words but saw no form; there was only a voice. (Deuteronomy 4:12 NIV)

Billye Avery talks of discovering her true voice in *An Altar of Words*. A women's health advocate, Avery was comfortable speaking to groups of people, but lacked confidence in her writing voice. Like Avery, sometimes the greatest barrier to finding our "authentic voice" is ourselves. Too often we "self-censure" before anyone else has the chance.

Many early church women such as Teresa of Avila and Julian of Norwich, whose writings and teachings influence us even today, struggled with the same conflicts about voice that we face. Overcoming the lack of respect for women's voices, barriers from established systems or authorities, and our own insecurities remain our biggest obstacles.

We must be willing to use what we have to get what we want. A key element of getting what we want and need is by using our voices. Voice, in this instance, refers not only to speech but also to whatever voice is uniquely yours. Your voice may express itself through working to better your community, nurturing and caring for your own or other people's children, cooking, organizing, painting, writing, singing, or some other avenue.

Where is your voice its strongest, its most powerful, its best?

Lord, today I celebrate and use my unique voice. Amen.

March 22   Stories Teach Us to Live

Then the disciples came and asked him, "Why do you speak to them in parables?" He answered, "To you it has been given to know the secrets of the kingdom of heaven, but to them it has not been given.... The reason I speak to them in parables is that 'seeing they do not perceive, and hearing they do not listen, nor do they understand.'" (Matthew 13:10-11, 13 NRSV)

The miniseries *Arabian Nights* tells of a sultan crazed with fear after surviving a murder plot by his wife and brother. His wife is killed, but his brother, who covets his title, plots revenge and war.

The sultan must marry again to retain his throne, but fears another plot. He decides to marry but then kill his bride on their wedding night. His chief counsel's daughter has a loving heart and agrees to marry the sultan, believing she can help him.

On their wedding night, the sultana begins a story hoping to keep the sultan engrossed until morning. As light dawns, she delays finishing the tale saying she's tired and must sleep. Enraged, the sultan calls for the executioner, relenting only after she promises to finish the story *tomorrow night*.

Each night she spins tales of proud warriors and ordinary men who are brave, heroic, and cunning; and each morning she resists finishing until the following night. A week passes and she still lives. The whole palace prays for her safety, creativity, and imagination.

Finally, she brings the long tale to an end and faces a different man than the one she married. Through her stories, he has learned to face his fears with courage, to use his skills and talents to his advantage, and to accept love. Like Jesus, the sultana used stories to teach about living and life.

God, I give thanks for my creative genius. I will use it to teach a new way to live. Amen.

March 23   Miracles

Splendor and beauty mark his craft; His generosity never gives out. His miracles are his memorial—This GOD of Grace, this GOD of Love. (Psalm 111:3-4 The Message)

BettyClare Moffatt writes in *Opening to Miracles: True Stories of Blessings and Renewal:* "I believe that our lives are a kaleidoscope, not a fixed line from birth to death. And a miracle ... can occur when you hold the kaleidoscope of your life up to the light and let all the patterns fall into place.... Each and every one of your experiences has contributed to the overall pattern of wisdom, clarity, and love you bring to your life.... It takes great courage to see your life as a kaleidoscope. Just as it takes courage to recognize the daily miracles in your life" (Berkeley, Calif.: Wildcat Canyon Press, 1995, p. vii).

Here is Moffatt's advice on how to make a miracle (pp. 210-11):

- Decide what you want.
- Ask for guidance.
- Ask what, if any, are the character defects, obstacles, and blocks that stand in your way.
- Be willing to change.
- Pledge your hands, your head, and your heart to this endeavor.
- Be willing to serve.
- Be willing to change.
- Forgive.
- Ask that light fill the vessel of your being.
- Ask what you can do specifically, concretely, now, to open to a miracle.
- Act on the wisdom you have received.
- Then rest.
- When what you wished for, hoped for, prayed for shows up in front of you, refrain from surprise.

When was your last miracle? Start work on one today.

God, help me recognize the great and small miracles in my life. Amen.

March 24   Welcome the Stranger

Do not forget to entertain strangers, for by so doing some people have entertained angels without knowing it. (Hebrews 13:2 NIV)

Angels unaware? My niece, Andrea, is certainly one. I knew and loved her before she was born. Within a week of finding out she was on her way, I bought her first gift. I had to take several deep breaths and remind myself that if I kept this up, I wouldn't make it to her birth. It was December. Andrea would be born in June. I had a while to go.

The big day arrived without much fanfare at my house, but for Andrea and her mom it was a different story. Andrea's entry into the world was an arduous, life-threatening one. The doctors didn't expect her to live past the first twelve hours, but she did; and slowly she got better. Only her parents and grandparents were allowed to visit her in intensive care, so she was almost a month old when I held her for the first time. Scrawny, hungry, and loud—we hit it right off! Like her, I too get out of sorts when I'm hungry.

Andrea turns three this year, and she is one of the bravest people I know. Every day she faces challenges that most of us take for granted, but she meets them with a radiant smile and a determined will.

I once believed that children were the learners and adults the teachers, but no longer. Through Andrea's love I welcomed a stranger and found my heart in the process.

Lord, help me follow your lead of putting out the welcome mat when encountering a stranger or an angel. Amen.

March 25   Sheroes

So let it grow, for when your endurance is fully developed, you will be strong in character and ready for anything. (James 1:4 NLT)

When times get tough, I look to my family for strength and inspiration. Both of my grandmothers faced hardships and challenges but succeeded against all odds. Leaning heavily on their faith, they raised their families as single working mothers. A laundress and a maid, my grandmothers maintained households full of children whom they loved and nurtured to adulthood on meager means. Although neither went far in school, both sent their children to college and on to better, richer lives.

Five of my aunts, who had never before traveled far from home, left tiny towns in South Carolina and moved north to begin new lives that included spouses, children, and new friends. Although likely frightened and unsure of the unknown, like millions of other women, they faced their fear and journeyed to new places to seek better opportunities for themselves and those they loved.

Although only three feet tall, my niece already has an incredible stockpile of courage, determination, and strong will. As a result of a difficult birth, she has needed to draw on these reserves to help her not only live, but also exceed many people's expectations. Through discomfort and frustration, she meets each challenge and refuses to give up.

These are my sheroes. Who are yours? What examples do they provide that help you endure difficulties and live more fully?

God of storms and calm waters, thank you for women who have modeled perseverance and faith. Give me strength and courage for my own journey. Amen.

So each generation can set its hope anew on God, remembering his glorious miracles and obeying his commands. (Psalm 78:7 NLT)

In 1994, Elaine St. James wrote *Simplify Your Life: 100 Ways to Slow Down and Enjoy the Things That Really Matter* (New York: Hyperion). Feeling that she and her husband were living a life controlled by "to-do" lists, time organizers, and five- to ten-year life planners, they decided to downsize their lives and began living more simply.

"For us, living simply meant reducing the scale, maintaining the comfort, eliminating the complexity, and minimizing the time demands of life" (p. 6).

In her quest for a simpler lifestyle, St. James found resources that talked about the philosophy of simplicity, but none that offered the practical help that she and her husband needed. So with each success, she wrote down the idea and noted their experience.

"If the two of us—for the most part rational and reasonable people—had gotten so caught up in the frenetically paced lifestyle and rampant consumerism ... there must be other reasonable people out there who had done the same thing" (p. 6).

What about your life? Are you comfortable with the pace and size of it? Has it grown out of control? Is God lost in the midst of franticness and manic energy?

Lord, in my frantic pace to catch up, stay even, and get ahead, it's easy to lose sight of you. Help me slow down, clear out, and let go so that you are more visible in all that I say, do, and am. Amen.

March 27   **Transformation**

He put before them another parable: "The kingdom of heaven is like a mustard seed that someone took and sowed in his field; it is the smallest of all the seeds, but when it has grown it is the greatest of shrubs and becomes a tree, so that the birds of the air come and make nests in its branches." (Matthew 13:31-32 NRSV)

In his book *Be-good-to-your-body Therapy,* Steve Ilg says that our bodies play a vital role in our spiritual and psychological realities. Faith Ringgold is a living testament to his assertions. Ringgold, an award-winning international artist who is well known for her story quilts, used art to recount and document her experience of losing one hundred pounds.

Ringgold, a former New York City schoolteacher, began her professional career as an artist in the 1960s. Her work includes soft sculptures, masks, paintings, performance, and story quilts. Never satisfied with the status quo, Ringgold constantly challenges herself to evolve by exploring and integrating different elements of art and culture that give voice to her unique life story. The transformation of her physical body is one example. For this work of art, she used acting, story, and quilting to examine the origins of her weight gain and the changes she made to lose it.

In the children's book *Talking to Faith Ringgold,* she says, "I am inspired by people who rise above their adversity. That's my deepest inspiration. And also I'm inspired by the fact that if I really, really want to, I think I can do anything" (New York: Crown, 1996, p. 3).

Lord, help me have a faith like the mustard seed that blossoms and grows unbounded. Amen.

March 28   Creativity

So God created humankind in his image, in the image of God he created them; male and female he created them. (Genesis 1:27 NRSV)

In *Seeing in the Dark: A Vision of Creativity and Spirituality,* Beverly J. Shamana writes: "What if creativity is ... a sacred presence that flows through our veins naturally, like our blood? What if God sees to it that we are endowed with this precious attribute at birth? What if creativity is already there, just waiting to be used?" (pp. 11-12).

What if, as Shamana suggests, creativity is just waiting for us to tap into and use? How would this affect the way you live? How would it change the way you think about yourself or those around you?

What if creativity is not some thing endowed to a select few but a gift given to all God's children? If true, would you make different choices in your career, lifestyle, home, relationships, family?

What if God expects us to be creative? How, then, do we live as Christians? Do we stop feeding the hungry, caring for the sick, or helping those in need and instead devote our time solely to artistic endeavors? Or do we use that same creative force that God used in creating us to do work that has meaning to us and our families and communities?

What if?

Creator God, help me use my innate creativity to live as you ask. Amen.

March 29   Killing the Beast

But you are a chosen people, a royal priesthood, a holy nation, a people belonging to God, that you may declare the praises of him who called you out of darkness into his wonderful light. (1 Peter 2:9 NIV)

> I want to declare that I am beautiful, I am charming, I am intelligent, I am talented, and as long as I believe it, Latoya Hunter will go places! . . . Now if only I can *keep this* up when I leave my room. (Tonya Bolden, ed., *33 Things Every Girl Should Know* [New York: Crown, 1998], p. 75)

Less than one hour after turning eighteen years old, Hunter wrote the above in an essay titled "You Could Be Your Own Worst Enemy." She writes insightfully of the significance of crossing this threshold while looking in the mirror and not seeing anything different.

"I just looked in the mirror and saw the same person I saw yesterday. There was not even a hint of new maturity or sophistication" (p. 74).

Hunter, though, is no ordinary teenager. An accomplished writer, she published her first book at twelve and started college a year early. Yet, like many women, young or old, she struggles with self-doubt despite her accomplishments.

"There has always been someone telling me that I just wasn't good enough. . . . The person was a beast that has existed inside of me for so long" (p. 74).

Hunter admits that if she is to become the "phenomenal woman" that Maya Angelou describes in her well-known poem, she will have to murder the beast "with the only weapon that could ever do the job—self-love. There is nothing more powerful" (p. 75).

Maybe we, like Hunter, should write to remind ourselves of who we are *and whose we are* so that when we go out into the world, we won't so easily forget.

God of heaven and earth, help me hold the love you shared through Christ inside me as I go out into a world that thinks little of you, and even less of me. Amen.

March 30   Getting On with It

Do you see what this means—all these pioneers who blazed the way, all these veterans cheering us on? It means we'd better get on with it. Strip down, start running—and never quit! (Hebrews 12:1 The Message)

Faith Hubley was a pioneer and trailblazer. An innovative filmmaker and animator, she, along with her husband, John, formed Storyboard Studios in

1955. They committed to making one independent film a year, despite the fact that a market for animated films was almost nonexistent. Hubley made twenty-one films with her husband, and another twenty-three on her own after his death in 1977. Seven of their collaborative efforts were nominated for Academy Awards, and three of them won.

Instead of using typical Disney-style animation, the Hubleys developed a less stringent and unique style all their own. Whereas Disney characters were drawn with hard edges and filled in with opaque paint, Hubley films featured an impressionistic style that incorporated watercolors and abstract images. Moreover, their ground-breaking work included celebrity voices and jazz music, as well as the improvised dialogue of their four children.

Hubley's persistence, courage, and perseverance paved the way for present-day animation. Before Hubley, most people associated animation with cartoons and kids. Using her creativity and unwavering faith, Hubley challenged this notion by making films that addressed topics of importance to her, such as the arms race, overpopulation, and children's rights.

What is God's call to you? How will you blaze a trail and get on with it?

Lord, help me use persistent faith to follow my heart and your call for my life and journey. Amen.

March 31   I Ask for Faithfulness

"I'm thanking you, GOD, out loud in the streets, singing your praises in town and country. The deeper your love, the higher it goes; every cloud is a flag to your faithfulness. Soar high in the skies, O God! Cover the whole earth with your glory!" (Psalm 57:9-11 The Message)

Do you know anyone who would voluntarily give up creature comforts to live and serve people in extreme poverty? Mother Teresa did.

"I do not pray for success. I ask for faithfulness," she said (*Quotable Women of the Twentieth Century,* p. 84). She worked to change the world one mouth, one person at a time, and she didn't even pray to succeed. It's hard to believe.

A small, frail-looking woman with a huge heart and an indomitable spirit, Mother Teresa challenged, "Do not wait for leaders; do it alone, person to person" (p. 130).

Millions were moved to action and wanted to follow her example. Some even talked of leaving their homes to move to Calcutta, India, to work alongside her. She reminded them that God's work, like God, is everywhere, and that where you do God's work isn't as important as actually doing it. She encouraged people to follow their hearts and God's leading, working in their own neighborhoods and communities.

The little lady with the shy smile and big heart continues to speak through her example of loving faithfulness. We can still hear her, if we listen.

God of the world, light my heart with the fire of faithful service to those I know well and those I don't know at all. Amen.

APRIL

Hope

Kelly Clem

April 1   **"The Sun Rose!"**

Early on the first day of the week, while it was still dark, Mary Magdalene came to the tomb and saw that the stone had been removed from the tomb. (John 20:1 NRSV)

I was pastor of Goshen United Methodist Church in the foothills of the mountains of Alabama. On Palm Sunday of 1994, our four-year-old daughter, Hannah, and nineteen other people in our church were killed in the middle of the service when an F-4 strength tornado demolished the sanctuary all around us. During that week, my family and congregation experienced suffering in ways we never could have imagined.

Days after the tornado, members of the congregation asked if we could continue our plans to hold an Easter service. *How could this be possible?* I wondered. Many of our members were in the hospital, immersed in funerals and arrangements, and, besides that, we had no church building in which to meet! Still, we all knew that we had to go on.

On Easter morning, the parking lot became our sanctuary. We gathered in the dark, sat on borrowed folding chairs using borrowed sound equipment, and faced the rubble of our sanctuary through an arch of stained glass windows that had arrived days before, a donation from a church in Texas. Strangers had sent stuffed bunny rabbits for all the children and donated Easter baskets, and family and friends had brought their loved ones out of the hospital to attend the service. All around us were signs of hope.

As we waited in the darkness, rays of rich amber and burnt orange colors began to creep over the mountains facing our church. Something happened to all of us that day. We were flooded with hope we never knew we could have.

After the service, when a television reporter asked how the service went, the strangest words came out of my mouth. "The sun rose!" That was what had stirred my heart the most: The sun rose on Easter! This was a new day. We had one another. We still had a church. Our daughter and the many other friends we lost the week before were sharing in that indescribable glory of resurrection with Jesus.

The sun rose! The Son rose! Hallelujah!

Lord, we, like the women at the tomb, are surprised and overwhelmed at the power of the Resurrection. You bring light into the darkest places. Each day's sunrise is another sign that life goes on. Amen.

April 2   God Brings Good

"Even though you intended to do harm to me, God intended it for good." (Genesis 50:20a NRSV)

Family envy. Lies. Deception. This is the fascinating story of Joseph's brothers whose scheme to get rid of him backfires. They throw him in a ditch and later decide to sell him to slave traders. Joseph makes the best of the situation and, over time, makes his way up the ladder to become the personal leader for the pharaoh. Joseph has gained tremendous power and influence. Now the tables are turned. He becomes the key person who could either help his brothers or let them die in a time of dire famine. He chooses the path of forgiveness.

Joseph permits his brothers to begin a new life in the prosperous land of Goshen, Egypt. But when their father, Jacob, dies, the brothers are still trembling in fear, knowing they are at Joseph's mercy. They come to their young brother, begging simply to live as his servants. Again Joseph has the last word. Do not be afraid, he says. Even though your motives were all wrong, look at what God did with the mess!

The fact that God can bring good from all circumstances gives us great hope. For the remainder of this month, we will explore the hope we have as Christians and how it can influence our lives.

Lord, when things aren't working out the way I think they should, help me remember that you are constantly at work in my life. I will be faithful and trust you with the results. Amen.

April 3   As Good as It Gets

For surely I know the plans I have for you, says the LORD, plans for your welfare and not for harm, to give you a future with hope. (Jeremiah 29:11 NRSV)

Three months after the death of our four-year-old daughter, Hannah, a woman came running up in a parking lot to speak to my husband and me. Tears began to well in her eyes as she said, "I know what you're going through. I lost my son twenty years ago, and you just never get over it." I felt a sinking feeling deep in my stomach. *Could it be true? Will life never get better?*

Melvin Udall, an obsessive-compulsive character portrayed by Jack Nicholson in the movie *As Good as It Gets,* has reached a breaking point. His psychiatrist's inability to see him without an appointment is the last straw. Leaving the office, he barges into the waiting room and asks the disturbing question, "What if ... this is as good as it gets?"

I have learned that though life may not get easier, the compounded richness of each day makes it better and better. Healing comes not because "time heals," but because God heals our broken hearts. We are offered the fullness of life each day. Will we let that life die on the vine, or will we nourish it? Is this day as good as it gets, or do you believe that life will get even better?

Lord, I know that I can choose my attitude. I will look back with gratitude on what I have learned and gained from my losses. I will look forward with gratitude for new beginnings. You have promised me a future with hope, and I will claim it. Amen.

April 4   A Hopeful Season

For everything there is a season, and a time for every matter under heaven. (Ecclesiastes 3:1 NRSV)

Years ago a friend asked me to speak at a women's seminar "The Seasons of a Woman's Life." When she told me the date, I felt a knot in my stomach.

This would be the one-year anniversary of my miscarriage. "I'll get back with you," I replied. The theme of seasons was attractive. I knew by the knot in my stomach, though, that I was still living in the winter of death of our hoped-for baby. We had moved from fall to winter. Maybe it was time to mark the beginning of a spring in our lives.

Sometimes what seems to be an insurmountable task becomes the best gift for helping us move forward. The timing was not a coincidence; I needed to claim God's presence in the current and future seasons of my life. I agreed to lead the seminar. I spent weeks considering the different seasons of a woman's life and the gift of changes each new season brings. When the day came, I found myself in church, surrounded by new and old friends who joined me in recognizing the beauty of the seasons' effects on our lives. Yes, I still had a knot in my stomach, but I felt God's presence, helping me face a mountain. When I returned home, my husband and I planted a tree in our yard with the firm assurance of a spring to come. Indeed, spring did come. Blossoms of joy, laughter, and new life returned.

God, I'm slow to see that life is changing all around me. I need to change my calendar when I see these signs and live into the season I'm in. I want to grow and be fully present to all of life. Amen.

April 5   Pansies

"This is indeed the will of my Father, that all who see the Son and believe in him may have eternal life; and I will raise them up on the last day." (John 6:40 NRSV)

"Who did that?" Hannah exclaimed, looking at the green chrysanthemum stems pushing their way out of the ground. I explained that last spring we had planted them, and when they died, part of the life stayed under the soil waiting for just the right weather to bring them back to life again. "Oh," she said, pondering the idea.

Several months later, a beloved church member died. She called him Mr. Marcus. I took her with me to the graveside service. After the service, I could tell she was working on a big idea. "So," she announced, "they put Mr. Marcus in the ground and then he'll come back up again." Confused, I asked for clarification. "Like the flowers, right?" she said. "Oh, yes, Hannah, like the flowers."

Hannah wanted to help plant some more flowers the following spring—pansies. They were just beginning to blossom when the warm weather gave way to colder weather and a tornado killed Hannah, destroying our church and much of our home.

It was painful to go back and visit our home, but at times we had to. Every time I went back, those pansies we had planted continued to bloom. It was as though I needed to be reminded that new life does return.

Dear God, as your Son was resurrected, we shall be resurrected. Thank you for new life! Thank you for children's innocent questions. Thank you for the beautiful colors of flowers all around me. Amen.

April 6   The Rainbow

God said, "This is the sign of the covenant that I make between me and you and every living creature that is with you, for all future generations: I have set my bow in the clouds." (Genesis 9:12-13a NRSV)

Our daughter Hannah took great pride in drawing and painting rainbows. She had learned a song in preschool to help her remember the colors, and she filled her drawings with every color she could get her hands on. Her room was filled with rainbows and signs of a little girl's wonder with the beauty of the earth.

In the days following her death, we went to the ocean to rest and get away from the crowds. We were eating out one evening in a restaurant with a sea-facing side of windows when we noticed that children were running to the windows and pointing eagerly. I guessed that they saw a school of dolphins jumping. But it was a rainbow, a complete bow spanning from one end of the sky to the other—and a double rainbow, at that. My heart stopped. This was what I was looking for: a sign of reassurance from God.

I excused myself from the table and ran to stand on the beach and marvel at the awesome sight. My husband, Dale, soon joined me, and we embraced and stood there in wonder, tears rolling down our cheeks. "Hannah is OK," I whispered. "She is OK."

Dear God, sometimes you send me a bird, sometimes a rainbow, sometimes a friend. But you always give me what I need so that I will not forget your promises. Thank you! Amen.

April 7   The Butterfly

For we know that if the earthly tent we live in is destroyed, we have a building from God, a house not made with hands, eternal in the heavens. (2 Corinthians 5:1 NRSV)

In 1994, as our congregation was portrayed as a group of victims, we realized we had to claim a better self-definition. We could see ourselves as victims (which we were), survivors (which we were), or overcomers—now, this seemed to fit a little better! We began to help one another live into a genuine identity of people who claimed the promises of new life after death—"Easter people."

As the months passed, we were anxious to move into our new church home. Still, we took our time with the building design because we knew that our new place of worship had to reflect who we were, not who we used to be. As we looked at the final drawings, Phil, one of the newest members of our church, exclaimed, "Hey, it's in the shape of a butterfly!" There was a moment of awe among the building committee as we realized that the building fit our new identity. We were the "Easter people," and the butterfly was our symbol!

Like the chrysalis awaiting transformation, during the time of transition we are sometimes painful, raw, and ugly. But the splendor of the butterfly, emerging victoriously from the cocoon, is a sight to behold!

Gracious God, through your Son, Jesus Christ, you have welcomed us into the family of Easter people! You bring life from death, joy from suffering, glory from anguish. Thank you for the butterfly that reminds us of the intricacy of your creation from what seems like death into new life. Amen.

April 8   Tangible Hope

She said to them, "Call me no longer Naomi, call me Mara, for the Almighty has dealt bitterly with me." (Ruth 1:20 NRSV)

The story of Naomi and her daughter-in-law Ruth is a deeply stirring reminder of the power of hope-giving presence. Because of a famine in the land of Moab, Naomi had to return to her homeland in Bethlehem. Ruth sacrificed to help Naomi in her grief and hardship. Naomi tried to send her back, but she refused. She knew her physical presence would comfort Naomi in the dark night of her soul.

Often those in grief and despair believe no one could possibly understand.

They put on a good face or distance themselves from others. Yet sometimes the greatest comfort is the physical presence of a friend.

In the months after the loss of our daughter, our church building, and our home, some tasks became increasingly harder for me. My friend Dorothy Ann gave me one of her days off, helping me sort through waterlogged and moldy papers from the out-box of my destroyed office. I could have done it alone, but I knew it would be emotionally unbearable. She sat with me in what seemed like a menial task, listening patiently as the papers called to mind stories of the past year of my life. Her gift of presence gave me hope to face an unknown future.

Lord, when I think I have nothing to offer, remind me that my presence is an offering. Thank you for giving me ears to hear, eyes to see, and the ability to sit still with a friend. Amen.

April 9 — Hope for the Poor

For the needy shall not always be forgotten, nor the hope of the poor perish forever. (Psalm 9:18 NRSV)

My dreams of making a trip to Africa had been quite different. Never mind that it was my husband's birthday; we joined the caravan of people serving soup and bread and offering medical assistance to the poor and homeless of Johannesburg's inner-city slums.

In one of our stops that evening, I talked with a woman whose name was almost like my own, and I learned that she had three children. Noticing that she lived in a tiny plywood hut complex, I innocently asked her where the children were. She stared blankly at me for a moment and, then, turning her gaze downward, she said, "I cannot even think about them."

I have not forgotten that look of despair. In spite of her situation, she continues to survive. The church, which has undertaken this ambitious project of feeding and caring for the poor, is bringing hope in ways we often cannot see. In silence, we stood together, two women worlds apart yet both experiencing tiny flickers of hope. She looked back up at me as I made my way to leave. I promised to pray for her. Ten years later, I still do.

Jesus, give me courage today to look into the eyes of everyone with whom I have contact. Help me find ways to share your powerful hope with the people who live in my neighborhood and around the world. Amen.

April 10   When We Cannot See Results

"If you love those who love you, what credit is that to you?" (Luke 6:32a NRSV)

Once there was a cranky lady who attended church. Kind words did not come from her mouth, and everyone wondered how a person could exude so much negativity. A young woman in the church named Penny decided to take on this woman as her personal faith project. Penny would occasionally write her a kind letter, sharing some encouraging words of scripture. The woman never acknowledged the letters, and though nothing about her seemed to be affected, Penny continued to write.

Over time, the old woman became more and more feeble, and her family was forced to move her to a nursing home. They spent hours in her home, sorting through and eliminating most of her possessions. Her son picked up a stack of letters tied together with a ribbon and asked if he could throw them away. "No!" she shrieked, grabbing them and clutching them to her chest. "These are my Penny letters!"

We don't always know the effects of the seeds of our faith. Jesus told the parable of the farmer who scattered seeds on various types of soil. We know that spreading our seeds on good soil usually produces growth, but what about the rocky soil of a hardened heart? Perhaps it's worth taking a risk.

God, I confess that when I do acts of love and kindness, I look for evidence that they are appreciated. I selfishly want to do things that I can see make a difference. Help me do your work faithfully and leave the results to you. Amen.

April 11   Adversity in Childbirth

For it was you who formed my inward parts; you knit me together in my mother's womb. I praise you, for I am fearfully and wonderfully made. (Psalm 139:13, 14a NRSV)

Birth is a blessing, a gift, a miracle. My birth, your birth—in God's image we are fearfully and wonderfully made.

Audrone was delighted to be having a baby, and this time it would be a girl. When her child was born with a deformed right hand, she plunged into despair, weeping for two weeks, wishing to die. God heard her lament and gave her the comfort to nurture her tiny child. Today her daughter is thirteen years old and is a daily reminder of God's grace, which helped Audrone overcome despair so great that it had led her to the brink of suicide. With her deformed hand, her daughter can hold a kitten, help around the farm, fight with her brother, and pick up hymnals after worship with nearly as much ability as any other child her age. Her shy smile and soft blue eyes ease the anxieties anyone feels when around her.

Audrone is one of the most enthusiastic Bible study participants I have ever been with—a person who has, through hardships, grown in her trust in God. She lives each day with faith and hope for her children.

Dear God, help me not to classify people; we each have our own life to live as best we can. Thank you for who I am. Thank you for every precious child who is born in my neighborhood hospital every day. May they grow up to be loved and adored. Amen.

April 12   Sailing on the Ark

Now hope that is seen is not hope. For who hopes for what is seen? But if we hope for what we do not see, we wait for it with patience. (Romans 8:24b-25 NRSV)

Noah built the ark on faith. But he sent the dove out in hope. It took a few tries, but finally one of the winged creatures he sent out returned with a hopeful sign: an olive branch. Hope is like a dove that flies out beyond our ability to see, scanning vast distances for a sign. When I picture hope, I imagine flying things—a butterfly, a dove, a kite. Hope soars high above the horizontal span of vision we so often believe is all there is to see. Hope flies like the dove sent from the confines of the boat's quarters in search of a new day.

As he built the ark on faith, I wonder how many people laughed at Noah. "A flood? Here? Who told you to do *what?*" His family was with him, and after many weeks at sea, I even wonder what his family thought when he sent the birds out. "Noah, the big dreamer," they might have teased. "What's a bird going to land on?"

How relieved they must have been to see that tiny olive branch in the bird's mouth. Hope has wings, and it soars upward in search of new vistas.

Lord, sometimes I let the panorama of floodwaters blur my vision. I find myself looking horizontally much more than vertically. Help me adjust my gaze and consider your possibilities. Amen.

April 13   Nothing Can Separate Us

For I am convinced that neither death, nor life, nor angels, nor rulers, nor things present, nor things to come, nor powers, nor height, nor depth, nor anything else in all creation, will be able to separate us from the love of God in Christ Jesus our Lord. (Romans 8:38-39 NRSV)

Olga had the misfortune of growing up in times of war, when chaos prevailed. She and her younger sister experienced the helplessness of their mother's death as she gave birth to their brother. The father was unable to support his family, and so he kept the younger daughter, found a family to adopt the baby, and sent Olga to live with a grandmother. The father remarried, and the stepmother abused Olga's younger sister terribly, eventually beating her to death. Olga ran away from the horror of her childhood and sought refuge—anywhere but home. Alone and hungry, she was picked up by strangers.

Through this ordeal, Olga was never taught about the Christian faith, though she remembered the Polish prayers of her grandmother. This was the tiny thread that kept her alive, hoping simply for a love she had never experienced. Though she does not remember her native Polish language, Olga never forgot the prayers her grandmother taught her. In spite of war and abuse, Olga never quit looking for love. She began to come to church. One day she found that love she sought—in God.

Lord, my life hasn't been easy. I haven't always experienced love. Help me keep looking for it. In you, I will find more than I ever dreamed. Amen.

April 14   Tiny Beginnings of Faith

I am confident in this, that the one who began a good work among you will bring it to completion by the day of Jesus Christ. (Philippians 1:6 NRSV)

Throughout Rasa's middle-school years, she read and absorbed all she could about how to be a good atheist. She learned how to poke fun at the weak, mindless Christians. Her textbook on atheism was full of excerpts from the Bible, and she read them with interest. Though she felt drawn to scriptures, she rationalized that she was only interested because it helped her better define the beliefs of an atheist.

Churches started to spring to life in Lithuania with the collapse of the Soviet Union. By this time, Rasa was a college student, still a devout atheist. One day she heard some Christians singing in an open-air amphitheatre.

She stayed to listen to the songs and to words of testimony. The next day, she went back. "I just like the music," she told her friends. Not long afterward, Rasa answered the invitation to give her heart to Christ. She and her roommates began to meet for prayer, and others in their university did, also. Today a movement that began one heart at a time is now the largest nontraditional denomination in Lithuania.

God, you are tugging at my heart because you have plans for my life. Sometimes I feel that tug, but I'm afraid to do anything about it. Thanks for not giving up on me. Amen.

April 15   What Are You Waiting For?

Hope deferred makes the heart sick. (Proverbs 13:12a NRSV)

She was only six years old, but she will never forget the day that German soldiers forcibly removed her from her home. An only child whose father had died, Zina lived in a village in Belarus that resisted the German invasion in 1941. As a consequence of their resistance, the whole area was ransacked and the young girl was by force separated from her mother and sent to the Salaspils concentration camp in Latvia. While there, she survived a poisoning attempt on her life as well as extreme hardships of hunger, loneliness, and imprisonment. Throughout this ordeal, Zina constantly recalled her mother's strong Christian faith.

After her release from the concentration camp, she became a foster child. All during this time, she wrote letters to her previous address in Belarus, not knowing any other way to locate her mother. One day, word reached her that her mother had received the letters and was looking for her. Her mother, Melanija, began a thousand-mile trek from their destroyed village in Belarus to Lithuania, grabbing free rides on the roofs of trains and trusting in the mercy of strangers and walking when she had to. On this arduous trek, Melanija carried a few belongings and her big leather-bound Bible.

Today Zina, a member of the church that I serve in Siauliai, Lithuania, holds her mother's Bible tenderly in her arms. "I would not be alive if it were not for my mother's faith. Faith was all I had to help me get through these difficult years." Then she smiles with a big grin and says, "God has been so good to me."

God, I don't want to lose faith in you! You have been good to me! Amen.

April 16   Hope When Fear Looms

[Martha] said to him, "Yes, Lord, I believe that you are the Messiah, the Son of God, the one coming into the world." (John 11:27 NRSV)

The service of mourning for her brother Lazarus was already underway. Martha offered to meet Jesus and explain that his visit was too little, too late. Martha wasn't like her emotional sister, Mary, who lavished Jesus with praise and adoration; for her, duties, facts, and etiquette were important. It was when Martha's orderly world seemed so hopelessly out of control that Jesus asked her to search the depths of her faith. From the whirlwind of chaos he provoked her to stand still and claim something stronger than grief: her ultimate faith in Jesus, the Messiah, the victor over death.

Sometimes our raw pain wants to have the last word. "Jesus, why didn't you help me when my family was suffering? Jesus, if you cared, you would do something about this problem I'm experiencing!" It is at this point that Jesus lovingly calls forth our statement of faith: "Yes, Lord, I believe." With faith, we can abide. We can endure seemingly insurmountable troubles with the knowledge that he is the one coming into the world. Lazarus's revival and Jesus' resurrection attest to his claims. Hallelujah! He breaks through the bandages and the shallow grave of death and gives life!

God, when we are suffering, you call forth our most basic statement of faith. I believe Jesus is the Messiah, the Son of God, the one coming into the world. Help me not to grieve as one who has no hope, but to carry the light of hope into my deepest darkness. Amen.

April 17   "Who Am I?"

"Do not be afraid, little flock, for it is your Father's good pleasure to give you the kingdom." (Luke 12:32 NRSV)

"Who am I?" sings JeanValjean, the prisoner forced ino labor camps during the days before the French Revolution, as portrayed in the Broadway musical *Les Miserables*. Though released from his sentence, he must live with a criminal's identity number branded on his chest.

Though he tries to make an honest living, he can't seem to escape from the brand of his past offense. Hopeless and destitute, he is befriended by a sympathetic bishop who gives him a meal and a place to sleep for the night.

The temptation is too great. He steals the silver table settings and slips away. After JeanValjean is caught by the police, the bishop chooses to cover the crime, claiming that the silver was a gift.

Though JeanValjean sells pieces of the silver, he never forgets the gift of the bishop's hope. He takes on a different name and identity, but he never gives up the last two silver candlestick holders. They become symbols of hope, reminders that he is no longer the man of his past. Valiantly, JeanValjean lives his life with the integrity and compassion symbolized in the silver candlestick holders.

What voices from your past threaten to lure you back into the destructive patterns of someone you once were? What kind of person do you believe God is calling you to be? Consider this today, and think of a symbol that can be a daily reminder of God's hopes for who you can be.

God, I often wonder, "Who am I?" I listen to so many voices around me who tell me that I am worthless, incompetent, unattractive, hopeless. But you have told me that I am your child, created in your image and called for a holy purpose. Help me live my life in response to who you have named me to be. Amen.

April 18   Hope for Others

Therefore be imitators of God, as beloved children, and live in love, as Christ loved us and gave himself up for us, a fragrant offering and sacrifice to God. (Ephesians 5:1-2 NRSV)

Vanda's village near the town of Pilviskiai was bombed by the Germans during World War II. She and her parents had fled in safety, and a few weeks later they returned only to see smoldering ruins where their house once stood.

She needed to return to school, but Vanda did not even own a pair of shoes. It was early spring 1944, and snow was on the ground. The trip to school was about three miles. When it was time to leave, her mother removed her own high-heeled shoes and placed them on Vanda's feet. They were too big, so she tied strings around them. Vanda walked in her mother's shoes to school, and nearly sixty years later she still remembers the compassion of her mother, giving all that she had to give.

Though her mother was a Christian, Vanda was an atheist for her childhood and adulthood. A missionary who met Vanda remarked to her daughter, "When she becomes a Christian, she'll be a powerful one!" to which her daughter laughed. It seemed so impossible. But at age sixty-five, the concept of Christ's unconditional love soaked into Vanda and, like Paul, the passion she once had to refute the claims of Christianity was transformed to spread the gospel. Vanda's faith is a by-product of unconditional love!

God, please help me set my own needs aside when I have a chance to share the gift of hope with someone else. It just might change their life for eternity! Amen.

April 19   Strength We Never Knew We Had

Now faith is the assurance of things hoped for, the conviction of things not seen. (Hebrews 11:1 NRSV)

"I'd never have the strength to face such a thing," we say to ourselves as we watch someone endure a tragedy. I said those words at the grave of my cousin's three-year-old daughter, Brianna, who died a slow and painful death to cancer. Yet, a few years later, when we tragically lost our daughter Hannah, I discovered that God gives us strength we never could have imagined.

At Hannah's funeral, I was comforted by my Aunt Dot, Brianna's grandmother. She didn't have to say anything. She had traveled more than six hundred miles simply to look us in the eyes and give a heartfelt hug. In that precious moment of meeting, I understood more than ever what her loss must have felt like. With her eyes she offered me a hope that gives unanticipated strength to face the dark hole tragedy leaves behind. Hope has kept me from staying in that hole.

In the days of my deepest discouragement, I need to catch hope again, to get a good dose of hope spreading through every cell in my body. It is the hope that my friends, family, and even strangers I've never met have lived out that gives me courage to continue the journey.

Dear God, thank you for the Aunt Dots in my life. Thank you for people who know when to say nothing and simply share an embrace. Thank you for every person who has given me reason to keep going. Amen.

April 20   Where Does God Figure In?

"Do you know the balancings of the clouds, the wondrous works of the one whose knowledge is perfect?" (Job 37:16 NRSV)

By the time my mother-in-law, JoAnn, knew she had breast cancer, it had spread to other parts of her body. The doctor delivered the news as her family sat with her. "How bad is it?" she asked. "Well," he said, "I would say 70 percent of patients with your diagnosis live two years, 20 percent live up to five years, and 10 percent might live longer." She paused to ponder the statistics and then said, "OK. I'll take the 10 percent."

Though the chemotherapy treatments were difficult, JoAnn lived as fully as she could. She continued to work, to make daily neighborhood walks with her buddies, and to spend time with her friends, her church, and her grandchildren. She refused to let her life be reduced to a medical statistic of probabilities. Though cancer finally claimed her life, she gave all the strength and energy she had to living. She believed that, any way she chose to look at the facts, one fact was indisputable: her life was in God's hands.

Job surveyed his losses, his lecturing "friends," his inability to understand, and he despaired of life. In the end, he found relationship with God and he was sustained. He had to learn to trust God with each day of his life.

Dear God, when I fear the bottom is dropping out of my life, I start resisting. I don't want my life to change! I don't want to suffer! Yet I know that you hold my future, and I want to trust you each day that I live. Hold me in the palm of your hands, and I will be assured that you are very near in these times. Amen.

April 21   The Gift of Generational Hope

I am reminded of your sincere faith, a faith that lived first in your grandmother Lois and your mother Eunice and now, I am sure, lives in you. (2 Timothy 1:5 NRSV)

Born to a Jewish mother who made a daring escape from a concentration camp in Poland, my friend Walla is a living example of hope. Though her mother suffered immeasurably, losing her husband and three sons, she began a new life in Sweden. Walla remembers that, though they were poor and alone, she knew she was loved and would be kept safe from harm.

In 1974, Walla was ordained a United Methodist pastor in Sweden. She has committed her life to serving the prisoners and outcasts of her own country as well as neighboring countries. Often she borrows an old truck or a van and fills it with charity gifts for the orphanages and churches.

One day as several of us were talking outside our church-sponsored medical clinic, I looked up to see that Walla had zeroed in on an elderly lady resting on a bench. Perhaps they conversed in Russian, or perhaps she simply gave the woman a language-free gesture of love. Minutes later, I saw her share an embrace and a good-bye with the woman the rest of us had never even noticed. In Walla, people see a message of hope.

Lord, I see those I expect to see, but maybe you could help me see those Jesus would see. You have given me hope. I want to pass it on. Amen.

April 22   Tenacious Faith

For the message about the cross is foolishness to those who are perishing, but to us who are being saved it is the power of God. (1 Corinthians 1:18 NRSV)

A few miles from our apartment is the Hill of Crosses, an ancient burial mound. There are at least one hundred thousand large crosses mounted in the ground, and as many as a million crosses in all. For more than a hundred years, Christians around the world have visited and left their crosses in the ground. When Lithuania was part of the Soviet Union, the crosses were a threatening image to the precepts of Communism. KGB and Soviet police loomed over the site. Beginning in the 1960s, fires were set to destroy the wooden crosses, and bulldozers buried the concrete and metal crosses. At least four times the site was leveled. Yet, miraculously, each time the crosses would reappear. The faithful would not be discouraged. They waited with active hope for the day in which there would be freedom of religious expression.

Today people travel from near and far to the site to take a prayer walk, sit for a while, or bring a cross. Some crosses are hand-carved from wood, some are metal, but all mark the many experiences of human need for prayer. The Hill of Crosses is a stirring reminder of the power of the symbols of our faith.

Jesus, when I wear a necklace or a pin with the symbol of the cross, I am reminded that I belong to your family. Yet, in public, your symbol makes a statement that still offends some people. Let me not be afraid to claim and share my faith. Amen.

April 23   Hearts Poured Out

Now while Jesus was at Bethany in the house of Simon the leper, a woman came to him with an alabaster jar of very costly ointment, and she poured it on his head as he sat at the table. But when the disciples saw it, they were angry and said, "Why this waste?" (Matthew 26:6-8 NRSV)

All week the work team from Alabama shivered from the cold and politely tasted the foods served to them. One relationship at a time, they began to make friends, share their witness, and receive hospitality from these people in a land very different from home. Their efforts were not wasted on the many lives they touched.

Michelle, the youngest member of the team, did not enjoy the food or weather. Nevertheless, she put her whole self into the experience. The group visited the Hill of Crosses and placed a cross from their church in the ground. From her pocket, Michelle removed a keepsake metal cross from a spiritual retreat she had attended several years earlier. After the church cross was secured in the ground, Michelle walked forward and placed her cross on top. I wondered, *Why would she leave something so valuable?* Then I remembered the woman with the alabaster jar of costly perfume; this was her fragrant offering to Jesus. She was experiencing a call to do more in the area of missions, and her heart was filled with gratitude.

The plane had hardly landed home in Birmingham before Michelle began making plans to return and give even more of herself to the people of Lithuania.

Dear God, I want my life to have meaning, no matter how old I am, how long I live, or where I am. I want to give back the blessings that have been given to me. And when I do, you always surprise me with even more blessings to share. Amen.

April 24   Rise!

"The kingdom of heaven is like yeast that a woman took and mixed in with three measures of flour until all of it was leavened." (Matthew 13:33 NRSV)

My mother makes the best bread. I have many of her recipes, but my bread never compares to hers. It's the yeast I have trouble with. A good bread-baker understands the importance of using the freshest yeast, adding water at the precise temperature, adding flour according to the humidity in the air, watching until the fermentation is complete, adding ingredients in the right way, and kneading the dough properly. Too much salt kills the yeast. Too much kneading makes it tough. Not enough kneading makes it lumpy. My mother can even show me how it's done, but I do not seem to have the patience to get everything just right. It's a fine art.

In *Season of Your Heart,* Marcina Wiederkehr says that "hope is like yeast and baking powder" (HarperSanFrancisco, 1991, p. 57). Just as a pancake made without baking powder tastes tough and rubbery, so also a life without hope is undesirable. However, with just a small amount of hope in Christ, mixed and kneaded with the expert hands of our creator, we can be formed into a remarkable creation.

Jesus, I need the aroma and the wonderful taste of your leaven in my life. You are creating something really special with me, and I don't always have the patience to see it! Fill me with hope. Knead me, Lord. Amen.

April 25   Scraps of Life

And all of them ate and were filled; and they took up the broken pieces left over, seven baskets full. (Matthew 15:37 NRSV)

The quilt my grandmother made me is a treasured heirloom. To anyone who will listen, I'll tell the stories of the dresses and outfits my mother lovingly sewed for me. There are more than pieces of my favorite clothes; there are those of my sister, my cousins, and other family members. Sewn together, the collection of fabrics reminds me that even with scraps, we can create something of lasting beauty and worth.

I don't quilt, but I do love to make books of the scraps of my life: ticket stubs from good shows, locks of my children's first haircuts, pictures from birthday parties, and handmade cards. The scrapbooks of today are not unlike the quilts of years gone by—a piecing together of the remnants of our lives into a meaningful whole, a comforting blanket of memories, a rich collection of the sacred moments of life.

The story of Jesus feeding the five thousand captures our imagination. How were there seven baskets of leftovers? How did the gift multiply? So it is with the scraps of my life. When I hold the completed product—my basket, my quilt, my scrapbook—I realize there is more here than I started with. I, too, have been filled. I am satisfied.

Jesus, you have a way of making miracles with the most ordinary things. I praise you for piecing and sewing together these treasures of my life into a meaningful whole. Thank you for the blanket of comfort and security you have given me. Amen.

April 26   How Long Must We Wait?

We also boast in our sufferings, knowing that suffering produces endurance, and endurance produces character, and character produces hope, and hope does not disappoint us. (Romans 5:3-5a NRSV)

Toni, Loni, and Honoratas grew up loving to go to church in the German factory community of Sanciai, Lithuania. With the advent of Communism, pastors fled for their lives and church properties were claimed by the Soviet government. Over the years, the church became a bar, a warehouse, a sports club, and a table-tennis hall. A beautiful house of worship was almost completely desecrated.

From their home nearby, with the curtains closed, these three women quietly held their own private worship services each week with a few neighbors. Often, Toni would walk past what was once her church and gently touch the building, offering a prayer that one day her church could be returned to its proper use. A woman shooed her away with a broom, and she eventually stopped touching the church; but she never stopped praying.

After the fall of Communism, the church was eventually reclaimed for its original purpose, though it was badly damaged. For the dedication service the sanctuary was filled with guests from all over the world who had participated in this joyous miracle. But no one was happier than Loni, Toni, and Honoratas, who had waited with hope for more than fifty years to see that glorious day.

Dear God, today we pray for those who cannot worship in freedom. We pray for those who wait with hope. Strengthen their faith. Amen.

April 27   Lord, Send a Ladder!

Cast all your anxiety on him, because he cares for you. (1 Peter 5:7 NRSV)

We were on a ski trip with family. We boarded the ski lift and enjoyed the ride as we moved high above the ground. When we reached the top, we set our feet down and glided gently down the arrival slope. My sister was in the chair lift behind us, and as she began to set her feet on the ground, she panicked. Afraid to let go or to stay on, she grabbed the bottom of the ski chair. As I turned around, I saw her dangling her feet wildly as the ski lift continued its ascent. Within seconds, the ski patrol was on the scene, shouting, "Hold on!" Soon the entire ski lift was shut down to allow the ski patrol to climb a ladder and grab her by the legs, gently easing her down to safety.

After we reached the bottom of the hill, we all had a bellyaching laugh. Sometimes we have to laugh at the way we make silly decisions we regret. In moments of panic we often get ourselves into trouble. We hope someone will come with a ladder to bring us to safety. The good news is that God's grace and love are always there to help us overcome our mistakes.

Dear God, sometimes I don't have time to think things through, and I have to live with a bad decision. Thank you for always being there for me. Amen.

April 28   Beyond Language

Likewise the Sprit helps us in our weakness; for we do not know how to pray as we ought, but that very Spirit intercedes with sighs too deep for words. (Romans 8:26 NRSV)

Learning a foreign language can be a humbling experience. Learning requires practice, and practice requires speaking aloud. Often, though, our words don't come out the way we thought they would. Children have laughed at my pronunciation in worship services, and strangers have turned their heads and walked away from my attempts to communicate. On the way to the post office, I rehearsed my query in Lithuanian: "Could I please buy an envelope?" But when I asked the question, I substituted the word "spider" (voras) for "envelope" (vokas). How silly this American must have seemed, waltzing into the post office to buy a spider.

I have grown accustomed to not always being understood; truly, I am delighted when I am understood in this foreign country. It is staggering to think about the complexities of our language and yet how God can hear every prayer offered, even by those who cannot speak.

Dear God, you are beyond language. I struggle to get the words right, to be understood, to communicate, but I know that you understand the language of our hearts. You always hear my prayers. Amen.

April 29   **Waiting**

I wait for the LORD, my soul waits, and in his word I hope; my soul waits for the
LORD more than those who watch for the morning. (Psalm 130:5, 6a NRSV)

In Spanish, the word for "to hope" and "to wait" is the same: *esperar*. Are
they one and the same in my faith language? As I wait, does my hope in
God's Word strengthen me? Am I empowered by hope to act? Or is what I
call "hope" simply waiting, ignoring life around me while I wait for a problem to go away, expecting that one day everything will work out just fine?
Am I poised to listen to the Holy Spirit's guidance when it's time to act in
hope?

My three-year-old niece, Amy, had been waiting for her mother to pay
attention to her. "Just a minute" was Connie's refrain for Amy's litany of
requests. Finally, Amy took on an active stance. She squared her face with
her mother's, shoved her hands on her hips, stomped her foot, and pro-
tested, "No more 'just a minute,' Mommy!" Amy knew what she wanted,
and she knew who could help her get it.

Hope gives us strength to wait. Hope keeps our waiting from being passive. With hope, we can step forward and claim God's promises, in God's
time.

God, I wait for a lot of things, but am I waiting with hope, or just passing
the time? Help me learn how to wait with hope, and how to do what needs
to be done as I look forward. Amen.

April 30   **Praising God in All Circumstances**

Why are you cast down, O my soul, and why are you disquieted within me? Hope in
God; for I shall again praise him, my help and my God. (Psalm 42:5, 11 NRSV)

My friend Patricia has had Job-like losses in her life: divorce, injury,
death of close family members, and financial struggles. As long as I have
known her, her losses have increased, yet her faith has grown stronger.
"When I feel like giving up," she once said, "I have learned to praise God,
no matter what."

Patricia stopped praying for patience a long time ago; she says she does-
n't think anyone could ever have the patience to endure what she's had to
endure. Still, she prays often and praises God all day long.

97

When we praise God, are we telling God that we agree with every circumstance? No, we are showing that we love God, not because of our present state of life but because of who God is. Patricia has a well of deep understanding that runs far deeper than her present situation to remind her that she is loved. No matter what, she knows that she has the ability to love God back. Praise emerges from a heart that is full. From my friend Patricia, I have learned that God's love isn't conditional, and no matter what circumstances we find ourselves in, love never fails.

Lord, I don't have the patience of Job. I'm not even sure that Job had the patience we attribute to him! But I thank you for friends who remind me to praise you for helping me to grow and to learn each day to depend on you more and more. Amen.

MAY

Making Time

Lillian C. Smith

May 1   **Making Time to Rest**

He said to them, "Come away to a deserted place all by yourselves and rest a while." (Mark 6:31 NRSV)

Does it seem that your life never slows down? Do you wish there were more hours in the day? Are there things you know you should do—things you really *want* to do—but you never have time for? If you answered yes to any of these questions, then this month is especially for you!

Let's begin with *rest*. Studies indicate that many of us are sleep deprived. Whether single, married, or divorced; with or without children; a domestic manager, an employee or business owner, or a minister: we women seldom get enough rest. In fact, rest almost has become a four-letter word! The old adage is true: A woman's work is never done. We juggle work, multiple personal and family responsibilities, and ministry or service. What's more, we often feel we have to work extra hard so that we aren't perceived as less qualified than our male counterparts.

The truth is, God wants us to rest. God actually values rest. In the creation story, God rested on the seventh day. Likewise, Jesus encouraged the disciples to rest after an active period of ministry. We need rest so that we can replenish our bodies, souls, and spirits. Resting reminds us that our value is not in doing, but in being children of the Living God. So, today, sistah friend, make time to rest!

Dear God, so often I'm weary but feel that I can't rest because so much has to be done. I hear your instruction to rest and will be faithful. Remind me when I fall short. Amen.

May 2   **Making Time to Rejoice in God's Goodness**

This is the day that the LORD has made; let us rejoice and be glad in it. (Psalm 118:24 NRSV)

"It is a great day, Mommy!"

This was the greeting my thirty-four-month-old son gave me first thing in the morning. What was so great about it? It had been a week from hell, and I wasn't feeling the greatness of the new day. As a pastor's wife, I was dealing with hurtful and deceitful actions of parishioners who were intentionally maneuvering to undermine my husband's leadership. At work, I felt pushed on every side. The responsibilities of being a spouse and mother were squeezing out any time for me. In the middle of all these challenges, my son's words were God's gift to me. They reminded me to stop focusing on the challenges of life and concentrate on the goodness of God.

In spite of all of the mess, God is still on the throne and is in the blessing business. As a child of God, I have the right and responsibility to be joyful. Today I choose to acknowledge God's resurrection power as more powerful than all oppressive forces. As God has helped me in the past, God will do so again. The psalmist knew that even in the midst of problems, God remains faithful. Dear sister, regardless of what confronts you, God wants you to live joyfully today and every day!

Dear God, I rejoice in the gift of this day and in your faithfulness and love, which undergird me amid life's challenges. Amen.

May 3   **Making Time to Fulfill Your Holy Assignment**

"For if you keep silence at such a time as this, relief and deliverance will rise for the Jews from another quarter, but you and your father's family will perish. Who knows? Perhaps you have come to royal dignity for just such a time as this." (Esther 4:14 NRSV)

As quiet as it is kept, God has an assignment just for you. It may seem to be a "mission impossible" and may even scare you. It may place you in opposition to what appear to be formidable powers. The situation may require you to give voice to the pains and injustices experienced by others. The reality is that you are in your particular situation of influence because God needs and wants you to accomplish this holy assignment. Like Esther, you have been prepared by God to "step up" and "represent" at this particular time. Like Esther, God needs you to help God's people. Don't shirk or run from it. Don't doubt your ability to do it. You don't go into the situation alone but with the leading and power of the Holy Spirit of our all-powerful God. People's lives are depending on your faithful response to this challenge. So, go ahead. If God is for you, who can be against you? Yes, it is a risk, but it is your time to shine God's love in the world. God has called you for such a time as this.

Dear God, I don't always feel like signing up for your holy assignments. They are difficult and sometimes scary. But your call is more important than anything else in life. Help me faithfully answer the call. Amen.

May 4 — Making Time for God's Direction in Your Life, Part 1

Trust in the LORD with all your heart, and do not rely on your own insight. In all your ways acknowledge him, and he will make straight your paths. (Proverbs 3:5-6 NRSV)

Have there been times when everything was going well? You thought you were where you were supposed to be and doing what you were supposed to be doing, and then, all of a sudden, it made no sense at all. It's almost like you ran into a wall that appeared out of nowhere, or life threw a curve ball you didn't see coming. When that happens, it's often hard to regroup and find direction.

For me, life is most frustrating and uncertain when it lacks understanding. Maybe a child has rebelled against family expectations. Maybe a family member has encountered serious health challenges. Maybe your job is going through reorganization, and you are unsure how it will affect you. Of course, you find yourself worrying and trying to figure the situation out. Guess what? God knew about the situation way before you and wants to guide you out of it. Save yourself time, energy, and stress. Take the matter to God.

Don't try to figure it out by yourself. Stop, pray, and ask for God's direction. Trust God more than your ability to work things out. Seek God's plan. God loves you and will make a way somehow.

Faithful God, help me know how to proceed with my life. Everything is so confusing now. I trust you to lead me now and always. Thanks for loving me so. Amen.

May 5   Making Time for God's Direction in Your Life, Part 2

Your word is a lamp to my feet and a light to my path. (Psalm 119:105 NRSV)

You are a gifted woman! You've got it going on in some areas of your life. But, believe it or not, your understanding is limited. It is minute in comparison to God's. Oh, how this reality slaps us in the face when the path that we chose— or that was chosen for us—leads us where the road ends in a somewhat perilous place. It's during times like this that life seems confusing and bewildering.

Stop thinking you have to do it all by yourself. God has promised to help you out if you allow God to do so. You have nothing to lose and everything to gain. Stop trying to control your life; let God handle it. God's better at it, anyway. God already knows how the story will end. You may not know where the path will lead, but the adventure will be well worth it. So, relax, seek God's direction, and get ready for God to surprise you once again. In the uncertainty of life, God's Word will be a lamp for your feet and a light for the path.

Dear God, you know what is going on and have my best interest in mind. Please get me out of this mess. Thank you in advance for your continued faithfulness. Amen.

May 6   Making Time for God Through Prayer

Pray in the Spirit at all times in every prayer and supplication. (Ephesians 6:18 NRSV)

P-R-A-Y-E-R. It is the spiritual bread that nourishes our souls. Prayer is the power that moves the heart of God and changes situations. Prayer takes us into the very presence of God and increases our intimacy with this special Love. Why is it that such an important task is often so low a priority in our lives? Our lives are so busy that it is sometimes hard to find time to pray. In the words of a spiritual uncle, Mr. Joseph Coleman, "If you are too busy to pray, you are just too busy."

Sister, we become weak without prayer. Daily prayer will make your day go more smoothly and help you better weather any unexpected challenges that will attempt to knock the wind out of you. Don't make another excuse. Just do it! Right now! Wherever you are, get quiet and pray. If possible, hide in a secluded place away from distractions, or go for a walk. Don't allow this day to end without a time of prayer with God. Today and every day, make time to pray.

Dear God, you are so patient and loving. Please forgive me for not always praying as I should. I love you and want to do better. Prompt me to pray, and remind me when I forget. Amen.

May 7   Making Time to Praise God!

Let everything that breathes praise the LORD! (Psalm 150:6 NRSV)

Breathe in. Breathe out. By those two actions, you have fulfilled the criteria in today's Bible verse. Today, make time to praise God. Why? God desires it, and so do our own spirits. Praise is defined by *Webster's New World Dictionary* as "to commend the worth of; express approval or admiration of; to laud the glory of, (God, etc.) as in song; glorify; extol." Praise is not something certain people do. Regardless of your denominational or church affiliation, praise is a calling and responsibility for all of us. Praise God with your spoken, signed, or written words. Praise God through your singing. Praise God with your dance and drama. You can do it in so many different ways. Clap! Shout! Lift your hands!

Scripture says that God inhabits the praises of the people. When you praise, you affirm the reality that, come what may, in the good and bad times, God is good. That kind of confidence and behavior confounds the enemy and keeps your mind on a faithful God. So, what is holding you back? If you need help, browse the psalms and recite those that praise our God!

Great God, I love you more than anything or anyone. You are an awesome, all-powerful, and excellent God. There is no one like you in all the world. I praise you today and will tell others of your goodness. Amen.

May 8   Making Time to Overcome

I can do all things through him who strengthens me. (Philippians 4:13 NRSV)

Equipped with an empty paper towel tube and a soft sponge ball, my almost three-year-old cornered me in the kitchen, insisting on a game of baseball. I'd throw the ball to him, and he'd attempt to hit it. An aspiring baseball player, he missed the ball more than he hit it. But the little tyke never gave up. Even when he would strike out, he'd hold onto the hope and expectation of being able to hit the ball once again. The times he hit the ball seemed to give him the resolve to keep trying. Armed with persistence and his ability to achieve the impossible, he wouldn't give up. "Let's try again, Mommy," he'd say. "I can do it."

My son's words and actions convicted me at a time when I wanted to throw in the towel and give up on a few fronts of my life. How often do life's challenges and attacks of the enemy cause us to want to give up? Sistah friend, we have all been there. But don't give up. With Christ, you have what it takes to go through and master any situation that comes your way. You can make it.

God, on my own I can't withstand all the harsh realities of life. But thanks to you and the sacrifice of your Son, I can do all things. Thank you for your overcoming ability and strength. Thank you for being with me in this situation. Amen.

May 9   Making Time for God's Peace, Part 1

Do not worry about anything, but in everything by prayer and supplication with thanksgiving let your requests be made known to God. (Philippians 4:6 NRSV)

Every now and then I hear Bobby McFerrin's whimsical and fun song, "Don't Worry, Be Happy." Just singing along with the video makes me feel happy because singing stops me from concentrating on life's challenges and pains. Life's problems always try to crowd out other thoughts, causing feelings of grief, fear, confusion, and anxiety. The negative thoughts crowd out knowledge and remembrance of a faithful God who is bigger than any problem the world can send our way. You serve a heavenly parent who cares for you. Like any mother or father, God desires for you to ask for help.

So, why not pray about the things that worry you? God is big enough to handle the situation and knows more about it than you'll ever know. Pray and rest in the knowledge that it will ultimately be OK. God has got the situation now. Choose not to worry. Choose to rest in God's faithfulness. Be at peace.

Great is your faithfulness, God. I'm tired of worrying about this situation that I lift before you now. I need you to enter into it and make things right. Thy kingdom come, thy will be done in this and other situations I give you. Thank you for your peace. Amen.

May 10 Making Time for God's Peace, Part 2

Finally, beloved, whatever is true, whatever is honorable, whatever is just, whatever is pure, whatever is pleasing, whatever is commendable, if there is any excellence and if there is anything worthy of praise, think about these things. (Philippians 4:8 NRSV)

Don't worry? How in the world am I not supposed to worry?

Though it is difficult, it is not impossible if you employ some divine strategies. First, remember what God has done for you in the past. Recall all the times when God answered your prayers. Write them down if you need to. Thank God for each of them. Then, think on what God says about your current situation. Read and meditate on the promises of God. Each time a negative, defeating thought enters your mind, respond with the goodness of God. If the bill collector is asking you for money that you don't have, thankfully remind God about the promise to "supply all of your need according to His riches in glory" (Philippians 4:19 NKJV). If people's manipulative and deceptive actions are attempting to railroad your destiny, remember that "no weapon formed against you shall prosper" (Isaiah 54:17a NKJV). Think on the good things of God. Sing a hymn of God's faithfulness. Train yourself to counter and replace the negative, life-defeating thoughts with what God has promised you. Think it, say it, believe it, and trust in it. Thank God for the peace, and let it overtake you!

God, as strange as it seems, I really am supposed to refrain from worrying. In your Word you've instructed me not to worry, so I'm going to try it your way. I choose to trust you. Remind me when I forget what I promise today. Amen.

May 11   **Making Time for God's Peace, Part 3**

Those of steadfast mind you keep in peace—in peace because they trust in you. (Isaiah 26:3 NRSV)

Has this ever happened to you? You have established a routine of regular prayer, Bible reading, and meditation. You feel connected to God and invigorated for ministry in a special way. Your life has balance, and you are living out the peace that the Bible speaks about. Then life gets busier, and the routine is put on hold for a day or two or three. And the peace you had seems to escape without a trace.

Many times God has awakened me to pray at 2:00 or 3:00 in the morning and I have chosen, instead, to continue sleeping. Then, later in the day, I encounter something for which I am unprepared. I have forfeited my peace because of my distractions.

A gift from God, peace can be defined as "wholeness, well-being, the absence of war, conflict and strife, and reflective of relationships among humans and between God and humanity." God intends for you to experience peace in all you do and in all situations—whether good or bad. It is difficult to trust in someone or something when your relationship is not continually being cultivated. It is easier to trust in God when prayer and Bible reading are continuously feeding your spirit and mind. Make time for God's peace in your life.

God, your peace does not mean that I won't have any problems; instead, it means that, come what may, you are still with me and in control. Thank you for your peace. Thank you for your joy. Amen.

May 12   **Making Time for Your God-ordained Destiny, Part 1**

For surely I know the plans I have for you, says the LORD, plans for your welfare and not for harm, to give you a future with hope. (Jeremiah 29:11 NRSV)

There are things in our pasts of which we are ashamed. We each can look back and be reminded of bad decisions and relationships, hurts, pains, and people who mistreated us. If we allow them, those mistakes and past hurts can sabotage our futures because they continually try to hold us in the past.

Friend, the past is the past. Leave it there. Before the beginning of time, God had a special plan for you. In order for you to live into your divine destiny, you've got to get rid of the baggage of your past. Lose it. Whatever it is, throw it away and get on with your life. That baggage is breaking your back. Those plans of others that were designed to destroy you have nothing to do with God, nor do they have power to influence your future if you align yourself with God's plan. According to God, your life has purpose, a future, and hope. Believe God's report and live into your future. Unlike others, God does not want to hurt you but to help you.

God, I give you my past with all my bad decisions and all the hurts inflicted upon me. Please cleanse my mind from the baggage that tries to keep me down. Help me to understand the freedom you give me to live out your purpose for my life. Amen.

May 13   Making Time for Your God-ordained Destiny, Part 2

Read Mark 5:25-34.

For she said, "If I but touch his clothes, I will be made well." (Mark 5:28 NRSV)

Dear sister, what is stopping you from getting to Jesus? The sister in this scripture faced public disdain and religious sanctions that restricted her actions. She had to use her limited strength to maneuver the crowds of people to get to Jesus. After suffering from hemorrahages for twelve years, she was exhausted by the problems she had had to endure. Her ill health had caused her to have an altered perspective of life. Still, she pressed on, for she knew God loved her and had promised her health and a better quality of life.

What is holding you back? Who is trying to stop you from getting to the very Lover of your soul? Your wholeness, health, and peace find their source in him. Your status as a daughter of the Most High God—a person worthy of respect, love, and honor—will be affirmed by him. If you are sick and tired of being sick and tired, press on. If illness threatens your very existence, press on. If societal or religious constraints try to hold you back, press on. Your future destiny is wrapped up in your contact with Jesus. Press on!

Dear God, I'm pressing through everything to get to you! I'm not going to let anything keep me back. Thank you for loving me. Thank you in advance for delivering me. Thank you for making me whole. Amen.

"You shall love the Lord your God with all your heart, and with all your soul, and with all your mind, and with all your strength." (Mark 12:30 NRSV)

What's love got to do with it? In relationship with our loving God, it is everything. Just as you demand expressions of love in romantic or familial relationships, so also God wants all your love. Imagine how you would feel if your child never told you that he or she loved you. God wants all or nothing.

Share your affection with God. As is true in any relationship, love grows when people spend time together and truly get to know the essence of the other person. One of the reasons marriages become dull, stagnant, and unhappy is because the partners have not placed a priority on continually cultivating their relationship. Your love for God will grow when you intentionally make time to learn about God through reading and meditating on the scriptures. Your love will grow when you make time to pray to your all-loving God. Your love for God will grow when you intentionally start telling God how you feel. Even if at first you feel awkward, tell God "I love you" every day!

After a while, the love you feel for God will gush out of your soul like a river.

Dear God, I love you! I adore you! There is no one like you in the world. Today I pray that all I do or say will demonstrate my love to you. Help me love you more. Amen.

May 15   **Making Time to Love Others**

"This is my commandment, that you love one another as I have loved you." (John 15:12 NRSV)

Let's be real. It's much easier to love God than to love some people. Some people can be mean and deceptive. Some have horrible dispositions. Some are downright unreliable. Some will use and abuse you. The scriptural commandment instructs us to love others. The instruction is not an option but a demand. This type of love demands that we want the very best for others. We do things that promote the well-being of other people. You say, "How can I possibly love so and so after what has transpired between us? You don't know what that person has done to me." You are right. I don't know, but God does. Love that person by first forgiving him or her. Love that person by praying to God and asking God to work in his or her life. Pray for that person's salvation and peace. Pray for that person to be delivered from the hurts and pains that have impaired his or her actions. Loving frees you from the prison of heartache.

God, you know this is hard. I choose this day to love_____. Please let this person know the depth of your love for her or him. Please open his or her eyes to see life as you do. And if reconciliation is possible, work your wonderful power. Amen.

May 16   Making Time to Love Yourself

"You shall love your neighbor as yourself." (Mark 12:31 NRSV)

In order to love someone else appropriately, you've got to love yourself first. Oh, sure, you have been told that you've got to take care of everyone else's cares and concerns. You've got to be the giver of the all-sacrificial love at your expense. Someone even may have told you that you are unlovable, and in response you entered into relationships where you lived into that self-fulfilling prophecy.

Take time to love yourself, my sister. Consider what is best for you. Concern yourself with your own well-being, just as you do for others. Make time to do things you enjoy. Read. Walk in the park. Go to movies or plays. Turn off the phone, lock the bathroom door, and take a bubble bath. Pamper yourself occasionally at the day spa. Radiate on God's love for you. You are worth it. You are precious; and when you understand yourself that way, you will be free to treat others even better than you did before. Once you do, people will alter their perceptions and actions toward you to adjust to your new attitude. Sister, love yourself!

Dear God, I confess that I haven't loved myself as much as I should. I always thought it was inappropriate to think that way. Help me love myself appropriately so that I can better love others. Amen.

May 17   Making Time to Appreciate How God Created You

I praise you, for I am fearfully and wonderfully made. Wonderful are your works; that I know very well. (Psalm 139:14 NRSV)

One of the hardest things for most women to do is to love themselves. That's understandable in this culture that attempts to make all women fit into the mold of a size-six figure. Let's be real: Professional models struggle to remain that size. It's difficult to love yourself when society tells you that your hair is too long or too short, too kinky or too straight; your hips or breasts aren't the right size; your skin color is wrong; your weight is a little off. What is a woman to do?

Sister girl, look in the mirror and see how beautiful you really are—externally and internally. Appreciate who you are in Christ. You are the handiwork of God, and God doesn't make any junk. Tell yourself that you are a beautiful woman, created and loved by God. Counter all the negative messages you've internalized and affirm the reality that you are fearfully and wonderfully made. Smile at yourself and let the beauty of God radiate into the world. The world cannot contain all your God-given beauty. The righteousness of God streams through you to the world. Enjoy who you are!

Dear God, stretch marks, age lines, and other imperfections notwithstanding, you created me and therefore I am good. No longer will I discount the beauty you have bestowed upon me. I thank you that I am wonderfully made. Amen.

May 18   Making Time for God's Provision

And my God will fully satisfy every need of yours according to his riches in glory in Christ Jesus. (Philippians 4:19 NRSV)

As I write this, the economy is down. Just reviewing the monthly financial losses in my pension statements would cause me to doubt my ability to ever retire and take care of my financial responsibilities. Emergency-room bills are about to make a visit to my house, and it's time to pay Uncle Sam. Downsizing is occurring right and left, and those who remain have to master the art of multitasking. We live in uncertain times. Like me, you probably find yourself occasionally with more bills than money, not knowing exactly what to do. One thing is for sure: Worrying about the situation is not going to change a thing. When you've done all that you can, it's good to remember that you have some divine help. You don't have to do it all by yourself. God will help you meet your needs.

There have been countless times when God has provided me with unexpected money to pay a bill. Go to God in prayer and ask for help. Expect God to show up and show out right on time. God will supply your needs.

Dear God, I am your child and need your help. Thank you in advance for supplying my needs in Christ Jesus. Amen.

May 19 **Making Time for Receiving Forgiveness from God**

"For if you forgive others their trespasses, your heavenly Father will also forgive you." (Matthew 6:14 NRSV)

In one Bible dictionary, forgiveness is defined as to "send away, remove or cover," which communicates God's intent and desire to eliminate sin. Sin always results in brokenness, with God and with others. Sin represents anything that usurps God's order for creation.

The prophets called the people to repent of their sins and turn back to the Lord. God instituted a system of sacrifices to effect forgiveness of sins. Ultimately, to end that system, Jesus became the final sacrifice and died a painful, horrible death on the cross for the sins of all humanity. Despite how good we think we are, we still need God's forgiveness. Our very relationship with the Divine is tied to the task of asking God to forgive us. Let's face it: We all rebel against the goodness and ways of God. Yet it's the mercy of God that covers and eliminates those sins so that we can better reflect God's original plans for our lives. Forgiven, we show the reflection of God to the world. The most important aspect of God's forgiveness is that it will not be granted in the absence of our forgiveness toward others. We can't have the one without the other. We need to grant it as much as God needs to grant it to us.

Dear God, please forgive me for those things I've done to sin against you. I desire to be in right relationship with you. Amen.

May 20 **Making Time for the Forgiveness of Others**

"And forgive us our debts, as we also have forgiven our debtors." (Matthew 6:12 NRSV)

There's nothing quite as painful as being betrayed or harmed by someone who is supposed to love you. I remember the pain I felt when I discovered that a man I dated had cheated on me. Blind to any signs of problems, I didn't understand when he broke up with me one weekend and brought his new girlfriend to the church we both attended the next Sunday. It was like he put a knife in my heart and twisted it. That kind of "in your face" behavior is hard to swallow, let alone forgive. But even in that situation, I was challenged to forgive him. Each and every time I prayed, "Forgive us our sins as we forgive those who sin against us," I was reminded of the divine directive to forgive.

God knows it wasn't easy, but one day I was genuinely able to say I had forgiven him. What freedom I felt. Forgiving someone was really possible! No longer did those emotions hold me captive. Peace had replaced anger, pain, and resentment.

Forgiving someone does more for you than it does for the other person, for it frees you to live an abundant life of joy. The harbored pain can eventually kill you. Forgiveness promotes reconciled relationships and ensures God's forgiveness of our sins. Give it a try!

God, I choose to forgive each person I name to you now. There are many people I need to forgive. Please remind me of people I've forgotten. Because you have forgiven me, I can do no less. Amen.

May 21   Making Time for Renewing the Mind

Do not be conformed to this world, but be transformed by the renewing of your minds, so that you may discern what is the will of God—what is good and acceptable and perfect. (Romans 12:2 NRSV)

The world's system is not as good as it's made out to be. Wrong is often touted as right. People are considered expendable. People are encouraged to get rich at the expense of others. Anything and everything is acceptable. A lie is not a lie. Personal integrity is not important. "If it feels good, do it" is commonplace.

The world's way of life is not God's way. It is directly counter to the way and will of God. To successfully make it in God's system, you must learn to transform your thinking. This world will have you operating with a messed up mind process, and if you are unable to get your mind straight, you will eventually suffer from spiritual schizophrenia. We know what the world says, but how do we know what God says? Make time to read the Bible. Participate regularly in a Bible study. Meditate and study the scriptures. For in them we discover health, hope, peace, and love in a world that promotes death, hopelessness, war, and hatred. God's way is always good.

Dear God, your ways are always good. Help me renew my mind by learning more about your ways. I want to know you better. Amen.

May 22   **Making Time to Work on God's Temple**
Inside of You

Do you not know that you are God's temple and that God's Spirit dwells in you?
(1 Corinthians 3:16 NRSV)

OK, sister friend, how's your temple? Is it tired and run-down? Is it getting regular exercise and appropriate nutrition? Is it in need of a spiritual tune-up? Is it well kept? Is it getting the appropriate diet of the Word? Does it reflect the beauty and righteousness of God? Does it need to be cleaned of any filth? Is it a place where the Spirit of God can reside in peace and glory?

The scriptures speak of the beauty of the Temple of Jerusalem. With elaborately designed furnishings made of stone, wood, and metals, it was spectacular. It had to be beautiful because it was there, in the place "designated as the house of God," that the Spirit of our all-perfect God resided.

How did you say your personal temple was looking? Make time to get things in order in your body, the temple of the Living God. You take care of everyone and everything else. Take care of yourself. Be intentional to continuously develop spiritually and physically. Do some spring cleaning to get rid of the spiritual clutter and junk. Make it look as the temple of God should look—spectacular.

Dear God, help me make the necessary improvements for this temple. May you always find a welcoming residence here. Amen.

May 23   **Making Time to Win the Race**

Therefore, since we are surrounded by so great a cloud of witnesses, let us also lay aside every weight and the sin that clings so closely, and let us run with perseverance the race that is set before us. (Hebrews 12:1 NRSV)

Ready! Set! Go! Those were the words my firstborn shouted before he proceeded to race with his mommy. The spiritual journey is a race, of sorts. The ultimate goal is to complete the course. The outcome of the race is not determined by a runner's swiftness alone. Instead, it is established by the person's resolve to complete the race even in the presence of opposition, physical and mental challenges, and unexpected obstacles. On the way to the finish line, various things and powers will attempt to stop your progress.

A friend of mine trained for months in preparation for a marathon. When the race was underway, she encountered numerous challenges—feet cramps, leg pain, and so forth. But she didn't give up. Somehow she completed the race. She walked a while. She ran a while. Though she wasn't the first one across the finish line, she completed the race nonetheless. Don't give up! Keep on running! Keep on striving! I know it's hard and it hurts sometimes. But don't give up.

Dear God, help me run this race set before me. When I become tired, give me the strength to continue the race. Amen.

May 24   Making Time to Claim Your Power

For the one who is in you is greater than the one who is in the world. (1 John 4:4b NRSV)

Do you know who you are? Do you know the extent of your strength? You've got a whole lot more in you than you know! Yeah, it may seem that all of hell has waged a frontal attack on your finances, family, relationships, health, or job. You may not know which way to turn or what to do, but you are not without the weapons needed for the battle you are in. God resides in you. God is bigger than any demon or problem that comes your way. Claim who and whose you are in Christ, and start talking to that situation. Take authority over it and demand that it bow in the name of Jesus. Don't just allow the problem to run over you. Claim your power and authority and challenge the mess. Don't be swayed by what you see but, instead, hold on to God's perspective on the situation. No weapon formed against you will prosper. Sin doesn't have dominion over you. You've got the power! You've got God's power. Now use it.

Dear God, you have given your children power over all of the works of the enemy. I now claim and operate in that power. Thank you. Amen.

May 25   Making Time to Experience the Impossible

"For nothing will be impossible with God." (Luke 1:37 NRSV)

"How do you do it? With a full-time and demanding ministry, small children, husband, aging mother, and a house? How do you keep it all together?" Those questions posed by a friend now ring in my mind. By all intents and purposes, I shouldn't have it all together. As I write this meditation it is 4:00 A.M., and I'm holding a teething ten-month-old who, for the moment, is asleep. The deadline for this project is upon me. Life has not slowed down, and my responsibilities seem to have increased. But somehow, I am able to keep things together. Is all in this life of mine perfect? Nope. But, what should be impossible somehow becomes a possibility.

My sister, God is good. God will always help you in a bind. Time and time again, God has helped me. What God has done for me, God will do for you. When your back is against the wall and it looks like all hope is gone, don't forget that God specializes in impossibilities. Try God! God likes to provide you with supernatural ability needed to overcome adverse situations.

God, without you this would all be impossible. Thank you for keeping and sustaining me. Amen.

May 26   **Making Time to Operate Under God's Power for Ministry**

"But you will receive power when the Holy Spirit has come upon you; and you will be my witnesses." (Acts 1:8 NRSV)

You are a together sister! You are a powerhouse of a woman. But that is just on your own personal strength and ability. Imagine what you could do under the power of the Holy Spirit.

To succeed in things spiritual, to fight this spiritual battle, you need spiritual power. We don't wrestle against flesh and blood but against spiritual powers and principalities in high places. They don't fight fair. You can't whup the devil using human intellect or power. You need the power of the Holy Spirit to break yokes of oppression and minister healing to others. You need the power of the Holy Spirit to communicate the love of God to others in ways that melt their hearts. You need that power, or anointing of the Holy Spirit, to proclaim with boldness that Jesus is Lord. Now, if Jesus operated under the power of the Holy Spirit, how can we think that we don't need the Holy Spirit? After the Resurrection, the disciples of Jesus yearned for that power, praying and waiting for that reality to become manifest in their lives. Pray that the Holy Spirit will come upon you and your religious community so that you can be bold witnesses of the gospel.

115

Holy Spirit, you are welcome in this temple. Come and dwell with me. Lead me in ministry. Amen.

May 27   **Making Time for Joy!**

Weeping may linger for the night, but joy comes with the morning. (Psalm 30:5b NRSV)

"Wilpas." Each time I'd see this e-mail address of a former campus ministry colleague, I'd always wonder what it meant. When I finally asked her, she explained that those letters stood for the words "will pass." She used that address to remind herself that all of life's difficult situations will pass. Storms come into our lives. Hardships try to beat us down. We may even feel that God doesn't hear our prayers. Things happen that make us want to cry. And sometimes it seems that we will never get out from under the pressure trying to break us. But, sister, this too will pass. You may cry tonight and tomorrow, but the time will come when you will laugh again. It may be raining today, but the sun has to come out again sometime. Nothing can or will keep you down forever.

Do you find yourself going through a difficult time right now? Is your heart breaking? This too will pass. Go ahead and cry right now. It's good to get it out. But know that it will soon be time to get ready for your joy!

God, I'm sure glad that troubles don't last forever. Thank you that the sun will shine again in my life. Amen.

May 28   **Making Time to Give God Thanks**

O give thanks to the LORD, call on his name, make known his deeds among the peoples. (Psalm 105:1 NRSV)

It was as if a lightbulb went on in my mind. As I attended a lunchtime board meeting in the executive dining room of a major bank and listened to an engaging discussion on community entrepreneurship, all of a sudden I asked myself: *How in the world did I get here?* Me. A descendant of people reviled in this society—slaves and free blacks as well as farmers, teachers, and doctors. I was there not because of any personal merit but because of God's favor and faithfulness to the prayers of my ancestors. Sitting there, I started to think about all that God had done for me throughout my life. After the death of my father, God enabled my mother to raise me and send me to college without any student loans. I've met two United States presidents. I'm one of the youngest program management staff at my agency. My ministry allows me to influence ministries on national and international levels. Silently I shouted, "Thank you, God!"

God is good and deserves our thanksgiving. I don't thank God enough. But today I challenge you to join with me in thanking God who has done so much for all of us.

God, thank you! Thank you! Thank you! You have done so many things for me. I just can't tell it all. Amen.

May 29   Making Time to Enjoy God's Love for You

For as the heavens are high above the earth, so great is his steadfast love toward those who fear him. (Psalm 103:11 NRSV)

If there is one thing you need to always remember, it is that God loves you. If no one else loves you, God does. If your parents turn their backs on you, and your friends forsake you, God loves you. If your significant other has tried to make you feel unlovable, God loves you. You are precious to God. Don't ever doubt that! God wants you to rest in the knowledge of that love. That love concerns itself with your welfare and future, your relationships and ministry.

Next time you go outside, close your eyes and turn your face up toward the sun. Feel the heat on your face. That is God's loving embrace on you. Sistah friend, the affection God has for you is limitless. Nothing will ever stop God from loving you. With that kind of love, you can face and do anything. How much does God love you? As high as the heavens are above the earth. How much does God love you? God loves you so much that his Son hung on a cross with arms stretched wide enough to embrace you in his agony. Now, that is love.

Dear God, it is good to know that you always love me. Thank you for your love. Amen.

May 30　　　　　　　　　　　**Making Time to Cultivate**
God's Gift in You

For this reason I remind you to rekindle the gift of God that is within you through the laying on of my hands. (2 Timothy 1:6 NRSV)

There is some truth to the old adage "Use it or lose it." If you don't exercise, your muscles will lose their tone. If you don't practice your craft, you will not improve. The same holds true in spiritual matters. We have to continually and intentionally cultivate our gifts. For God's gift in you to increase in strength and power, you have to nurture and develop it. Take time to learn about your gift. Take time to use it. Every person who ever did anything great for God had to start somewhere. Everyone had to start small by taking baby steps. Everyone with the gift of administration had to learn to administer. Every person with the gift of healing had to lay hands on someone and trust that something was going to happen.

What gift is in you? Sure, the prospect seems a bit unsettling. You may even doubt your ability to produce, but you can do it. God has not only gifted you but also invited you to be on God's team. Go ahead!

Dear God, thank you for trusting me with this special gift. I commit to nurture and cultivate it. Amen.

May 31　　　　　　　　　**Making Time for "In the Meantime**
Experiences"

But those who wait for the LORD shall renew their strength, they shall mount up with wings like eagles, they shall run and not be weary, they shall walk and not faint. (Isaiah 40:31 NRSV)

Every woman has found herself in a waiting period. We wait in line at the grocery store. We wait for a mail-order item to come. We wait to give birth to a baby, or to hear of the birth of a child we're adopting. We often wait for God to touch our situations. Waiting is difficult and often painful. To say that God operates on our schedule would be a lie. There are times when it seems that God has forgotten our plight and has turned a deaf ear to our situation.

What are we to do in the meantime? We are to wait in expectation for God to do something. We are to trust in the Lord with all our strength, not leaning to our own understanding. We are to pray and sing with the knowledge that God is still concerned about our situation and will be faithful. We are to feed our spirit with the Word. We are to joyfully wait for God to show up and show out.

As we wait, let us rest in our knowledge of our faithful God. In the end, we will find we have new strength that will help us respond to all life will throw our way.

Dear God, in my periods of waiting, help me expectantly know that you will still show up. You have been faithful to me in the past, and I thank you that you will do the same in the future. I love you and will remember your faithfulness at all times and in all seasons. Amen.

J U N E

Altars Along the Journey

Nancy Nikolai

June 1   **Building Altars**

"Then let us arise and go up to Bethel; and I will make an altar there to God, who answered me in the day of my distress and has been with me in the way which I have gone." (Genesis 35:3 NKJV)

There were many reasons people in the Old Testament built altars. They built them to thank God and give him the glory, to commemorate and celebrate God's faithfulness, and to pass on those stories of God's goodness for generations to come. They were tangible reminders of moments when God made his presence known to them.

We may not have altars of stone, but if we are traveling with the Lord as our companion in this life, we will have plenty of "altars" along the journey. There will be instances in which God intervenes in our life as only he can. It is those moments we must capture somehow and share with those we love so that the moments will not be forgotten.

This month I have the honor and privilege of sharing some of my "altars" with you, which I have collected on this adventure with our incredible Savior. It is my hope and prayer that you will be inspired to "build" your own.

Dear Father, bring to mind the many things you have done in my life, and give me opportunities to tell others about them. Amen.

June 2   **Hospitality to Strangers**

Let brotherly love continue. Do not forget to entertain strangers, for by so doing some have unwittingly entertained angels. (Hebrews 13:1-2 NKJV)

My mother once told me a true story that happened in my home church. A bedraggled, dirty looking stranger came into the fellowship hall where church members were enjoying a weekly fellowship meal together. He was quietly ushered to the kitchen where he was fed and then led out the back door to the alley behind the church.

A guest preacher was to speak at the service following the meal, but as time for the service approached, the preacher had not yet arrived.

As the congregation sang the first hymn, the indigent whom they had fed earlier came down the aisle and stood in front of them. The music stopped. The man removed his dirty overcoat to reveal a nice suit. He wiped his face and hands clean and combed his hair back. He was not an indigent at all but the guest preacher who was to speak that night; however, the message had been given without saying a word.

Dear Lord, help me remember that every person is precious in your sight and needs to be treated with respect, dignity, and kindness. Amen.

June 3   The Empty Pews

Now thanks be to God who always leads us in triumph in Christ, and through us diffuses the fragrance of His knowledge in every place. For we are to God the fragrance of Christ among those who are being saved and among those who are perishing. (2 Corinthians 2:14-15 NKJV)

I woke up to a sickening smell. As I walked sleepily into my grandmother's kitchen, I asked her what the horrible odor was. She explained to me how the dog had chased a skunk under the house during the night and we were all now suffering the consequences of his actions.

As our family prepared to go to my grandmother's church that Sunday morning, we did everything we could to stifle the putrid smell. Nothing worked. We would have to go to the small community church as we were!

My grandparents, parents, brothers, sister, and I took up a whole pew. However, even at the age of eight, I quickly realized other people's subtle reactions to our plight. The pews in front and behind of us were completely empty, and church members made sour faces or held their noses after walking past us.

It's a humorous memory now, but it also provokes a more serious thought. As Christians, we are to have the aroma of Christ. What kind of aroma do you convey to others? Could it be anger, jealousy, gossip, or impatience? Or do you exude the fruitful fragrance of the Holy Spirit?

Lord, help me remember that I represent you in this world. Let people be attracted and drawn to you through me. Amen.

June 4   The Treasure of Older People

When I call to remembrance the genuine faith that is in you, which dwelt first in your grandmother Lois and your mother Eunice, and I am persuaded is in you also. (2 Timothy 1:5 NKJV)

"Momma, can I go over to Mayfield and Dewey's?" The answer was almost always yes. They were a sweet elderly couple who lived across the street and loved me as if I were their own granddaughter. The feeling was mutual, and almost every day, my dog, Judge, and I would make the trip to their house to get a piece of candy and talk for a while.

As the years passed, they applauded and encouraged me, counseled me, laughed at my silly jokes, and helped me remember what was truly important in life. But most of all, they believed in me. They truly had an impact on my life, and over the years I have thanked God for the gifts he gave me in my relationship with them.

My parents and my husband's parents live far away now, so I have prayed through the years that God would place older people in our children's lives to love and cherish them. He has been faithful to do so, and I know their lives will be richer because of it.

Lord, thank you for the treasures we have in older people. Help us be patient, listen to their stories, and gain wisdom as a result. Amen.

June 5   Fear of God

"And do not fear those who kill the body but cannot kill the soul. But rather fear Him who is able to destroy both soul and body in hell." (Matthew 10:28 NKJV)

The moment I arrived in the Irish Channel, I knew I was in a different world. The mission where I would be spending the summer was located near the St. Thomas housing project, in the inner city of New Orleans, Louisiana. The mission was a nice brick building, but there were bars on the windows. The upstairs door, which led to the area where I would eat and sleep, had two deadbolts installed. To say I was out of my comfort zone would be a huge understatement.

I felt fairly safe despite the security precautions taken around me, until the third night I was there. At about nine o'clock that night, I heard something that sounded like a firecracker going off. I was told the next morning that a teenage boy had been killed in the park across the street because of a "drug deal gone bad." I was now afraid for my life and seriously questioning my reasons for being there.

After praying earnestly about the situation, I felt God's peace in staying there. I knew the safest place to be was in God's will.

Lord, thank you for your protection. Thank you also for the opportunities you give me to love those who are different. Amen.

June 6   Tough Love

"Behold, I send you out as sheep in the midst of wolves. Therefore be wise as serpents and harmless as doves." (Matthew 10:16 NKJV)

There I was in the middle of the inner city of New Orleans. Being a small-town girl, I was experiencing new situations and having to learn very quickly about my new environment. It was culture shock.

My second day at the mission, I learned what my responsibilities would be. I would conduct a Bible school for forty or so first and second graders all by myself. Being an optimist, I thought I would be very sweet to these underprivileged children, and they would respond with thankfulness and fascination with what I had to teach. Oh, how naïve I was! They ate me for lunch, so to speak.

That afternoon, I went into the missionary's office with tears in my eyes and told her I could not do it. I was ready to go home. She taught me about loving children enough to give them boundaries, and being consistent in enforcing the consequences, a lesson I never forgot as a teacher or a mother. I stayed, things got better, and I learned being a Christian sometimes means having a tough love.

Lord, please give me the courage and wisdom to handle difficult situations when they arise. May I handle them as Jesus would. Amen.

June 7   Making Christ Known

That if you confess with your mouth the Lord Jesus and believe in your heart that God has raised Him from the dead, you will be saved. For with the heart one believes to righteousness, and with the mouth confession is made to salvation. (Romans 10:9-10 NKJV)

One of the most wonderful experiences during my summer in New Orleans was when I had the privilege of sharing this verse with the children. Many of them responded, praying to receive Jesus Christ as their Savior, but only after I had spent several weeks building a relationship of trust with them. They knew I loved them and cared about their future.

As the summer drew to a close, I knew God was prompting me to change my major at college from mass communications to elementary education. At the time I didn't understand why I was being drawn to do this, but in later years I would see how the Lord would weave all these experiences into the tapestry of my life.

I also renewed my commitment to follow wherever the Lord would lead. I now knew I could trust him, even with my very own life. My number one desire was, and still is, to confess Jesus Christ so that others can come to salvation.

Dear Father, thank you for your salvation and the privilege to proclaim your son, Jesus Christ, to a lost and dying world. Amen.

June 8   The Binder of Wounds

The sacrifices of God are a broken spirit, A broken and a contrite heart—These, O God, You will not despise. (Psalm 51:17 NKJV)

During my last semester in college, my friend Ronda told me about a guy she met at church whom she thought I should meet. When I met Pete, I knew he was special, but I was dating someone else. On the day of graduation, my boyfriend and I ended our relationship. I was brokenhearted, but I knew God was in control.

After graduation, I became a teacher in the same town. It was Valentine's Day, and I had had a rough afternoon. Wanting to avoid all the couples, I told Ronda I was going to a lecture at the university. She exclaimed, "No, you're not. You're going to go to a movie with Pete!" I laughed as she picked up the phone and dialed his number. I thought she was kidding as she asked into the phone, "Hey, Pete, how would you like to go to a movie with Nancy?" and then handed me the receiver. Then I heard his voice: "So, which movie do you want to see?"

After that night, Pete and I started spending more time together as friends. As our relationship grew, the Lord began to heal the huge wound in my heart and restore my hope.

Lord, thank you for being there during my times of heartbreak. Help me trust in your loving care so that you may heal me. Amen.

June 9   A Bright Future

"Do not remember the former things, Nor consider the things of old. Behold, I will do a new thing, Now it shall spring forth; Shall you not know it?" (Isaiah 43:18-19a NKJV)

Pete and I had been spending time together for several weeks, and even though I was very attracted to this tall, dark-headed, and handsome man, I had other plans. I was in the interview process of a missions program in which I would spend two years in Bukoba, Tanzania, in East Africa.

As I went to the headquarters for my final interview, we were given time to go pray about our decision. I prayed, "Lord, it's very simple. If you don't want me to go to Tanzania, just place a brick wall in the way. Otherwise, I'm going." I prayed this because I felt sure that this missions program was what God wanted me to do. He wanted me to sacrifice everything for him, and that must mean he wanted me to go to Africa, right?

When I returned home, Pete realized his time with me was short. By the next week, we were talking about marriage, and I knew God had answered my prayer. Pete was the man I had always dreamed of—and my brick wall. God's plan for my future was definitely best!

Lord, thank you for caring about my hopes and dreams, and for knowing what is truly best for me. Amen.

June 10   Purpose Under Heaven

Do not be afraid of sudden terror, Nor of trouble from the wicked when it comes; For the LORD will be your confidence, And will keep your foot from being caught. (Proverbs 3:25-26 NKJV)

When Pete and I had been married for two weeks, I was told I would be working at an inner-city school. I probably surprised the administrator by saying, "Great!"

My experiences in New Orleans prepared me for a lot of the situations I faced. I was not shocked easily, I quickly earned the respect of my students, and I prayed earnestly for my precious third graders and the challenges they faced every day.

I was not prepared, however, when a fourth-grade girl from our school was kidnapped and brutally murdered. The murderer was still at large, and I found myself on my knees in prayer on behalf of the children of that school. One day, shortly after the incident, a student raised his hand and asked, "Mrs. Nikolai, where do you think she is?" All my students looked at my face in search of an answer. Holding back the tears, I told him, "I believe, if she knew Jesus as her Savior, she is in heaven." Many of my students, being Catholic, nodded in agreement; and I've since prayed that the impact of that moment will prompt them to know the Savior in a personal way and come to have the peace and confidence that only he gives.

Dear Lord, when I experience a death or loss, give me the words to comfort others in the midst of my own grief. Amen.

June 11   God Our Provider

My brethren, count it all joy when you fall into various trials, knowing that the testing of your faith produces patience. (James 1:2 NKJV)

My husband, Pete, had been unemployed for six months. We both felt that God was encouraging us to continue trusting him, but it was a challenge to have faith when we needed to provide for ourselves and our nine-month-old baby boy.

Then an unexpected blessing occurred. I began to feel the signs of pregnancy. Even though we did want a second child, the timing was awful—or at least I thought. I went to a local crisis pregnancy center, where I had been a counselor, and took a pregnancy test. I came home with tears of joy and yet fear of the unknown.

As I told my husband the bittersweet news, he held me tenderly and said, "We'll look back nine months from now and see how the Lord has provided." We laid everything before the Lord, and God rewarded our faith. Two weeks later Pete had a wonderful job, and a month later we found out that insurance would pay most of the pregnancy and delivery expenses. Pete was right. Nine months later we were able to look back and praise God for his faithfulness!

Lord, thank you for your incredible provision, and thank you for building my faith in you through the hard times. Amen.

June 12   The Little Prayer Warrior

For I will pour water on him who is thirsty, And floods on the dry ground; I will pour My Spirit on your descendants, And My blessing on your offspring. (Isaiah 44:3 NKJV)

I was pregnant with our third child. One night, I awoke at four o'clock in the morning and began praying for the child I was bearing. I felt the clear impression that God was speaking to me about our son: "He will be a prayer warrior." As I kept this in my heart after our son, John, was born, there were several times I saw him fulfill what the Lord had told me about him.

When John was four years old, I had a terrible wreck as I was driving alone in our car. I was blessed to come out of it alive and without injuries. However, the car was totaled. After talking to the police and EMT personnel, I shakily sat in our other vehicle while Pete took care of details. All four of our children surrounded me with questions of concern, but John went further. He laid his precious little hand on my shoulder and prayed, "God, thank you Mommy is OK, and help her not be scared anymore. In Jesus' name. Amen."

Lord, help me recognize and pray for the gifts you've given my children and loved ones. May they glorify and honor you. Amen.

June 13   Hide-and-Seek

Where can I go from Your Spirit? Or where can I flee from Your presence? If I … dwell in the uttermost parts of the sea, Even there Your hand shall lead me, And Your right hand shall hold me. (Psalm 139:7-10 NKJV)

When my children were all babies, it would intrigue me when they started playing peek-a-boo. They would sometimes keep their hands over their eyes, thinking I could not see them if they could not see me. When they first started playing hide-and-seek, I would try not to laugh as they told me where they were going to hide, or as they hid in the most obvious places. They also loved to hide under the covers in the morning when I first awoke, squealing with laughter as I tickled them.

Do I play the same games with God? Are there times when I think he does not see me or understand my thoughts? Do I shut my eyes to his precepts, thinking that if I do, they don't exist? Do I lack trust when he doesn't answer my prayer my way, in my time?

I think we all play these games and others with God at one time or another, but they are not games. They are misconceptions of who God is, and I realize how ridiculous they are when I look at my life through his perspective.

Lord, help me live my life before you honestly, and help me be constantly aware of and thankful for your watchful care. Amen.

June 14   The Great Shepherd

Yea, though I walk through the valley of the shadow of death, I will fear no evil; For You are with me; Your rod and Your staff, they comfort me. (Psalm 23:4 NKJV)

Our third child, John, was only six months old and I was staying at my parents' home with the children while Pete was out of town on business. Then I received a call from Pete.

My very healthy husband had become sick and had been admitted to a hospital in Denver. The doctors could not find what was wrong, and he became more and more incoherent every day. The third night Pete called, he could barely talk. I knew I had to get to Denver, even though we did not have the money. That night, I was praying for Pete when God stopped me. I heard in my heart, "Do you want him to live?" "Yes, Lord, of course, I do!" I answered. "Then pray for him to live," he said. I fell on my knees immediately.

I didn't realize it then, but Pete was fighting for his life. He had a small pinhole-sized leak in his appendix, and the poison had been leaking into his body for four days. However, because of the uncharacteristic way the organ had ruptured, it had the doctors puzzled. God spanned the miles to prompt me to pray at just the right moment. I discovered firsthand that our God truly is with us through the valleys.

Dear Lord, I praise you that you are an all-knowing God, and that you are with me even when I must look death in the face. Amen.

June 15   God or Chariots?

Some trust in chariots, and some in horses; But we will remember the name of the LORD our God. They have bowed and fallen; But we have risen and stand upright. (Psalm 20:7-8 NKJV)

The morning after Pete's disturbing phone call, I received another call from the vice president of the company Pete worked for. He told me that I needed to be there with Pete, and that they were flying John, our six-month-old baby, and me to Denver. They would handle all the other arrangements. Although I was concerned, I had a peace, the kind that passes understanding.

As John and I were getting settled on the plane, a gentleman wearing a very expensive suit boarded and sat next to me. He began asking me questions about John, and we started a conversation. He spoke most of the time, and the topic of conversation seemed to dwell on his expensive house, wealthy friends, numerous possessions, and triple-digit income.

When the plane began to land, he asked, "So, what brings you to Denver?" As I told him the events leading up to that day, saying that at that precise moment my husband was having exploratory surgery, his jaw dropped. "How in the world are you handling this so calmly?" he asked. I then had the opportunity to tell him about my relationship with Jesus Christ, and how I knew everything was in the Lord's hands.

Look for your opportunity to "remember the name of the Lord" today.

Lord, give me a love for those who are lost. Help me remember not to place my trust in my possessions, but in you. Amen.

June 16   God Renews Strength

He gives power to the weak, And to those who have no might He increases strength. Even the youths shall faint and be weary, And the young men shall utterly fall, but those who wait on the LORD Shall renew their strength. (Isaiah 40:29-31a NKJV)

Pete had just come out of surgery and was in the intensive care unit. When I walked into the room, I now realized how bad the situation was. He looked gaunt from not eating in four days, and he had tubes coming out of everywhere. The doctor told me that if they had not gone in when they did, Pete would have died within the hour. He was in very good shape going into this, and that is what saved his life.

The fight was not over yet. Pete still had the poison all in his body. My visits were limited to twenty minutes three times a day, and all I could do was let him know I was there. Every morning I woke up, got on my knees, and prayed for several hours. As I did, the Lord showed me verses to strengthen my faith in him.

One day, I went to a nearby town to get away from it all. As I sat on a restaurant patio, I felt a wonderful cool breeze, and I knew it was the Lord telling me, "I love you, and it will be OK." Pete did recover, and we both learned what a precious gift this life is.

When we're so weak and weary that we think we can't go on, our Lord is always faithful to renew our strength.

Lord, help me depend on your strength and not my own. Thank you for being there in my desperate times of need. Amen.

June 17   Respecting Those in Authority

Obey those who rule over you, and be submissive, for they watch out for your souls, as those who must give account. (Hebrews 13:17 NKJV)

I was driving what I thought was the speed limit, but I was in a school zone. A policeman was right there to stop me. I was given a citation and told I would have to appear before a judge in one week. All the way home I answered my young children's questions about why the policeman had given me that piece of paper, and why he had not taken me to jail.

When my time came to appear in court, I was very nervous. I went early in the morning, and there was only one other case in front of mine. The lady ahead of me argued with the judge and stomped out of the courtroom, putting him in a really bad mood to hear my case.

As I approached the bench, the judge asked me if I was pleading "contest" or "no contest." I spouted out what I had rehearsed: "Guilty!" As the judge grinned slightly, he stated my speed as lower than it actually was. When I corrected him and told him I was actually going faster, he looked at me for a second and said, "I'm throwing out this case."

Respecting authority is not limited to the courtroom. Ask God to show you where you need to respectfully submit to authority in your life.

Lord, help me be respectful to authorities even when I may disagree with them, and help me always be truthful even when it may hurt. Amen.

June 18   The Lord's Work

The eyes of your understanding being enlightened; that you may know what is the hope of His calling, what are the riches of the glory of His inheritance in the saints. (Ephesians 1:18 NKJV)

As I sat in an auditorium seat at a church camp, I remembered how years before, in that same seat, I had surrendered my life and services to the Lord, fully expecting to be sent to Africa or some far-off place as a missionary.

Here I was, fifteen years later, coming to the same camp to learn how to start a prayer ministry for the schools in my area. Now, I was a mother of four beautiful children and a wife to a wonderful, godly man. However, sometimes I had wondered if I had missed my calling. God gently reminded me that I had been in the center of his will all along. I felt such a peace, comfort, and joy as I praised God for his faithfulness in guiding me through all those years. He had given me the desires of my heart while showing me the needs of those in my own community.

Lord, thank you for the privilege of serving you. Amen.

June 19   The Bully

Plead my cause, O LORD, with those who strive with me; Fight against those who fight against me. (Psalm 35:1 NKJV)

My oldest son's fifth-grade teacher asked me during a parent-teacher conference to watch for signs of someone bullying my son. She suspected a large boy in the class, but my son James would not tell her anything out of fear of being ostracized. After arriving home, I laid my concern before the Lord and asked him to reveal any problems to me.

That afternoon, James came home in tears, which was very uncharacteristic for him. He explained how this large boy had, indeed, been singling him out, and how it was becoming worse and worse. I asked him, "What do you think you should do?" He answered, "Mom, I know if I say or do anything back, I'll get in trouble and my reputation will be ruined; but I'm just tired of it." I reassured him that my prayer group would lift him up the next day. He replied, "Mom, pray hard."

Within three weeks the bully was suspended from school for a variety of reasons, and the problem was resolved. What a powerful lesson this was for all of us.

Lord, help me remember that you genuinely care for me and my loved ones and our concerns. Thank you for hearing my cry for help. Amen.

June 20   True Treasures

I will bless the LORD at all times; His praise shall continually be in my mouth. (Psalm 34:1 NKJV)

Pete and I were excited. It was our first vacation to take with only our family. Up until then, we had taken trips to see our parents, who lived in Minnesota and Arkansas. Those were wonderful and special times, but we also felt the need to spend some special bonding time alone with our children.

We planned it carefully, choosing a cabin in the Great Smoky Mountains near Gatlinburg, Tennessee. It had a front porch, complete with a swing, rocking chairs, and a game table.

I will never forget our first night there. As the sun began to lower in the sky and show the beautiful hues on the horizon, we experienced a breathtaking view of the mountains from the front porch. Pete and I sat cuddling on the swing as we watched our children chase fireflies, the children oblivious to the event that was taking place. It was a treasure-filled moment. So rare, but perhaps that's what makes them so precious.

Father, thank you for the times of love, laughter, peace, and joy we experience in this life. Help us savor them. Amen.

June 21   There's No Place Like Home

You number my wanderings; Put my tears into Your bottle; Are they not in Your book? (Psalm 56:8 NKJV)

My parents had remodeled my grandparents' home and had moved in, yet they still had many things in their previous home where my siblings and I had grown up. Things needed to be sorted, and the house needed to be cleaned. I offered to help them out. They watched my children, and I set myself to the task alone.

I only had three days to work, so I tried to ignore my feelings and accomplish my goals. But God had another reason for me being there. With every object I sorted came a story, a memory, a visit to my past. Finally, I picked up a toy wooden hammer from a carpenter's bench, one of the earliest toys I remembered playing with. It was dented, dirty, scratched, and, well, ugly, but it was the final straw. As memories, love for that old house, love for my family, and thankfulness to God flooded over me, I sat in the middle of the floor and cried, grieving the end of that era in my life.

Lord, thank you for understanding us and knowing how hard it is to let go sometimes. Thank you for seeing us through all the changes in our lives. Amen.

June 22   Praying for Children

Pour out your heart like water before the face of the Lord. Lift your hands toward Him For the life of your young children, Who faint from hunger at the head of every street. (Lamentations 2:19b NKJV)

Five years ago, I found out about a ministry called "Moms in Touch" that organizes prayer groups for moms to pray for their children's schools. There was not one of these groups for my children's school, and after praying about it, I felt the Lord leading me to start one.

Through the years I have prayed with my sisters in Christ on behalf of our children and all the children and faculty at the school. We have prayed for all kinds of situations, and we have seen God answer our prayers in incredible ways.

It is so wonderful to hear another mom praying for my child. Oftentimes, a mom will pray something I never would have thought of praying. As we have come before the Lord each week, we've grown to love one another's children, as well as the other children attending the school.

A thought occurred to me as we were praying for the children at the school one day. We may be the only persons who have ever lifted some of these children up in prayer. What a blessing we can be in our own corner of the world!

Lord, help us be aware of the spiritual needs of the children around us, and constantly be in an attitude of prayer when those needs are made known. Amen.

June 23   Submit and Resist

Therefore submit to God. Resist the devil and he will flee from you. Draw near to God and He will draw near to you. Cleanse your hands, you sinners; and purify your hearts, you double-minded. (James 4:7-8 NKJV)

Three of my friends and I had decided to meet and start an accountability group. The first week, we prayed this prayer: "Lord, please show me anything in my life that is hindering me from being everything you want me to be, and remove it."

As I prayed that prayer every day that week, the Lord pointed out several things I needed to remove from my life. One was not so easy to root out, though, and I asked God to help me eliminate it. As I sought God in my weakness, I felt his presence there to protect and strengthen me. I also drew near him by poring over his Word and learning what he had to say about my problem.

I also asked for God's forgiveness every time I failed. I followed what the verse for today says, and, as I got serious with God about this particular sin, I found myself struggling less and less with it. He also gave me friends in whom I could confide and ask for prayer and accountability. God is faithful to his promises.

Dear Lord, please don't let me be double-minded, thinking I have no sin in my life. Thank you for drawing near when I seek you. Amen.

June 24   Important Work

"And whoever gives one of these little ones only a cup of cold water in the name of a disciple, assuredly, I say to you, he shall by no means lose his reward." (Matthew 10:42 NKJV)

I like to say that I am a home manager instead of a stay-at-home mom or homemaker. For years, I struggled with how the outside world saw my position in the home. I watched many friends of mine become very successful in their careers, accomplishing many impressive goals. Although I was genuinely happy for them, it left me thinking deep down, *What have I accomplished? What do I have to show for the education I received?*

When I went to God's Word, he reassured me that what I am doing is, indeed, worthwhile and important in his eyes. God notices everything I do for my family. A task as simple as getting a glass of cold water for a thirsty child is important to the Lord. When I get up in the night with a sick child, when I go without a new outfit so that one of my children can go to camp, when I put down what I think is so important and have a tea party with my six-year-old, that takes sacrifice; and no sacrifice goes unnoticed before God. He sees and rewards.

Lord, thank you for reassuring each of us in the jobs you have chosen for us. Help us notice and appreciate the sacrifices made for us. Amen.

June 25   A Lovely Woman

As a ring of gold in a swine's snout, So is a lovely woman who lacks discretion. (Proverbs 11:22 NKJV)

I had just finished a household job and was looking to see what was on television. Being unfamiliar with what was on during that time, I decided to switch channels. As I did, I saw a beautiful talk-show host; and so I stopped to see who she was and listen to what she had to say. It was shocking to hear the vulgar language she spoke and to see how rudely she behaved toward her fellow hosts and guests.

As I witnessed these things, I realized that my opinion of this woman had changed. She was no longer beautiful to me. I could sense the animosity toward her by those who were the victims of her scathing language.

As I silently prayed for her to come to know Christ, I thought how she must grieve the Creator, who gifted her with such beauty. She may as well have been wallowing in the mud.

Lord, help us remember to treat the gifts you have given us with care, and to be true women of beauty, inside and out. Amen.

June 26   Breakfast with Sarah

"You shall teach them to your children, speaking of them when you sit in your house, when you walk by the way, when you lie down, and when you rise up." (Deuteronomy 11:19 NKJV)

As my eleven-year-old daughter, Sarah, thoroughly enjoyed her biscuit covered with grape preserves, I thought about how quickly she is growing up. It seems to be getting harder to keep up with the changes. She is enjoying spending more time with her friends these days, which I know is a natural progression into the teenage years.

It had been a while since the two of us had spent time alone together, and I realized that I needed to be more proactive in this area. Simply having time together or having her come tell me that she wants to sit and talk will happen less and less as she gains more interests. I may even have to schedule an appointment! But I will, if that's what it takes to spend time with her and to show her, as well as my other children, that they are an important priority in my life.

Recently I have started taking one child with me each night when I go for my evening walk. Now they ask, "Mom, is it my night to go walking with you?" I need to ask God to help me find more creative and inexpensive ways to combine activities to include each of my children, one at a time. Perhaps you need to pray this request as well.

Lord, help me be there for each of my children and to have the kind of comfortable relationship that encourages open communication. Amen.

June 27   The Closed Door

Therefore, my beloved brethren, let every man be swift to hear, slow to speak, slow to wrath; for the wrath of man does not produce the righteousness of God. (James 1:19-20 NKJV)

On a hot day in June, I was finally getting the opportunity to cook supper. All my children were playing in the backyard, and Abby, my youngest, had been in and out of the backdoor many times within the last ten minutes for no apparent reason. This would be all right except that I would have to open and close the door for her each time, which took me away from my task in the kitchen.

As my patience was wearing thin, I heard another knock on the backdoor. It was Abby, again, with her nose pressed against the glass. I said, loud enough for her to hear, "Go play!" As I went back to my work I heard another knock. I looked at her with a slightly stern expression. "Go play!" I said.

The third knock came, and as I opened the door, I said with an exasperated tone, "What, Abby?" As a pout came over her face, she pulled out some yellow field flowers and said with the same tone, "Here, these are for you!" Instead of following the advice from today's verse, I had done just the opposite.

Today, may we be quick to hear, slow to speak, and slow to become angry.

Lord, help us take the time to listen to our children. When things are difficult, help us be patient. Amen.

June 28   Common Bond

But the wisdom that is from above is first pure, then peaceable, gentle, willing to yield, full of mercy and good fruits, without partiality and without hypocrisy. (James 3:17 NKJV)

Our oldest son, James, was bored. His neighborhood friends all had plans, Pete and I were busy, and Abby, our youngest, was the only sibling at home that day. After complaining a little about the situation, he went upstairs and retrieved an old storybook, which had belonged to my father. He brought it back down and interrupted Abby's playtime, which she welcomed. It wasn't every day that her older brother actually chose to spend time with her.

Instead of playing together, which would be hindered by their age gap, he explained why the book was special and tenderly asked her if she wanted him to read to her. I smiled as I stood in the other room overhearing their conversation. She gladly sat and listened as James read many of the fascinating old stories to her. It was a seemingly uneventful moment, which I hope they will both remember with fondness.

Lord, please help our family take the time to build relationships with one another. May we always be close, no matter how different we are. Amen.

June 29   Letting Others Down

For I know that in me (that is, in my flesh) nothing good dwells; for to will is present with me, but how to perform what is good I do not find. (Romans 7:18 NKJV)

"Yes, Jan, I'd be glad to pick them up and take them to school in the morning." As I got off the phone with my neighbor, I was distracted by a pressing need of one of my children, and I forgot to write a reminder to myself.

The next morning, I arose quickly, got ready, and rushed out the door with my children to our minivan. As I fought traffic and finally arrived at school, it hit me like a load of bricks: I had forgotten to pick up my neighbor's children. I felt so awful. As my children went to class, I went to the school office, dreading what I had to do. I told the kind secretary what had happened, and she told me not to worry. The children would not be counted tardy. I called the children and assured them I was on my way, and apologized profusely to their parents later.

At times like this when I could kick myself, I remember the words of Paul. God knows I am but flesh.

Lord, thank you for your mercy, grace, and patience. Help us extend the same to one another, especially when we let one another down. Amen.

June 30   Delight in the Lord

Delight yourself also in the LORD, And He shall give you the desires of your heart. Commit your way to the LORD, trust also in Him, And He shall bring it to pass. (Psalm 37:4-5 NKJV)

"Lord, what do you want me to do next year?" I prayed. I had felt for some time that God was leading me to part-time work, but I had no idea where. For eleven years I had been at home with my four children, and now my youngest was about to enter kindergarten.

As I waited, the Lord's response to my prayer surprised me. "What do you want to do?" I really wanted to go into broadcasting, a career dream I had given up a long time ago. As I released my heart's desire to the Lord and laid it at his feet, I felt a peace come over me.

Since that prayer a year ago, I've seen God open incredible doors. I've had two internships at local television stations, and I'm about to begin free-lance work. My schedule even works out, so that I'm able to be home by the time my children get off the bus in the afternoon!

It pleases the Lord to bless us. He loves us so. If we delight ourselves in him, committing our way to him and trusting him completely, he *will* give us the desires of our hearts. Then we will have more stories to tell of God's goodness, and more altars to commemorate his faithfulness.

Father, thank you, for caring about our dreams and desires. Let them come into line with your will for our lives. Your timing is perfect. Amen.

J U L Y

The One to Whom We Pray

Anne Hagerman Wilcox

July 1 **Our Ever-listening God**

In my distress I called to the LORD; I cried to my God for help. From his temple he heard my voice; my cry came before him, into his ears. (Psalm 18:6 NIV)

This month will be an opportunity to explore the passionate attentiveness of our God. So often when we explore prayer, we look at the techniques and attitudes of the one praying. Focusing on the *petitioner* certainly brings crucial insights to our prayer lives. However, this month I'd like to "turn the tables" and explore prayer by watching the *Listener*.

Psalm 18 provides this kind of perspective as David finally rests from the intense conflicts with several enemies and from the jealous personal pursuit by King Saul. This psalm is a creative, joyous song focusing on the One who hears.

Throughout David's life, we know that he physically fought many national enemies who scoffed at his God and his king to whom he was deeply loyal. Though these types of battles took tremendous courage and faith, I suspect his darkest most difficult battles were fought in the face of King Saul's jealous pursuits. David knew the wounds of hand-to-hand combat as well as the emotional wounds of disloyalty and betrayal. For both battlefields, he sought an ever-listening, ever-eager-to-act God.

Dear Lord, we all experience battles in this fallen world. Some are physical; some are emotional. Open our hearts not only to your ability to hear us, but also to your loving eagerness to respond to our cries. Amen.

July 2   A Plethora of Imagery

The LORD is my rock, my fortress and my deliverer; my God is my rock, in whom I take refuge. He is my shield and the horn of my salvation, my stronghold. (Psalm 18:2 NIV)

A poet's main task is to create unforgettable imagery. David, however, chooses to begin Psalm 18 with a personal declaration. Because God has seen him through many battles, David shouts, "I love you, O LORD, my strength" (v. 1). Then he begins to weave the wonder of imagery.

The next verse finds the warrior-poet working with every image he can possibly use to illustrate what he means by "my strength." The repetition in these verses is a poetic device called *Hebrew parallelism*. The Hebrew poet's job was not only to create unforgettable imagery, but also to repeat the imagery creatively in various comparisons or contrasts.

First, David uses the image of a rock. David knew firsthand the strength of this weapon in battles with lions, bears, and a man named Goliath. Then he uses images of fortresses and strongholds—places that surround the warrior, protecting him even from behind where he cannot anticipate attack. He completes this verse with images of a shield and a horn, which provide frontal protection and a way to call for help in the heat of battle. From every direction, David has experienced God's protection and camaraderie in battle.

Lord, in the battles we face today, some obvious and some beyond our awareness, be our front-runner and our rear guard. We join David in the confidence that you will become our strength. Amen.

July 3   I Call, and I Am Saved

I call to the LORD, who is worthy of praise, and I am saved from my enemies. (Psalm 18:3 NIV)

We are all desirous of immediate answers. The idea that I can call upon God and be immediately saved appeals profoundly. However, David's psalm is written in hindsight. The years of living in caves, running for his life, and trying to escape without harming his chief pursuer, King Saul, were probably years when answers did not seem immediate to David.

Just as many psalms ask, "How long, O Lord?" In Psalm 12, we hear

David despair that any godly person is even left on earth: "Help, LORD, for the godly are no more; the faithful have vanished from among men. Everyone lies to his neighbor; their flattering lips speak with deception" (Psalm 12:1-2 NIV). *Everyone* lying to his neighbor was probably a slight exaggeration, but that was how it felt to David. Psalm 12, therefore, is just as revealing as Psalm 18. Both feelings—that God saves the moment I call, *and* that all is lost—are the authentic feelings from the trenches of human experience.

Lord, when the heavens seem silent, open our eyes to your choreography of our lives, for nothing escapes your ultimate purposes—and nothing escapes the attentive ways you hear, act, and are moved in response to our cries. Amen.

July 4   The Cosmic Warrior

The LORD thundered from heaven; ... He shot his arrows and scattered the ene-mies.... The valleys of the sea were exposed and the foundations of the earth laid bare at your rebuke, O LORD. (Psalm 18:13-15 NIV)

In verses 4 through 6 of this psalm, David paints his darkest hours. In verse 4 he says, "The cords of death entangled me; the torrents of destruction overwhelmed me" (NIV). As David looks back over these times, now knowing their outcomes, he finds that only the imagery of a cosmic warrior can capture how profoundly he was rescued from such life-threatening events and such days of despair.

David's realization of God's unique interventions creates images in verses 7-19 that would tax even the most proficient special-effects team if this psalm were ever put to cinema. This cosmic warrior's anger shakes the *entire* earth. Smoke even rises from his nostrils, not to mention the fire and coals that explode from his mouth. This warrior was also capable of splitting open the heavens to burst upon the battlefield for a dramatic rescue. What do we make of all this? God will stop at nothing to answer the cries of his beloved people.

Lord, our view of your passionate desire to intervene for us is too small. We love your gentleness and your mercy, but we also love your warrior's heart that responds with all power when we cry out during the battles of our day. Amen.

July 5   His Delight

He brought me out into a spacious place; he rescued me because he delighted in me.
(Psalm 18:19 NIV)

After painting the storm of God's warrior-like interventions, David brings us to the calm after the rescue. In verse 16, we find that not only does David's Lord have power over the entire earth; he also reaches down to take hold of one hand. He exercises omnipotence and, at the same time, individual intimacy. Despite the constant global concerns that need his intervention, he also gives himself for the needs of the individual. He uses the way of power when that must be, and yet with power he intertwines the way of gentleness.

When the enemies are routed, God brings David to a "spacious place." Everyone can finally breathe more slowly and more deeply. For this place of calm, the poet has saved his most incredible insight. In the latter part of verse 19, we discover that God not only rescues because he's capable and powerful and hears us; he also rescues because he *delights* in us. We are treasured beyond our wildest dreams.

Lord, how do we respond to One who delights in us? Bring to our countenance today the beauty of being treasured by the King of kings. Bring to our step a confidence that knows our rescue will come at Love's perfect time. Amen.

July 6   What Does It Mean to Be Blameless?

For I have kept the ways of the LORD; I have not done evil by turning from my God.
(Psalm 18:21 NIV)

In verses 21 through 24, David seems quite certain of his own righteousness. I'm not so sure I'd be that confident in myself—especially in the midst of the battlefield. So what is he really saying?

In verse 21, he claims that he has not turned away from God. This certainly does not mean he didn't question—and question intensely—many of the difficult circumstances he faced. His other psalms record his tremendous struggles. What he must mean here is that, after pounding on the chest of God, he still looked to him for direction. Verse 22 seems to confirm this idea by showing his deep commitment to obey the scriptures. Verse 23 appears to explain a purposeful avoidance of sin on David's part—something that heartbreakingly was not observed later in his life as he deeply wounded Uriah and Bathsheba's family. The last verse of this section ends with an assurance that the Lord has rewarded David for purposefully committing himself to righteousness.

Therefore, after closer inspection, it appears that these verses are not arrogance, but a rehearsal of David's intent to follow a righteous path.

Lord, keep us from overconfidence in our own righteousness. Keep us also purposeful in our pursuit of a life aligned with the winsome, life-giving righteousness that you modeled to us during your life among us. Amen.

July 7   Both Serpent and Dove

To the faithful you show yourself faithful, ... but to the crooked you show yourself shrewd. (Psalm 18:25-26 NIV)

This One to whom we pray is not only God; he's someone we want very much to be around. He is winsome in his graciousness, but he is never naïve. His mercy comforts us; his "no tolerance" of evil protects us. He is the author of righteousness, and yet he knows the ways and the motives of evil. Don't misunderstand me; his knowledge of evil does not come by participation but by the searing perception of One who is Truth. He is not surprised by the tactics of the crooked; he is never caught off guard. Therefore, his faithfulness and purity lead us close and his shrewdness protects us from the crookedness without and within.

These images created by David always remind me of Christ's words to his disciples in Matthew 10:16. As he commissioned them for ministry, he said, "I am sending you out like sheep among wolves. Therefore be as shrewd as snakes and as innocent as doves" (NIV).

When we petition our Lord, we speak to One who shows himself shrewd in the face of evil—as well as One who is faithful and pure. He has called us to be the same way—not just nice people, but wise, shrewdly wise, in this world of ours.

Lord, give us wisdom to integrate the serpent and the dove in discerning balance. Amen.

July 8   Bending a Bow of Bronze

He trains my hands for battle; my arms can bend a bow of bronze. (2 Samuel 22:35 NIV)

Some of my favorite childhood memories revolve around learning archery. My bow was plastic at first, and my aim was pretty pathetic. However, I had a lot of inspiration since my father was a bow hunter. He would practice diligently at our backyard target—especially the weeks before hunting season. When his skills were honed once again, he would spend part of each September tracking pronghorn antelope in Idaho.

He always let me have a turn at the target with my small bow and arrows. Then I would watch him diligently work at his preseason training. As the weeks of practice continued, I would marvel as the muscles in his arms grew steadier and as each arrow found the bull's eye consistently. Therefore, David's image of learning archery was not lost on me. Being able to bend a bow of *bronze* would require diligent training and would result in being highly equipped and strengthened for any battle.

This One to whom David prayed had used the difficult circumstances of David's life to make him effective in the heat of many battles. The rest of the psalm celebrates the results of his training. He was victorious and was able to praise God among many nations.

Lord, train us for the battles of our era—and the battles of our personal journeys. Your love knows we will need to be highly equipped and strengthened. Amen.

July 9   The Wisdom of Consultation

Then the man and his wife heard the sound of the Lord God as he was walking in the garden in the cool of the day, and they hid. (Genesis 3:8 NIV)

As we move in our prayer exploration to other parts of the Old Testament, I can't help wanting to begin in the beginning.

Every time I read Genesis 3, I want Eve to say to the serpent, "Wow, that's pretty convincing. I've never seen anything so sensible and enticing in my whole life. I'm going to wait, though, before I actually *act* on all this. I want to run it by the One who put me here in the first place. He should come strolling through here any minute. I'll ask him then and get back to you."

I can't help thinking, if only she had consulted! We also have "opportunities" presented to us that are not what they seem. At first, it seems so perfectly tailored to meet our legitimate needs. However, the One to whom we pray yearns to show us how to meet our deepest needs and desires in ways that will bring life, not death, to ourselves and to others.

Dear Lord, prompt us to meet often with you. We want to be people who have no reason to hide—from you or our loved ones or our community. Most of all, keep us from hiding from ourselves. Amen.

July 10   The Living One Who Sees Me

God heard the boy crying, and the angel of God called to Hagar from heaven and said to her, "What is the matter, Hagar? Do not be afraid; God has heard the boy crying as he lies there." (Genesis 21:17 NIV)

So much is "wrong" between Sarai and Hagar in chapters 16 through 21 of Genesis. Arrogance, blaming, jealousy, and dishonor are only a few of the problems between these two women. However, through the life of Ishmael, we are given evidence of the attentive nature of our God.

The first time Hagar found herself in the desert (Genesis 16:4-15), her haughty attitude had run head-on into Sarai's pride. The second visit to the desert came when Ishmael's haughty attitude sparked a bonfire of jealousy from Sarah (Genesis 21:1-20). During both of these exiles, God revealed his incredible attentiveness to us when our prayers have no words—only desperation and tears.

During the first desert exile, God found Hagar and gave her the name Ishmael for her child, meaning, "the Lord hears." When Hagar was in the desert the second time, it must have seemed as though the God who hears had become deaf. This time there was no hope—only tears. Both Hagar and her son despaired. However, the attentive One was close at hand, providing water for their immediate need and hope for their future.

Lord, when we can only weep, open our eyes to the God of Hagar—One who watches closely enough to meet needs we have no strength to discern. Amen.

Before We Have Finished Praying

"By this I will know that you have shown kindness to my master." (Genesis 24:14b NIV)

Genesis 24 records a fascinating prayer. The petitioner is the chief servant of Abraham's household, and his task is monumental. He is to find a wife for Isaac—not just any young woman, but someone from Abraham's relatives.

In verse 12, the servant begins to pray "in [his] heart" (Genesis 24:45 NIV). He calls upon the God of Abraham, which proves he is aware of addressing the one, true God. He petitions for success that God may show his faithfulness to Abraham.

He goes on to ask for a sign to help discern which woman he should choose for Isaac. Asking for signs in prayer is tricky business. God is never limited by our need for him to communicate in prescribed ways. However, in this case, the servant discovers God's eagerness to answer. Before the servant is even finished praying, God brings a young woman who is gracious in hospitality and gives this faithful servant the evidence he needs. The servant is not hasty, but follows up the sign with perceptive questioning. When the questions reveal that he has indeed found a young woman from Abraham's relatives, he worships the God "who has not abandoned his kindness and faithfulness to [Abraham]" (Genesis 24:27 NIV).

Lord, guide our hearts away from assuming you need to be convinced or coerced. Instead, may we pray today to One whose eager love answers even before we have finished praying. Amen.

July 12   **Unloved but Not Forgotten**

When the Lord saw that Leah was not loved, he opened her womb. (Genesis 29:31 NIV)

How heartbreaking Leah's marriage is in Genesis 29. What would it feel like to be the woman used to deceive the bridegroom (Genesis 29:25-27)? Though our customs do not permit such a wound, there are many other ways women of our era know the pain of being unloved. Comfort comes from knowing that the Lord has made us to be cherished by one another; and that when this commitment is withheld or betrayed, God sees and acts.

God was extravagant with Leah. He couldn't seem to bless her enough. *One* son in that era and that culture would have eased her misery. *Two* sons were definite evidence that God saw her need. *Three* sons were sure to make her husband realize her value. And *four* sons were "over the top"!

Leah was very aware of God's gracious actions on her behalf. She named the first son Reuben, which sounds like the Hebrew for " he has seen my misery." The second son was Simeon, meaning "one who hears." After the third son, Leah was sure her husband would honor and value her; so his name was Levi, meaning "attached." Finally, with the fourth son, Leah had healed enough to simply rejoice. Therefore, he was called Judah, meaning "rejoice."

God of Leah, heal those of us who know the wound of being unloved. We look to your wondrous extravagance to rebuild our lives. Amen.

July 13   But You Have Said . . .

"But you have said, 'I will surely make you prosper.'" (Genesis 32:12 NIV)

Jacob's prayer in Genesis 32:9-12 is a petition of distress. This former deceiver had every reason to be worried. After Jacob stole his brother's birthright, Genesis 29 informs us that Esau carried a grudge against Jacob and was plotting his murder. Under these circumstances, Jacob left home. In chapter 32, Jacob—the deceiver—was about to return home and face his victims again.

First of all, Jacob divided his large family and servants into two groups in hopes of saving some of them. Then he prayed. As the prayer unfolds, we find Jacob calling on the God of his fathers and rehearsing the instructions and promises this God had given him. Verse 10 reveals a definite change of heart in Jacob over the years. Instead of grasping and deceiving, Jacob humbly recounts the abundant faithfulness of the One to whom he has prayed all these years. We also see his raw honesty in verse 11. Jacob is terrified.

Despite these odds, Jacob resets his focus. He prays, "But you have said . . ." In other words, because the One to whom he prays has spoken, Jacob can move forward from deceiver to believer, from grasper to receiver, and from controller to relinquisher.

God of Jacob, keep what you have said before us. May we embrace changes of heart that help move us forward—even in the face of fearful possibilities. Amen.

July 14   **Through Times of Injustice**

The LORD was with [Joseph]. (Genesis 39:21 NIV)

As if it were not enough to be sold into slavery by his brothers, Joseph had to deal with more injustice in Genesis 39. Potiphar's wife behaved outrageously, Potiphar took her lies as truth, and Joseph reaped the consequences of someone else's immorality. We're left with the question, *What did God—the One to whom Joseph prayed—do?*

Sometimes I think it's fascinating to look at what did not happen. The deceitfulness of Potiphar's wife was never uncovered. Potiphar believed Joseph's integrity could not be trusted. As far as we know, the truth never did come to light. Instead, the one who had resisted temptation and had spoken for a pure heart before God was not rescued from prison. He was thrown into it.

In verses 21 through 23 of Genesis 39, we discover that while Joseph suffered this injustice, the Lord was with him. When God seemed absent, nothing was farther from the truth. These verses report that the Lord was not only there companionably; he was actively showing Joseph kindness and causing those around Joseph to see him in a favorable light.

At the end of this passage, in case any reader still questions what our God does in the face of injustice, verse 23 says *again* that the Lord was with Joseph, actively giving him success.

God of Joseph, injustices surround us. Help us perceive your gracious care during those times. Amen.

July 15   **In the Land of My Suffering**

Before the years of famine came, Joseph had two sons. (Genesis 41:50 NRSV)

Fortunately, Joseph's story does not end in jail. Near the end of Genesis 41, we find him creatively testifying to God's faithfulness as he names his sons.

As the first son is born, Joseph reflects on the past. Though he was taken from his first family, Joseph has now become the father of his own family. In that realization, Joseph names his firstborn Manasseh, which sounds like the Hebrew idea for forget. Joseph says he chose the name "because God has made me "forget" all my trouble and all my father's household" (Genesis 41:51 NIV). We know from later chapters of Genesis that Joseph did not

150

literally forget his first family. The idea of forgetting used here probably meant that this son brought enough joy to give relief from the ache over his former family and his former troubles.

As the second son is born, Joseph reflects again on what has transpired in his life. This time the son is named Ephraim, which sounds like the Hebrew expression "twice fruitful." Joseph explains the name was chosen because God had made him fruitful in the land of his suffering.

God of Joseph, we look to your companionship as we endure seasons of suffering. Because of the names Joseph was able to give his sons, we also look to you for relief from heartache and for tangible evidence of fruitfulness in the land of our suffering. Amen.

July 16   Goodness—God's All-powerful Intent

"You intended to harm me, but God intended it for good." (Genesis 50:20a NIV)

At the end of his life, Joseph gives us further insight into the heart of the One to whom we pray. Joseph had every reason to feel bitterness toward his brothers, yet he saw Another One creating good out of their evil intent.

In Genesis 37, the jealousy of Joseph's brothers is exposed. Roots of being favored less and gaining less recognition seem to have grown this intense sibling conflict. Add to that Joseph's dreams, which indicated a future superior social position, and you have the makings of dangerous resentment.

In a sense, these older brothers interpreted Joseph's calling and gifting as threatening to their own positions. The possibility of losing center stage seemed to justify lies, betrayal, and talk of murder. Never once did it occur to the older brothers that God was preparing their sibling to bring life and goodness to them all.

However, there was Someone else who had gifted and chosen Joseph. He was able to redeem the jealous, selfish impulses of Joseph's brothers. Joseph could see clearly that "it was not you who sent me here, but God" (Genesis 45:8 NIV). Though the purpose God had for Joseph threatened even his closest family members to the point of immoral acts of jealousy, those plans could not be thwarted.

Lord, we praise you for making your intent of goodness stronger than any intent of evil. Amen.

July 17   Send Someone Else

But Moses said, "O Lord, please send someone else to do it." (Exodus 4:13 NIV)

In addition to the profound interaction Moses enjoyed with the Lord, this frantic plea in Exodus 4 is added to the prayers of Moses. Despite his curiosity about the burning bush and his obedient response of, "Here I am," Moses is a shining example of hesitancy.

One has to admit his concerns are not unreasonable. He simply asks, "Who am I to do this?" and, "Who's going to ever believe this one?" Of course, God is ready with graphic replies. First, the burning yet not consumed bush continues. Then, a staff turns into a snake. Next, a hand goes from leprous to healthy, and finally, water to blood ends the miraculous demonstrations.

Despite these wonders, Moses turns to the practical. He really doesn't have the gifts for the job. As Moses continues to try to convince God that he's unqualified, the Lord's irritation builds. With piercing rhetorical questions, God asks, "Who gave humans a mouth? Who makes a person deaf or mute? Who gives sight or blindness?" In other words, God is saying that this task is not just about a human named Moses. It is also about the capabilities of the One who has called Moses.

Lord of the Exodus—and of my life—pry open the fingers that clutch my inadequacies. May I release them to your all-wise stewardship and say, "Here I am," instead of, "Please send someone else." Amen.

July 18   The Wonder of His Concern

"When they heard that the LORD was concerned about them and had seen their misery, they bowed down and worshiped." (Exodus 4:31 NIV)

So far beyond the people's awareness, the Lord was orchestrating Israel's deliverance. Their daily lives of bitterness, hard labor, and being used ruthlessly continued on relentlessly as if no one saw and no one cared. However, intricate plans were being constructed to ease their suffering and bring them safely to peace and abundance. Plans extending back through former generations were now being choreographed to achieve fulfillment in their generation.

When Moses appeared with the message from an all-seeing, all-compassionate God, the people regained hope. They were able to stop their intense labor and bow down. They were able to lift up weary hands and worship. The possibility that all this bitterness had not gone on in isolation and had not been meaningless was almost too good to be true. This time hope seemed authentic—not like the false hopes from before—and it was confirmed by miraculous signs and sincere reports from both Moses and Aaron. Maybe, just maybe, the suffering would end.

Lord of history, increase my awareness of your faithfulness throughout all generations. Give me the courage to endure or give me the strength to move ahead if your saving hand is signaling my era. In all of this, may I live in gratitude for the richness of your presence in the days ordained for me. Amen.

July 19   Why?

Moses returned to the LORD and said, "O Lord, why have you brought trouble upon this people? Is this why you sent me? Ever since I went to Pharaoh to speak in your name, he has brought trouble upon this people, and you have not rescued your people at all." (Exodus 5:22-23 NIV)

The One to whom we pray welcomes angry accusations from the reality of our perspective. Moses had believed God, and now look. Things were worse, not better. If Moses had not maintained a vibrant relationship with God, this crucial prayer might have remained unspoken. It might not have been recorded for our encouragement.

Many are the times in life when our anticipation of events or our expectations of timing leave us with the very same prayer on our lips. We sign up for miraculous success, not for more suffering in order for the bewildering purposes of God to continue beyond our understanding. We feel cheated that more endurance is required in an already impossible set of circumstances. Like Moses, the only honest thing to do is scream, "Why?" Authentic relationships are those that can take the fury of the beloved and not lose the relationship. "How could you not be—or do—what you promised?" our hearts should rail in protest, for that is the honest way of prayer—and of relationships that last.

Lord, give us enough honest intimacy with you to question you—even vehemently—when life from our perspective calls for it. Amen.

153

What other nation is so great as to have their gods near them the way the LORD our God is near us whenever we pray to him? (Deuteronomy 4:7 NIV)

Before the people of Israel enter the promised land, Moses begins his farewell speeches recorded in the book of Deuteronomy. Because of the disbelief of the generation he led out of Egypt, neither that generation nor Moses will be allowed to enter the good land so long awaited. We know from chapter 3 of Deuteronomy that God gives Moses a panoramic view of the land, but Moses will not enjoy the final goal of entrance into that land.

Despite this disappointment, Moses makes an incredible statement about the uniqueness of following the God of Israel. He could have emphasized the power of God shown in the rescue from Egypt. He could have recounted the pillar of fire by night and the cloud by day, or the way God faithfully fed the people in the wilderness. Instead, he calls their attention to the way God is *near* when they pray to him.

It is the hearing, seeing, and acting in response to his people's needs that distinguishes this God of Israel. He is everything these Old Testament characters have testified to as they have named their children, as they have wept, and as they have seen him answer even before their prayers had ended.

Lord of the patriarchs, may we pray differently today, knowing that you are indeed near. Amen.

"O Lord, the great and awesome God, who keeps his covenant of love with all who love him and obey his commands, we have sinned and done wrong." (Daniel 9:4-5a NIV)

Daniel's prayer in Daniel, chapter 9, is insightful as we continue to explore the character of the One who hears us pray. In this prayer that encompasses fifteen verses, Daniel primarily brings the concerns of his entire nation to God. He makes it clear that the One he is approaching has never changed or broken any of his promises. Daniel continues throughout the prayer to rehearse the ways in which this faithful God has been who he said he would be—in the face of obedience and through the consequences of disobedience.

As we approach this same promise-keeping God with our national needs, we must include ourselves—as Daniel did—with those who need his merciful restoration. Despite his integrity shown by wanting not even to defile himself with food in the land of captivity, Daniel understands his part in the collective sin of his nation and his community. Therefore, he does not elevate himself above others or pray in a condescending tone. He knows well that the One to whom he prays is quick to hear the repentant heart and swift to answer a sincere desire for purity.

Lord, because of Daniel's example, help us approach you with global concerns by first acknowledging our own participation in the sin that continues to wound the world. Amen.

July 22   Consequences Guaranteed

"Therefore the curses and sworn judgments written in the Law of Moses, the servant of God, have been poured out on us, because we have sinned against you."
(Daniel 9:11b NIV)

As we pray, we often think that consequences for disobedience belong only with Old Testament peoples. However, both testaments clearly show that the Lord disciplines those he loves. However, it is always crucial to explore the question, *Why does God insist on real consequences for disobedience?*

As I write this, the world is mesmerized by the cinema versions of J. R. R. Tolkien's *Lord of the Rings*. In this fantasy trilogy written by a devout Catholic, a concept emerges that may help answer the question of God's careful correction of his children. Through the power of the ring to corrupt, the idea emerges that evil has within itself the seeds of its own destruction.

Evil and disobedience destroy; the One to whom we pray wants us to live. Daniel was keenly aware that the people purposefully turned away. They didn't just forget; they didn't have a bad day. They intentionally ignored all the prophets God sent to call them back to *life*. God is not arbitrary—he gives decades of warning. However, his righteousness—and his desire for us not to self-destruct through evil—requires a day of reckoning.

Lord, let us not toy with your commands. May we see, like Daniel, that real disobedience reaps real consequences—and may we feel how desperately you ache for us to choose life. Amen.

"For your sake, O Lord, look with favor on your desolate sanctuary. Give ear, O God, and hear; open your eyes and see the desolation of the city that bears your Name." (Daniel 9:17b-18 NIV)

In verse 17, Daniel reveals a concern that goes beyond personal and national sin. He treasures the reputation of God. He is well aware of the incredible rescue God achieved for his people from Egypt, and he recounts the deserving honor God received for displaying such power at that moment of history. However, the present captivity makes it look as if the God of Israel thinks nothing of abandoning his people, or as if he isn't strong enough to protect them. Daniel prays for the misrepresentation to end and for the former wonder the surrounding nations have had for the God of Israel to be restored.

Daniel's three friends, Shadrach, Meshach, and Abednego, certainly help restore that wonder as they choose to remain loyal to God, which results in an extraordinary rescue from the fiery furnace (Daniel 3:17). As incredible as this display is, Daniel's concerns are even wider. He desires the whole plan of God to be restored. He longs for the sanctuary and the city of worship to be restored so God and his people might enjoy the unity of obedience and love—instead of the distance resulting from disobedience and captivity.

Lord, guide our prayer life to reflect your wider concerns for the world and for future generations. Amen.

"We do not make requests of you because we are righteous, but because of your great mercy." (Daniel 9:18b NIV)

Daniel is keenly aware that the sinfulness of his nation deserves the consequences he and his generation are now experiencing. He appeals not to God's approval of his repentant petition, but solely to God's mercy.

In C. S. Lewis's fictional work titled *Till We Have Faces,* the main character, Orual, envisions a day of reckoning as her life ends. With intensity, she speaks with her former beloved tutor as she traverses the life-after-death world. As they examine murals that replay her life, she asks him, "Are the gods not just?"

He poignantly replies, "Oh, no, child. What would become of us if they were?"

Orual has spent her entire life writing an angry treatise against the gods for their injustice related to her life and her loves. Her tutor's answer reveals that we live *only* because there is tremendous mercy extended to us. Without that mercy, none of us could stand in the courts of "the gods."

The point is that mercy is profoundly extended to us in ways we don't even realize and for reasons beyond our comprehension. Daniel seemed well aware that we live because the One to whom we pray is a merciful God.

Lord, the extent of your mercy goes beyond our comprehension. May we always be aware that the hope we have for answered prayer rests solely on your great mercy. Amen.

July 25   May He Send You Help

May the LORD answer you when you are in distress; may the name of the God of Jacob protect you. (Psalm 20:1 NIV)

Psalm 20 reveals a petitioner wanting the characteristics of God that he has discovered to be experienced by another individual. In ways that almost summarize the study we have done in prayer, the psalmist yearns for specific qualities of this listening God to be evident to the one needing prayer.

The petitioner asks for the Lord to *hear* when the other is in distress. He asks for a rescue to come to the one in need. He also asks that God *remember* the former times of faithfulness on the part of the one in need. The psalmist then continues to ask not only for help, but also for *extravagant support*. The petitioner has watched God bless abundantly—in the tradition of Leah with her *four,* not just one or two, sons.

This last request is phrased as giving the one in need the desires of her heart and making all her plans succeed. Then the one petitioning will begin a fitting celebration. Desires met and hopes realized are reasons for this unselfish petitioner to pull out all the stops.

There is also a deep awareness that out of the myriad of things humans choose to trust in, the most dependable is the name of the Lord.

Lord, as we experience your incredible care, may we pray powerfully and joyfully for this same care for others. Amen.

July 26   **When the Wicked Seem the Strongest**

In his arrogance the wicked man hunts down the weak, who are caught in the
schemes he devises. (Psalm 10:2 NIV)

The One to whom we pray seems absent as Psalm 10 erupts. It begins
with the strong complaint that God remains hidden when he is most needed.
This prayer continues with descriptions of the wicked that are all too familiar. These ones who seem stronger than our Helper are people who have no
room for God. Consequently, they curse, lie, and threaten all the while they
are gaining prosperity.

If that isn't enough, they boast that they will always be happy and
never know troubles. Meanwhile, the victims of these schemers are
helplessly crushed. These perpetrators of pain and loss think that God
does not see and will never call them to account. The strength of the evil
ones prompts the psalmist to create the image of a lion waiting in cover
to pounce on its unsuspecting victims. All seems lost in the face of such
schemes.

And yet, the psalmist draws comfort from remembering that God hears
the desires and needs of the afflicted. Trouble and affliction move him to
profound action. Confidence that God will indeed act on behalf of the weak
returns, and the wicked are strong no more.

Lord, we live in times when the wicked seem too strong. Keep us confident
that you hear and will call evildoers to account at the same time you bring
relief to their victims. Amen.

July 27   **Purity Doesn't Pay—or Does It?**

Surely in vain have I kept my heart pure; ... you destroy all who are unfaithful to
you. (Psalm 73:13, 27b NIV)

The heart cries in the psalms are so refreshingly honest. Psalm 73 looks
deeply at times when those who disregard God seem to have no struggles.
In fact, they seem to have escaped the "burdens common" to the rest of us.
The diligence to keep a pure heart seems to yield a life of oppression and
punishment. Meanwhile, those who could care less or who continue in disobedience seem to have it easy.

The psalmist questions this economy that appears to show preference to those who disregard God. As the prayer continues, the psalmist looks more closely beneath the surface of appearances. As time goes on, these out-of-balance scales begin to reveal crucial results. Sudden destruction awaits those far from God. Though they seem to have life now, it is a counterfeit. It exists as deceitfully as a mirage.

Finally, the psalmist realizes what he desires more than anything. He started his complaint by wishing for the absence of burdens and human ills. Now he realizes that nearness to God is what he desires above all else. He wouldn't trade it for any of the mirages billed as a life of ease without God.

Lord, help us desire you above all else today; then we will experience our other desires with the greatest joy, discernment, and delight possible on this earth. Amen.

July 28　　　The One to Whom We Pray, Prays for Us

"Father, the time has come." (John 17:1a NIV)

In the final four days of exploring prayer, we must turn to John 17. Here we can view the One to whom we pray as he prays for us in his last hours on earth. Much of his heart is revealed as he brings his strongest concerns to the Father in these final moments with his disciples.

The first concern of our Lord's is timing. The prayer begins with, "Father, the time has come." Earlier in John's Gospel when Jesus was pushed to demonstrate his power more publicly, he responded, "The right time for me has not yet come" (John 7:6 NIV). All this seems to prove that God orchestrates with precision the work he does on earth.

Christ goes on (verses 1-5) to speak of faithfully finishing the work that he and the Father lovingly designed—work that provides eternal life for us. These verses also capture Christ's yearning to be home, to be reunited with the Father. Therefore, we are given a taste of the intimacy and togetherness that must be so vital to the love between the Father and the Son.

Lord, we long to put our complete trust in your timing. Give us the needed courage and strength to complete the work you have designed for our life-time. May our yearning to be reunited with you guide that work and infuse it with joy, endurance, and wonder. Amen.

July 29   **Welcomed into the Heart of Things**

"I pray for them. I am not praying for the world, but for those you have given me, for they are yours. All I have is yours, and all you have is mine. And glory has come to me through them." (John 17:9-10 NIV)

Christ's prayer expresses deep honor concerning the disciples. They were gifts belonging to the Father, which he entrusted to the Son. The Son, in turn, deeply valued, carefully trained, and fiercely protected them.

When Christ concludes that these disciples have brought him "glory," I am reminded of C. S. Lewis's definition of glory. In his essay "The Weight of Glory," Lewis's definition includes "good report with God, acceptance by God, response, acknowledgement, and welcome into the heart of things."

This prayer reveals how joyously Christ is bringing his disciples alongside himself to return to the Father. These valued men are on "the inside"—welcomed into the heart of the Godhead.

How needy we all are as human beings to be so treasured. We have all felt the sting of not being included; some of us bear the deep wounds of abandonment. In Christ, as Lewis would say, we are "welcome[d] into the heart of things. The door on which we have been knocking all our lives will open at last."

Lord, we need to know how much you want us—and that you are inviting us to belong to you in deep and everlasting ways. Amen.

July 30   **Our Strong Protector**

"My prayer is not that you take them out of the world but that you protect them from the evil one." (John 17:15 NIV)

Another deep concern of Christ in this final prayer is for the disciples' protection. While Christ was with them on the earth, he watched over them. Now that he's leaving, he calls upon the Father for their protection.

First, he acknowledges that one of the disciples was lost. This heartbreaking betrayal was anticipated—not orchestrated or designed—by the Godhead. Therefore, it could not thwart the purposes of God even though it deeply grieved the heart of God.

Next, Christ longs for the full measure of his joy to be in the disciples. In the same breath with this joy, Christ acknowledges the difficulty of the place where his people must remain. They will be hated; therefore, they will need the shield of joy.

Finally, Christ asks these disciples to be sanctified—meaning "set apart." They are to be cared for specially—as well as used in special ways. In a world where the father of lies prowls relentlessly, truth must set these followers apart. Christ knows that truth is the hardest to discern when surrounded by lies. Therefore, again, his fierceness calls for them to be set apart by truth.

Lord, the evil one attempts to invade our lives in such brutal, deceptive ways. Help us draw comfort from the fact that you see all, hear all, and pray for our protection before the Father. Amen.

July 31   Christ's Deepest Desire

"May they be brought to complete unity to let the world know that you sent me and have loved them even as you have loved me." (John 17:23 NIV)

In the last verses of this prayer, Christ expresses his deepest desire for his disciples, and for us—"for those who will believe in me through their message" (John 17:20 NIV). Above all else, the One to whom we pray wants us to love and be loved by divine passion. He wants the *eternal* and *perfect* love enjoyed within the Godhead to be ours!

According to verse 24, he wants us to be with him—forever. Closeness is one of his chief concerns. He is so desirous of our company that moments before the torture of injustice and crucifixion begin, he is thinking of us!

He also gives us the chief characteristic of this divine love. Unity and oneness infuse every part of the relational Godhead. We catch whispers, maybe even glimpses, of these qualities in our healthiest relationships. However, he prays that we would be brought to *complete* unity—not only for our own hearts, but also for a world needing to see evidence of his reality.

Lord, this perfect love and complete unity are your deepest desires for us. As we journey in a world filled with anything but those qualities, may we somehow redeem our sphere of influence knowing your unceasing prayer undergirds our quest. Amen.

AUGUST

The Strength of My Life

Marie Schockey

August 1   **The Source of Our Strength**

The LORD is my light and my salvation; Whom shall I fear? The LORD is the strength of my life; Of whom shall I be afraid? (Psalm 27:1 NKJV)

*I*n Mexico, where my husband and I work as missionaries, there are so many things to be afraid of, and yet we do not see fear in the eyes of the people who know the Lord. They have learned to come to him as little children and to trust that he will supply whatever is necessary to meet their daily needs.

While walking one day in a neighborhood where we were building houses, a woman with six little children sent one of them to invite me to her home. She lived in a fourteen-by-fourteen pallet house with cardboard wrapped around it and a dirt floor. She was doing her laundry in a metal tub, using a washboard, while her children played in the dirt at her feet. My assumption was that she wanted information on how to get one of the many houses we were building in her *colonia* (neighborhood) that week. After I arrived at her home and introductions were made, her request was not for a house but for a Bible. She had a strength in her life that did not allow her to fear, as we probably would *(How will I feed my family? How will I keep them warm?)*. Her strength was in the Lord Jesus. Her desire was to really know him. And the most important thing to her at that time was to have his Word in her possession, for that was the source of her strength.

This month we will explore the source of our strength and what it means to be strong in the Lord. When God is our strength, we have nothing and no one to fear.

163

Lord, help me put my trust in you and not fear the things that surround me. Help me look to you daily to meet all my needs. Amen.

August 2   Let Go

Do not be anxious about anything, but in everything, by prayer and petition, with thanksgiving, present your requests to God. And the peace of God, which transcends all understanding, will guard your hearts and your minds in Christ Jesus. (Philippians 4:6-7 NIV)

A friend's only child was dying from a genetic disease. Her mother had prayed with faith, believing. She had gone to healing services. She had confessed her sin. All in all, she had tried to do everything *she* could to see her daughter healed.

Finally, one day she called me and asked, "How do I let go?" The year before, our five-and-a-half-year-old son had gone home to be with the Lord. What we had learned during his illness was that we couldn't bargain with God. He asks, "Do you trust me with part or all of your life? Are you willing to give all your life to me, including everyone and everything in it?" With this realization, we stopped pleading and begging and prayed, "Lord, not our will but yours, and give us strength to go through it."

In my friend's case, letting go meant that God healed her daughter by taking her home with him. Sometimes strength is not how well or how long you hang on, but how freely you let go.

Lord, help me trust you not only with my life, but also with everyone and everything surrounding me. Amen.

August 3   Choose to Trust

Trust in the LORD with all your heart and lean not on your own understanding; in all your ways acknowledge him, and he will make your paths straight. (Proverbs 3:5-6 NIV)

We can give our children verbal instruction and show them how things are done, but our actions, attitudes, and behaviors speak louder than our words. When our middle son was sick with a blood disease, he trusted that we knew what was best. We desired him to be unafraid, so it was important for us to model our trust in the Lord

One day the doctor told us that, though it had never happened before, the Lord had told her to tell us that time was short. While driving home that day, I looked at my young son and said, "Are you ready to go live with Jesus?" We had talked about heaven often and how wonderful it would be. His response was, "Mom, I am ready today; I know you don't think it's fair 'cause I get to go first." I said, "It's OK if you go first because you have lots of pokes [needles] and bleed [effects of the illness]." He said, "It's OK, Mom, you'll get to come pretty soon." And with that said, he turned and looked out the window.

Through it all, he trusted us while we put our trust in the Lord. It's not always easy, but it's a choice we make.

Lord, help me put my trust in you and be an example of Christ to my family—not only in my words, but more important, in my actions. Amen.

August 4   Be Still

In returning and rest you shall be saved; in quietness and in trust shall be your strength. But you refused. (Isaiah 30:15 NRSV)

I have a hard time being still, and I don't always recognize the need for down time. To get my attention, the Lord moved me to a new city and state. Making new friends was an adventure. I felt as if I was back in high school. *What if they don't like me? What if I don't like them?* I missed the closeness of old friends and the security of those relationships.

My confidence and identity were challenged. The good thing was that it brought me to my knees before the Lord, and my relationship with him was renewed. Once again he became my best friend. I rediscovered that God is my strength and my security, and that in him I can do all things. My confidence returned, and I began to enjoy the adventure that God had set before me.

Today I have a renewed commitment to spend quiet time each day waiting on God and listening for his direction. I am thankful that I have learned to "be still, and know that [he is] God" (Psalm 46:10 NRSV).

Lord, help me come before you with a quiet heart, free of the schedules and routines that can take over my time and thoughts. Help me focus on you alone. Amen.

August 5   Lay Your Burdens Down

[Cast] all your care upon Him, for He cares for you. (1 Peter 5:7 NKJV)

My husband and I ran a home for teenage girls for ten years. One girl lost her father when she was eight years old. The family was not allowed to talk about it because it hurt too much. Over the next four years, they moved a lot and stayed with relatives. During this period, she was abused by two uncles, her grandfather, and, finally, her new stepfather. She arrived at our home a hurt, lonely, overweight, angry, and insecure twelve-year-old.

Through the weeks she watched how we treated one another, went to church with us, and listened to us pray for one another. After a few months, she began to ask how she could have joy in her life. Soon after, she committed her life to Christ. It took time to fully let go of the hurt, forgive the people who caused the pain, and move forward with her life; but today she is a different person.

Often we think that being strong means we have to handle everything on our own. We struggle through tough situations and "stuff" the pain. We think no one will understand, and we suffer alone. But the Lord wants us to lean on him and move forward with our lives, not letting the past dictate our future. Will you lay your burdens down?

Lord, make me whole again. Help me trust you and forgive those who have caused me pain so I may be free of bitterness and full of joy. Amen.

August 6   Resist the Devil

Your adversary the devil walks about like a roaring lion, seeking whom he may devour. Resist him, steadfast in the faith, knowing that the same sufferings are experienced by your brotherhood in the world. (1 Peter 5:8b-9 NKJV)

The sufferings we experience are most difficult when we are in the midst of them. It's hard to see an end to it all, and even more difficult to see any good in it. Yet the Bible tells us to "count it all joy when [we] fall into various trials" (James 1:2 NKJV). How *do* we count it joy when our marriage is falling apart, our husband has lost his job, we're going bankrupt, or a loved one has died?

The devil is real, and he is seeking to destroy us. His goal is for us to turn our backs on God. His ploy is to conquer and divide and hurt us when we are down. He knows his time is short, and he will use any means to get to us.

We must remember that this world is temporary and our real home is in heaven. No matter how much we hurt right now, it *will* pass. "Trust in the LORD with all your heart, And lean not on your own understanding" (Proverbs 3:5 NKJV). It's hard to do at times, but those are the times when it is most important to lean on the strength of the Lord.

Heavenly Father, help me come to you when I am suffering and lay my burdens down at your feet. Help me trust you completely with my life and those I hold dear to my heart. Amen.

August 7   Praise Him

The LORD is my strength and song, And He has become my salvation; He is my God, and I will praise him. (Exodus 15:2 NKJV)

My worst nightmare was when my four-year-old son was diagnosed with a terminal disease. It started with a bloody nose that trickled but wouldn't stop. After a week in the hospital and many tests, he was diagnosed with aplastic anemia, a blood disease that affects the immune system.

One night when he was very ill, I asked the Lord, "Are you going to take my son?" I heard an answer almost immediately: "Yes, I am; prepare!" Strangely, I didn't feel fear—only peace. Though I did second-guess what I heard, thinking that perhaps God meant my son would die when he was older, I knew in my heart that the time would not be long.

We spent a lot of time together, went to Disney with "Make a Wish," and took a lot of pictures and videos. We imagined what heaven would be like and told him how lucky he was to get to go first. We explained everything, not wanting him to be afraid. In the midst of it all, I would find myself in the shower, singing praises to the Lord. I found my strength in the joy of the Lord (Nehemiah 8:10).

Even in difficult times when there is no joy in the situation, we can be filled with the joy and peace of the Lord that passes all understanding (Philippians 4:7). We can choose to worship the One who created us, knowing that he loves us and our children more than we can imagine.

Lord, help me choose you in the midst of my pain and sorrow. Help me see that, with you, each day is a new day. Help me lift my voice in song to you and wait for your joy. Amen.

August 8   Trust God to Defend You

Praise be to the LORD, for he has heard my cry for mercy. The LORD is my strength and my shield; my heart trusts in him, and I am helped. My heart leaps for joy and I will give thanks to him in song. (Psalm 28:6-7 NIV)

Some years ago, my husband, Nolan, and I were youth workers at a church. One day our boss came to me to talk about a situation involving the crisis pregnancy center. Recently I had been visiting with one of the center's staff members at church, and I had mentioned that I had taken a young girl to a public health clinic instead of to the center. I didn't explain, however, that the girl had asked me not to take her to the center because she didn't want this very individual, who knew her family, to know that she might be pregnant. This person went to her boss and said that they needed to stop me from working at the church if I was taking girls to "planned parenthood." She called my boss several times, hoping to get me fired.

The easy way out would have been to tell this person the "whole story," but that would have betrayed a confidence I had promised to keep. So I stood firm, trusting God to defend me. Fortunately, I had a boss who was more interested in the truth than hearsay. The Lord heard my cry for mercy. I trusted in him, and he protected me.

We know the enemy will attack us, but it is even more difficult when the attack comes from within the Body of Christ and we are unable to defend ourselves. We must trust in the Lord to reveal what he chooses and move forward in his strength.

Lord, help me always trust you and be obedient to you, allowing your justice and mercy to reign in my life. Amen.

August 9   Make God Your Refuge

God is our refuge and strength, an ever-present help in trouble. (Psalm 46:1 NIV)

Spring in Juarez, Mexico, is generally very mild, yet there are unbelievable winds. Because there are very few trees and almost no grass, the sixty-mile-an-hour winds blow sand everywhere—and into everything. At times the sandstorm is so bad that it's difficult to see five feet in front of you.

We work in this weather no matter what, because if we don't, the family living in a pallet house with cardboard walls will not receive their new home before it's time for the mission team to leave. Though we suffer for a few days, they live in these circumstances every day. We see them go about their daily lives with no concern for their living conditions. A mom waits for a bus, shielding her daughter's face from the full force of the wind. A father holds his young son against him so that the dirt blowing in his own face will not penetrate his son.

Isn't that just like our heavenly Father? Whatever our situations may be, he shields and protects us from the brunt of the storm until we've matured to the point that the storm no longer affects our "walk." Whatever the storm may be, God is our shield and our strength.

Father God, thank you for being my shield and protector in the midst of the storms of my life. May I turn to you and hide my face in times of trouble. Amen.

August 10   Persevere When You're Weary

He gives strength to the weary and increases the power of the weak. (Isaiah 40:29 NIV)

It's hard being a mother, especially in the early years. The chores never seem to get done, and someone always needs something from you. Whether you work outside the home or stay home with the children, you're exhausted by late afternoon; and you still have to put dinner on the table, clean up, give baths, and read bedtime stories. By 9:00 P.M., you just want to fall into bed! Thankfully, it isn't always going to be that way; it does get easier in some ways—and more difficult in others.

Three years before we had our own children, we chose to take in teenage girls. We did this off and on for the next ten years. Our lives were a bit chaotic and challenging at times, yet we knew we had a responsibility to the Lord to make a difference in these children's lives—to direct them to the Creator and love them freely so they would catch a glimpse of God's love for us.

The time our children are in our care passes so quickly. They are really God's children, and he has entrusted them to us for a time. We must cherish the time and use it wisely.

Lord, in the midst of my day, remind me to thank you for the children you have entrusted to my care. When I am overwhelmed, help me see them as blessings rather than burdens. Give me strength to persevere through the difficult days. Amen.

August 11   Remember That You Can Do All Things Through Christ

I can do all things through [Christ Jesus] who strengthens me. (Philippians 4:13 NRSV)

I grew up in a dysfunctional home. My mom had three husbands, and my alcoholic dad was on his third wife by the time I was graduated from high school. At age eleven, I had a strong sense that I needed to take care of him or he might drink himself to death. This protective feeling carried over into my adult life. Four months after I was married, my husband and I began to take in troubled teenage girls. Later we became foster parents and started a group home for teenage girls.

In my early twenties, I was trying to be a mother to teenage girls without any support of my own. I would take walks in the woods by our home and ask, "Lord, do you know what you're doing? Because I don't know what I'm doing." He gave me not only the strength to go through each day, but also the lessons I needed. The Lord used the classes we were required to take for licensing purposes to reveal my unhealthy behavior. I realized I was a caregiver in all my relationships. I needed to be needed.

Today I have a life full of healthy relationships. I still take care of others, but I have friends and a husband who help me keep a balance in my life. Best of all, my identity is not in what I can do for others but in who I am in Christ.

Lord, help me remember that, in you, all things are possible, and apart from you, most things are impossible. Amen.

August 12   Know That the Lord Rejoices in Your Victories

O LORD, the king rejoices in your strength. How great is his joy in the victories you give! You have granted him the desire of his heart. (Psalm 21:1-2a NIV)

The Word says that when we seek God's will, he will give us the desires of our heart. Sometimes we don't think he is listening because we don't get what we desire immediately. But God is not our magic fairy, waiting to grant our wishes. When we have a desire, we first must see if it lines up with his Word. Would this desire glorify God? Then we must realize that there may be a training period.

For most of my Christian walk, I desired to be a missionary. I was so intrigued by the way they lived their lives totally sold out for God, trusting completely in him. Our journey started out with different ministries, and there were a lot of changes and growth along the way. Twenty years later, my husband and I are now full-time missionaries living the desire of our hearts. Looking back, I see that all the Lord taught us we now use in our ministry in Mexico.

God desires to set us up for victory, not failure, and he delights in our victories. If we're not careful, our impatience and unwillingness to listen to his still, small voice can set us up for failure and, in time, make us unwilling to step out on faith so that the Lord may use us.

Lord, help me seek your will for my life and know that the trials you allow in my life are meant to shape and mold me. Amen.

August 13   Release Those You Love

Precious in the sight of the LORD is the death of his saints. (Psalm 116:15 NIV)

The Bible says our life on earth is temporary and our real home is in heaven. To be absent from the body is to be present with the Lord. In heaven, there will be no more crying, sorrow, pain, or death. Why, then, are we so reluctant to release those we love to the Lord? Do we really believe that there is a time to be born and a time to die, and that our sovereign God knows the appointed times?

I know how difficult it is to lose loved ones. My own son went to be with the Father sooner than I would have chosen, and I lost my mother to cancer shortly after she gave her life to Christ. My father also died while I was on my first mission trip. He would not allow me to talk about my walk with Christ or my desire for him to know Christ also. It's especially hard to let go when we are pretty sure our loved ones never chose Christ. We have to trust that the Lord is just and fair, and that he gives every individual every chance possible. We also must remember that only he knows a person's heart, and so there is always hope.

Lord, help me know in my heart that you love those you have placed in my life more than I could ever imagine, and help me remember that my ways are not your ways. Amen.

August 14   Look Out for Others

Let each of you look not to your own interests, but to the interests of others. Let the same mind be in you that was in Christ Jesus. (Philippians 2:4-5 NRSV)

For ten years, Nolan and I took in teenage girls who had been removed from abusive or possibly abusive situations. They were scared and were not allowed to return home or talk to their families until their cases went to court. For the first time in their lives, they were in a safe environment, but it took a while for them to realize this and adjust to the new rules. The most important thing we could do for them was to accept them just as they were, not expecting immediate change.

This is how our heavenly Father accepts us when we first come to him. We are elated to know him for the first time but still may have baggage that our sinful nature has left us with. Our loving Father gently works with us, changing our desires to match his will.

We, too, need to be accepting of others, especially those who are new Christians or who are struggling in their walk. Instead of pointing out all they need to change, we need to be encouragers, drawing attention to how far they've come and pointing them to the Word of God.

Lord, help me see how patient you have been with me in all my struggles so that I may have patience with those who are just learning to look to you for strength. Amen.

August 15   Practice Your Faith Through Prayer

You do not have because you do not ask. (James 4:2b NKJV)

We know how important it is to exercise. Unless we continue to work our muscles, we begin to lose the strength we had. So it is with the faith the Lord has given each of us. People who "exercise" or practice their faith see God's hand in their lives, which prompts them to pray expecting an answer.

I remember the first time I was aware that God had answered my prayer and there was no way it could have been a coincidence. One day I was sitting in church, and it was time for the offering. We had just accepted three teenage girls in our home, and they needed new underwear. As I pulled out our checkbook, I whispered to Nolan, "We only have our tithe money in our account; do I pay the tithe or use it to get the girls new underwear?"

He said, "You better pay our tithe."

As I wrote the check, I sent a prayer up to God: "OK, God, these girls need underwear, so I'm going to trust you for the money."

Later, as we got up to leave, a lady I had met in church once before came up to me and asked, "Do any of the girls in your home need underwear?"

I had never experienced an answer to a specific prayer that quickly. It was a faith-building miracle in my life.

As we see God answer our prayers, our faith grows, leading us to pray even more expectantly.

Lord, strengthen my faith and help me trust that you not only hear my prayers but also answer them when I ask in your will. Amen.

August 16   Trust in Him Forever

You will keep him in perfect peace, Whose mind is stayed on You, Because he trusts in You. Trust in the LORD forever, For in YAH, the LORD, is everlasting strength. (Isaiah 26:3-4 NKJV)

Becoming a new mom as a fairly new Christian was a challenge for me. Coming out of an alcoholic environment, I knew what I did not want to be as a parent, but I wasn't sure how to make changes in my behavior. The most important thing I learned was that I needed to rely on the Lord and ask him for guidance before looking to others for answers. I needed to keep my mind focused on him and trust in him completely. As I did this by reading God's Word, along with Christian books, which spoke to my heart and made sense, the Holy Spirit worked in my life and cleaned out the "garbage." Fellowship with other Christian women and couples at various stages in their walks also taught me a lot.

There were times I wondered if I was making progress, but looking back, I can see that I was—and still am, for we are always growing. Today Nolan and I have two godly young adult sons, and we have been blessed to help many other young people in our lives. To think that we may have been a godly influence in their lives, directing them to Christ, is awesome.

Lord, like Noah, who obeyed your command to build the ark over a period of 120 years, help me keep my commitment to you by keeping my mind stayed on you, my everlasting strength. Amen.

August 17   Let God Restore Your Soul

He restores my soul. (Psalm 23:3a NKJV)

Years ago on this date, we laid to rest our five-and-a-half-year-old son. The first few months after the funeral were a fog of mechanical days; we struggled to live with the emptiness inside—the hole left in our hearts. I remember thinking one day that life would get back to normal someday. Then I thought, *What is normal?* Our lives would never again be the same, and would we really want them to be?

I will never completely understand all we went through until I am with the Father, but I do know this: To have gone through this trial and experienced the "valley of the shadow of death" and come out on the other side unchanged—*that* would be the real tragedy. God gives us choices, and we had a choice. We could become bitter and withdraw from the Lord, or we could choose to draw near to him. That did not mean we would not hurt. It meant that we would allow our heavenly Father to comfort us, teach us, and use what we had learned to walk others through the journey of grief.

We treasure the short-lived joy we had on earth with our son and the memories we still have, and we look forward to a blessed reunion in heaven.

Lord, help us remember that this home on earth is temporary and that "normal" is only a state of mind. The only thing permanent is eternity with you. Amen.

August 18   Look for God's Blessings

The LORD gives strength to his people; the LORD blesses his people with peace. (Psalm 29:11 NIV)

God allows us to see certain needs for a reason. At times, it is so we can pray. At other times, it is so we can be the "network persons" who set up solutions as the Lord provides or directs.

Miracles abound all around us; it's just that most of the time we are too distracted to see them. Here in Mexico, we see God's hand daily. One of the orphanages we visit had run out of food. This orphanage is way out of the city and off the beaten path. One day, while the children and directors were sitting in a circle praying, a large black sedan pulled up. Out stepped some very nicely dressed people who asked the director if he knew of anyone in the area needing food. They were headed farther into Mexico and had too much food to carry. When they opened the trunk, it was full of rice, beans, tortillas, and other items, which they gave to the orphanage. Then they were on their way, never to be seen again.

The Lord loves to bless us—even when we don't deserve it!

Lord, help me pray, believing you will answer; and help me look for the daily miracles you do in and around my life. Amen.

August 19   Show Mercy

For judgment will be without mercy to anyone who has shown no mercy; mercy triumphs over judgment. (James 2:13 NRSV)

The circumstances we face with our children are often analogous to our relationship with our heavenly Father. Ever get through scolding your children for something, only to see them fall into the same trap once again? You may think to yourself, *Will they ever learn?* Later you may spend some time with the Father and have to confess once again an attitude or behavior you thought was long dealt with.

Fortunately, our Father doesn't think that way. He is loving, patient, kind, and full of mercy. His Word says that once we ask for forgiveness, he forgives and forgets. Jesus' death on the cross has paid for our sins in full—past, present, and future.

Do you show mercy and forgiveness, just as it has been freely given to you? Showing mercy doesn't mean that there are no consequences for sin, or that discipline and guidelines can be disregarded or rejected. It means that we forgive without bringing up the past and respond lovingly, basing our action or response on the situation at hand—just as Christ does for us.

Lord, help me be sensitive to the way I handle the sins of others, just as you are with me. Amen.

August 20   Determine Your Role in the Body

For as the body is one and has many members, but all the members of that one body, being many, are one body, so also is Christ. (1 Corinthians 12:12 NKJV)

One of the things we teach groups in the "boot camp" part of the mission trip experience is how important teamwork is. We share a common goal, yet not much will be accomplished if we all try to do the same job. The same is true in the Christian experience. Sometimes we admire the gifts of others, yet when we try to imitate them, we find ourselves frustrated and worn out. The reason is usually that we were not given the same gift.

Nolan and I both have a passion for teenagers, but we have different gifts; so we approach our passion in very different ways. His gift is discernment, and he is very task-oriented; so he tends to be the teacher. My gift is exhortation, so I tend to be the counselor or relational person. We love being in the mission field, which is our calling; yet we could not do our work without those who partner with us as prayer warriors, financial supporters, and temporary workers. Together we form a team. With any part of the team missing, it would be virtually impossible to accomplish the job.

What is *your* role in the Body of Christ?

Lord, help me determine my passion and the gifts you have given me, so that I may use them to your glory. Amen.

August 21   Stop Making Excuses

But each one is tempted when he is drawn away by his own desires and enticed. (James 1:14 NKJV)

We've all heard the old saying "The devil made me do it." The truth is, that's an excuse for sinful behavior. Making excuses is a sign that we're not using the strength Christ has given us and need discipline in our lives. The Word says we are drawn away by our *own* desires and enticed. It's all about the choices we make on a daily basis.

When children are placed in foster care, they are removed from their homes, and the abuse stops. However, when they are able to be on their own, learned behaviors can creep back into their lives. They need continual loving guidance. Likewise, when Christ pulls us out of the world and we enter his family, there is a noticeable change; yet, if we're not disciplined, we can begin to "backslide." The Bible is our best instruction book for growing in Christ. Each day we need to renew our minds, our attitudes, and our responses to stress and difficult situations by reading the Word of God and practicing what we learn.

God has paid our debt. We are no longer slaves to sin. Let's claim our freedom and quit making excuses.

Lord, thank you for paying the price for my sins. Help me start new every morning, renewing my mind in your Word so that my past does not rule my future. Amen.

August 22   Accept the Gift

For by grace you have been saved through faith, and that not of yourselves; it is the gift of God, not of works, lest anyone should boast. (Ephesians 2:8-9 NKJV)

Have you ever received a gift when there was no holiday or occasion to warrant it, and you knew you had done nothing to earn it? We are usually surprised and pleased, but we're suspicious of the motive behind the gift. *Does this mean he loves me? What offense is she trying to make up for? I need to remember to give something in return, or she won't think I appreciate her also.* And so our thoughts go.

Christ's gift, however, is free, though it cost him his life. We don't deserve it; we never will. We can't earn it, and yet we must choose to receive it. Along with the gift come abundant blessings that God chooses to give. The days I am at my worst and deserve nothing, he chooses to bless me; and I find myself on my knees in tears, asking his forgiveness because I'm unworthy of his love. Nevertheless, I am so consumed by his grace in my life. The thing that I can do for him, however, is turn my life over to him, obey him, serve him, and love him with all my heart.

Lord, I accept your gift of grace. Let all I do be to the glory of God so that I may boast of you only and not of myself. Amen.

August 23   Become as a Child

"Assuredly, I say to you, unless you are converted and become as little children, you will by no means enter the kingdom of heaven." (Matthew 18:3 NKJV)

Ruby lives in one of the *colonias* where we work in a one-room, dirt-floor, cardboard shack with her mom and dad and three siblings. She is five years old; and for most of those years, she has been left to sit—sometimes for the entire day—in her broken-down wheelchair. Some days her mother leaves with the other children for the day while Ruby stays at home alone, sitting in her wheelchair, soiled and dirty. Her mother believes there is no hope for her. The incredible thing about Ruby is that she always has a smile on her face, ready for any attention or love that might come her way. She expects nothing and is glad about everything.

God tells us he will supply our needs. In reality, we have very few needs. Ruby's needs are often met by Christian neighbors who are concerned for her welfare, as well as by other Christians the Lord brings into her life.

It's not easy to come to the Father as a trusting child, but herein is our strength. When we trust God as a little child, we discover that his way is simple and his burden is light.

Lord, I lift up Ruby to you, and others like her. Help them be an example to me when my burdens begin to weigh me down, so that I will turn my burdens over to you. Amen.

August 24   Appreciate God's Provision

Better is the poor who walks in his integrity Than one perverse in his ways, though he be rich. (Proverbs 28:6 NKJV)

The people in Mexico have very little, but most take pride in caring for what they do have. Many days I am humbled by what I see.

One day, after I had spent seven hours at a self-service laundry doing thirty-five loads of clothing on my day off, I was exhausted. A group had given us clothes to be given to the needy, but they needed washing first. A few days later, while I was in an area where we work, I spotted a woman doing her laundry. She was using three five-gallon buckets, and she had a smile on her face. I may not have my own washing machine as I did in the United States, but at the self-service laundry I can do several loads at once without having to haul and heat water. Once again the Lord was showing me the integrity of the poor as I watched this woman take care of what she had by the means available to her.

We can be so demanding of what we think we deserve or "need" when it is really a "want" that, if fulfilled, would soon be replaced with another. God tells us that he cares for us and will supply our needs. Do you appreciate what he has given you and care for it as a precious gift from above?

Lord, help me see that if I have you, I am rich in spirit. Help me not to complain about what I do not have but to give thanks for what I do have. Amen.

August 25   Step Out of the Boat

And immediately Jesus stretched out His hand and caught him, and said to him, "O you of little faith, why did you doubt?" (Matthew 14:31 NKJV)

Have you ever felt a tug to do something that was not the norm? You said to the Lord, "Use me, Lord," and soon an opportunity came. Perhaps your church was planning a mission trip, or you heard of an opportunity to serve in your church or community. You felt a tug on your heart; but before you could even consider it, your mind was flooded with reasons why it wouldn't work.

We, like the disciples, can stay in the boat all our lives and play it safe, or we can trust the Lord when he calls our name, keep our eyes on him, step out of the boat, and walk on the water. It is amazing the miracles God does in our lives when we trust him rather than our own understanding. If we refuse to listen to the tug of the Holy Spirit, refusing to give up control of our own lives, we can miss out on the blessings God wants to give us. So, go ahead: Step out of the boat onto the water, and remember to keep your eyes on Jesus!

Lord, I want you to be in charge of every part of my life. I need help in letting go of my insecurities so that I can walk by faith. Amen.

August 26   Be Content

Not that I speak in regard to need, for I have learned in whatever state I am, to be content. (Philippians 4:11 NKJV)

Our home in Colorado Springs was modest in size, about twenty-five hundred square feet. There were days I wished it were bigger because of all the people we entertained and the "strays" (youth) we would bring home to live with us. My perspective changed while building a home for a Mexican family with five children. This 22-foot-by-22-foot home was divided into four rooms. It had a concrete floor and four unfinished walls. The ceiling was the unfinished plywood of the roof. Yet on the last day of construction, the father went inside, raised his hands to praise the Lord, and began to cry, repeating, "Father, it is so *big!*"

One thing I've learned working in a foreign country is that less really is better. Less means more time with family and less time cleaning. Less means that I don't have to find time to fit God into my agenda. We all have the same amount of time in a day; our contentment is determined by how we use that time and measure our success.

Lord, help me know what is really important to you—not what the world dictates as success. Amen.

August 27   Be Consistent in Your Parenting

Train up a child in the way he should go, And when he is old he will not depart from it. (Proverbs 22:6 NKJV)

As parents, we must be consistent in the way we train our children. From the time we bring our children home from the hospital until the time they depart from our homes, we must model Christ in our lives. We also must allow the Holy Spirit to convict us of our sin and make us aware of needed changes in our lives. Then we have a choice to make: to confess our sin, receive forgiveness, pay the consequences of our sin, and move on; or to ignore our sin and hope it will "go away." Choosing the latter affects our attitude, our relationship with Christ, and our contentment—with ourselves and others. Eventually, we become bitter, finding fault in others to guard ourselves from being discovered.

We need accountability just as our children do. As long as we are on this earth and sin abounds, we will be subject to temptation; and when we fall into the trap, we want a chance to repent, to receive loving forgiveness and fair discipline, and to move forward. Our children need and want the same. So, set boundaries and stick to them. Be consistent!

Lord, help me be consistent and fair in the way I train my children, just as you are with me. Amen.

August 28   Give Generously

He who has pity on the poor lends to the LORD, And He will pay back what he has given. (Proverbs 19:17 NKJV)

Some time ago we were given a digital camera to keep better records of the families and groups we work with in Mexico. Most of the families in Mexico do not have the luxury of family photos; I was so excited to be able to take pictures of them with the groups who came to help them.

One day I went to a home to take such a picture. When I arrived, it was so hot that the baby was naked and the other children had on only shorts, as did the father. They were embarrassed and began to look for clothing to put on. While I was talking to the mother about the heat and why she wasn't using their fan, the father slipped outside. She told me that they could not afford to pay the $3.50 per month that their neighbor charged to hook them into his wire so that they could have electricity. By then the father had returned and was in the corner, working on something. As I began to set them up for the photo, the father offered me something they had denied themselves: ice water. He had gone to the very neighbor who had "cut them off" and asked for some ice for his guest. Upon returning, he had chipped the ice out of the butter-tub container and put it into a glass of water for me.

My intention was to bless them with a photo, but I was blessed by their humble generosity.

Lord, help me always be sensitive to the needs of the poor, and help me remember that you bless me so that I may bless others. Thank you for the joy I receive in giving. Amen.

August 29   Serve in Love

Though I speak with the tongues of men and of angels, but have not love, I have become as sounding brass or a clanging cymbal. (1 Corinthians 13:1 NKJV)

All we do means nothing unless we do it in love. To do otherwise is just going through the motions.

Being a stay-at-home mom was one of the most difficult jobs I've ever had, yet one of the most rewarding. One day, at the height of my frustration, I met Nolan at the door with these words: "I have to get out of here for a little while." After I returned later and the kids were settled in for the night, Nolan asked, "What has you so frustrated?"

Nolan is an electrician by trade, so I said, "Imagine that you wired a house. It took all day, but at the end of that day you looked at the job you did and were proud. The next day, all your wires were pulled out, the fixtures were broken, and everything you had done was a mess. You felt you were expected to say nothing and calmly redo the job every day. Would you get a little frustrated?"

Life can seem that way if we're just going through the motions. That's why it's so important to start our day with the Lord. If our focus is on Christ, we'll see clearly and be able to reap joy—joy of time well spent with family and friends, of having a home, of taking opportunities to share Christ with others. Without Christ, the love is missing. With Christ, every day is an adventure of serving him in love.

Lord, help me see the many blessings you have given me and realize that caring for others is a way I can show my love for you. Amen.

August 30   Love Him

We love Him because He first loved us. (1 John 4:19 NKJV)

When we spend time in God's Word daily, we build a personal relationship with him, realizing how much he loves us; and, through prayer, we are able to follow his guidance in our lives.

Many people come to our ministry in Mexico for various reasons. Some come to serve; some come to see a different culture; some come to get away from home; some come to be with friends because it's the "cool" thing to do; and some come to be obedient, because they prayed to follow God's will and this is where he led them.

If we're not in God's Word, we can only guess what he desires of us by watching what others who claim to know him do and choosing what we think is God's will for us. That can lead to problems if the person we follow is not following the Christ of the Bible or our perception is way off. The outcome will not be of Christ, nor will it meet our expectations.

Many people walk away from Christianity, saying it's not what it's cracked up to be. Yet they never took the time to build a relationship with Christ, to fall in love with the Creator who first loved us. Do you love him?

Lord, help me keep falling in love with you as the years go by, and help my relationship with you get deeper and deeper. Amen.

August 31   Hide God's Word in Your Heart

My son, give attention to my words; Incline your ear to my sayings. Do not let them depart from your eyes; Keep them in the midst of your heart; For they are life to those who find them. (Proverbs 4:20-22a NKJV)

The Word of God is alive and will not return void (Isaiah 55:11). If we will share the Word of God with others as the Holy Spirit leads us, he will prepare their hearts to receive it. We don't have to "candy coat" it or "make" others believe; we need only share the truth.

As a new Christian, I worried about how to share Christ with others when I knew so little myself. It wasn't long, though, before I was sharing, and it didn't bring fear to my heart anymore. What made the difference? I began to study God's Word and hide it in my heart. I had to have a willing heart to do as the Spirit led. For me, opportunities arose at the park, in line at the grocery, or anywhere I might be doing a normal, everyday task. It wasn't something I had to dress up or make easy to digest; I had to say what the Spirit urged and learn to be quiet when the words stopped. I also learned that we're all different, and God delights in using us the way we are.

Get before the Father and ask him to give you a willing heart and to use you; then trust that he will do just that.

It has been great spending August with you. God bless!

Father, help me hide your word in my heart and gladly share your love and mercy to all you place in my path. Help me take the blinders off and see what you see. Amen.

SEPTEMBER

God's Healing Love

Hilda Davis

September 1   **God's Love Heals in All Seasons**

I will turn the darkness into light before them and make the rough places smooth. (Isaiah 42:16b NIV)

While working as chaplain in a cancer clinic, I became especially fond of the wife of a man who had cancer. The wife could not understand how God would allow a man as loving as her husband to have terminal cancer. He was beloved in his church and his community. She told me she could no longer hear God.

I spent a lot of time listening to her, and I recommended a book by Renita J. Weems titled *Listening for God: A Minister's Journey Through Silence and Doubt* to let her know that silence is one of the seasons of our faith walk. Weems writes, "Finally, I admit that most of the spiritual pain I have experienced over the years has been the result of my failure to surrender to the season in which I found myself" (New York: Simon & Schuster, 1999, p. 21).

The book helped her understand that our ability to feel God's presence changes. She found that sitting in her garden and watching the sunrise helped her manage the change of season in her own life. Eventually, she found the light in the darkness—God's healing love for them. Though, in her life, healing did not mean a cure for the cancer that eventually took her husband's life, healing did happen when she could once again find comfort in the presence of God.

This month you will be encouraged to reflect on your personal story and how you have experienced God's healing love in the midst of the seasons of your own life. God's love is present in *all* seasons. Sometimes we simply have to wait for the light.

O loving God, who brings light in spite of the darkness, let us know that your presence keeps us even in the rough places. Amen.

September 2   A Love That Never Changes

For everything there is a season. (Ecclesiastes 3:1a NRSV)

September is my favorite month. It is a time for beginnings and endings. It is the beginning of fall, a new season. The sultry summer days are gone and the air is becoming cooler. All of nature begins to announce that it is time for a change. Many who have had a hot summer or a drought welcome the change. Fall is a season that announces the end of the hectic yet laid-back pace of summer and the beginning of a more focused, businesslike rhythm of autumn. We are ready to find rest in the routine.

God has created the seasons to help us mark our days. In some ways it is reassuring to know that regardless of what season we are in, there will be a change; at the same time, we may feel a little anxious—unsure of what is next. Though we cannot know what change is coming, God's love is the constant in the changing seasons of our lives. God's constant love allows us to move through the seasons of our lives comfortable in the knowledge that though we are sad to see the summer pass away, we can find healing in what is to come with the fall.

Dear Lord, thank you for the movement of the seasons. Keep me in your healing love, which never changes. Amen.

September 3   God's Love Heals Mind, Body, Spirit

… and a time for every matter under heaven. (Ecclesiastes 3:1b NRSV)

I have spent almost thirty years learning about the different ways God heals us. In my twenties, it was a time for athletics. I took aerobics, I jogged, and I tried to add modern dance to my list of activities. I felt that if I kept active, I would stay well and live well. As it turned out, I had a diseased appendix, which was related to the stress I had placed upon my body, and I had to have an appendectomy. I had time for my physical well-being, but I did not take time for my mental well-being. As I have grown older and learned more, I have slowly understood that there is a time for everything.

God has given us bodies to care for, but we are also to care for our minds and our spirits. As I have begun to pay closer attention to my spiritual healing and my emotional well-being, my body seems to grow stronger. When you find yourself spending more time on one part of your life while the other parts need attention, listen for God's voice and pay attention to the other parts of your life that need healing.

O God of healing love, let me hear your voice so I will know when I need to balance my time in order to keep myself well in mind, body, and spirit. Amen.

September 4   God's Love Gives Us Rebirth

... a time to be born. (Ecclesiastes 3:2a NRSV)

Jesus told Nicodemus, a ruler of the Jews, that he must be born again to see the kingdom of heaven. Nicodemus apparently was confused because he asked Jesus how a man could enter his mother's womb again. How can a man be born again? Nicodemus had every reason to be confused. If there is one time to be born, how can we be born again?

We learn as we read further in John 3 what Jesus meant. Not only are we born of the flesh, but we also are born of the spirit (John 3:6). So, just as we care for our flesh and seek for signs of healing when we are ill, let us also watch for signs of illness in our spirits. Does it take too much effort to spend time reading scripture? Is there no time in your schedule to give time to the church or another place in need of volunteers? Are you too busy to pray for yourself and others? If you had to think about any of these answers, it is time to be born again. It is time for a spiritual birth.

O God of rebirth, help me find time to seek you and allow your love to give birth to healing for my spirit. Amen.

September 5   God's Love Brings New Life
from Death

... and a time to die. (Ecclesiastes 3:2b NRSV)

In the Gospel of John, Jesus told his disciples that in order for a grain of wheat to be fruitful, it must die (John 12:24). If you are a gardener or have ever planted anything, you can get an image of a seed being buried, watered, and fed. The old form of the seed now must die for the new life to begin.

In her best-selling book *Kitchen Table Wisdom: Stories That Heal,* Rachel Naomi Remen looks at the lives of people who have chronic diseases and recognizes the strengths they develop once they are able to make some changes in their beliefs about their limitations. Remen, a physician who lives with a chronic illness herself, has a particular sensitivity to the difficulty of letting go of beliefs that are more limiting than the actual disease. She writes, "We may need to let go of our beliefs and ideas about life in order to have life" (New York: Riverhead Books, 1996, p. 75).

Think about what beliefs you have that prevent you from being fruitful. Are there ideas that must die, that must be let go, in order for you to live more fully? It is time.

Dear God, give me the courage to know that it is time for me to let go of beliefs that are not life-giving. Amen.

September 6   God's Love Offers Presence

... and a time to heal. (Ecclesiastes 3:3b NRSV)

"Heal me, O LORD, and I shall be healed; save me, and I shall be saved: for thou art my praise" (Jeremiah 17:14 KJV). I remember the first time I heard this verse. I was having a bad day and a woman at my church asked me what was wrong. I had just left the doctor's office where I had complained of pains in my side. The doctor had ordered some tests, causing me to wonder what was going on. I was worried.

So, when she asked what was wrong, I was ready to talk. I was feeling weary, worn, and weepy. She looked at me, reached out, and gave me a hug. We sat down, and she let me talk for a few minutes. Then she gave me this verse from Jeremiah. I was touched. My spirit felt peaceful. As I recited the verse to myself, I felt the presence of God.

Healing happens from the inside out. It is also a good thing when someone cares enough to take time to touch our minds and spirits and, at the same time, bring healing to our bodies.

Dear God, when I see someone who appears to be suffering, help me reach out in love and bring your healing presence. Amen.

September 7   God's Love Focuses on Wellness

. . . a time to keep. (Ecclesiastes 3:6c NRSV)

Some of us have made promises to ourselves—and perhaps to others—to improve our health. Fall is a good time to keep those promises by beginning an exercise program if we haven't already. The weather is cooler and the children have returned to school. Now the rhythms of our days are more structured and organized. This is the time to keep those promises to begin walking at the mall or to sign up for a membership at the local health facility. When we make our health a priority, we create wellness in many parts of our lives.

God cares about our physical bodies, which is why Jesus spent so much time healing people. The woman with the flow of blood had a dream to experience health, and she knew where to go for her healing. She had a goal that helped her overcome crowds and years of disappointment to reach her healer. Jesus' healing love for this woman made him stop and care for her physical healing as well as her spiritual and emotional healing.

Dear God, who stops and cares for us whatever our issue, help me keep my focus on wellness—for myself and for others. Amen.

September 8   God's Love Leaves Old Baggage Behind

. . . and a time to throw away. (Ecclesiastes 3:6d NRSV)

Recently I went to a women's retreat. We were a group of women who were coming to be refreshed, to hear a word that would touch us in our dry places and bring healing. We shared stories of strength and weakness, of despair and hope, of the death of old dreams and the birth of new ones.

On the last day of the retreat, the leader talked about the woman at the well, the Samaritan woman, who was so excited about hearing of the waters of eternal life that she left the pot she had used to gather the well water and ran to tell others of the new life promised by Jesus. The leader told us to "leave our pots" at the retreat. She suggested we leave behind the "baggage" that weighs us down—past hurts, broken relationships, and disappointed dreams.

We were encouraged to step into a new life. God's healing love had restored and refreshed us. We did not need our old "baggage." Neither do you!

Dear God, help me leave behind old baggage and receive new life and healing love in you. Amen.

September 9   God's Love Speaks Boldly

... and a time to speak. (Ecclesiastes 3:7d NRSV)

There are many stories in the book of Acts of bold women who spoke out and made a difference in the early church. One woman gained her freedom by speaking boldly.

Paul and Silas were followed for several days by a "slave girl" who was speaking the truth about who they were. As she followed them, she announced that they were "servants of the most high God" (Acts 16:17 KJV). This slave girl could not stop speaking about what she knew. Before now, she had spoken only when her owners had told her to speak. But, when she saw Paul and Silas, she could no longer stay silent. Suddenly she began to use her voice to speak the truth that God had placed in her heart. When she spoke the truth, she was set free from her owners.

As women, we often are asked to "keep silent" or to not say exactly what is on our minds. Yet, when we are able to speak the truth from our spirits, we gain our freedom in Christ.

Holy God, give me the courage to speak boldly about what I know: your healing love. Remind me that I can praise you and bring healing to myself and to others. Amen.

September 10   God's Love Is Unconditional

... a time to love. (Ecclesiastes 3:8a NRSV)

When my daughter was little, I would ask her, "Who loves you?" She would happily begin to call out the names of family and friends whom she knew loved her. At the end of the game I would hug her and say, "You are so loved."

We have strong feelings of joy when we hear the words, "You are so loved." It's no wonder when we read the description of love found in 1 Corinthians 13: "Love is patient; love is kind; ... it is not irritable or resentful; ... It bears all things, believes all things, hopes all things, endures all things. Love never ends" (vv. 4-8a NRSV).

Imagine God asking you, "Who loves you?" Begin to name the people who love you. Now think about the qualities they show to let you know they love you. Are these qualities found in 1 Corinthians 13?

As you enjoy and appreciate the feelings of loving and being loved, think of God who loves you and delights in you simply "because." This is unconditional love. Play the game with yourself. Say, "Who loves me?" Then answer, "God does." You are so loved!

Dear God, in those times when I feel unloved and unlovable, remind me that you love me and that I am "so loved." Amen.

September 11   God's Love Comforts and Rejoices

... a time to mourn, and a time to dance. (Ecclesiastes 3:4c, d NRSV)

Today is my birthday. However, since the tragic attack on our country on this day in 2001, it has been a day of both sadness and joy. I did not lose a loved one in the devastating attack; however, I, along with the rest of the world, lost a sense of safety and security. Many changes have been made to rebuild confidence in our country's defense system; yet, despite the changes, we know that healing takes time.

How long it takes to mourn is a personal decision. A friend in her nineties recently told me that she continues to grieve her husband who died thirty years ago. She happens to be one of the most joyous, vibrant, and loving people I know! Her sense of loss does not keep her from honoring life. On this day of national mourning, it is important to take time for the memorials as well as the celebrations.

God reminds us that there is a season for all things. I will never forget the tragedy that happened on this day. I will also remember that just as there is a time to mourn, there also is a time to dance. God's love brings healing to our pain and rejoices with us in our celebrations.

Loving God, who stands with us as a healing presence, give me grace to stand with others during times of joy and seasons of sorrow. Amen.

September 12   God's Love Forgives

... and a time for peace. (Ecclesiastes 3:8d NRSV)

Forgiveness wouldn't be so difficult if we didn't have to forgive people who were mean to us! That's why forgiveness takes determination. It's just not easy to overlook past hurts. Yet one of the best ways to achieve healing and peace is to forgive.

I stood at the altar with someone who promised to love, honor, and obey. Then, almost before the ink was dry on the marriage license, that same person was calling me names and dishonoring me in painful ways. I find it hard to forgive him. However, today I am determined to begin the process one more time. I have forgiven before, only to be reminded of my pain and become angry all over again. Today, I will remember the times I have disrespected God and have awakened the next day, forgiven. I will remember the times I have not loved God with my whole heart and have been given the gift of taking another breath. I am so grateful that God loves me just as I am.

Think about how much God loves each of us, and remember that God doesn't ask that we forget—only that we forgive and allow ourselves to heal.

Dear God, grant me your healing love so that I can find healing by forgiving others. Anoint me with your peace as I grow in the grace to forgive. Amen.

September 13   God's Love Brings Peace

For the mountains may depart and the hills be removed, but my steadfast love shall not depart from you, and my covenant of peace shall not be removed, says the LORD, who has compassion on you. (Isaiah 54:10 NRSV)

As we've spent time in the book of Ecclesiastes, we've seen that our lives change just as the seasons change, yet we can trust that God's healing love never changes. The knowledge of God's steadfast, unchanging love gives us peace. Over the next several days, the book of Isaiah will continue to show us God's healing love through its message of hope and peace amid change.

Today we're reminded that God has compassion for us and promises to give us peace. The peace we receive from God in times of change brings healing to our bodies, minds, and spirits. We need God's healing peace today more than ever before. We have so much going on in our lives: working high-pressure jobs, rearing children while caring for aging parents, juggling multiple responsibilities, maintaining relationships with friends and loved ones. For our health's sake, we must set aside time in the midst of all that is going on to meditate and connect to our Source.

It's important to remember that the peace of God is ours—always available. We can have the same peace that quieted storms and healed broken spirits by learning to relax, rely on God and God's Word, and rest in the assurance that God's Word can be trusted.

God of peace and unchanging love, I pray that your peace will bring calm to my constantly changing, always demanding life. Amen.

September 14   God's Love Creates a Peaceful Life

Peace, peace, to the far and the near, says the LORD; and I will heal them. (Isaiah 57:19 NRSV)

Take a moment to sit quietly and think what it would mean to have peace in your life. You may need to end a relationship that is no longer working. You may have a special relationship that needs some attention, some kindness. You may have an opportunity to offer peace to someone who is hurting. Or, you may need to embrace the special relationship you have with yourself.

Begin practicing biblical affirmations each day to remind yourself of how special you are and to motivate you to begin needed lifestyle changes. Take a small step toward peace—such as simply increasing the amount of water you drink each day. Peace can be very near.

Today, find what you need to create a place of peace and healing. You may have a corner of your room where you can create an altar. Place objects you enjoy on your altar (candles, green plants, a fountain), and spend time there in relaxation. Or you may find peace in a park or beside a lake. Select a place where you can go often. Find renewal and healing in your own sacred space.

O God, help me find time to sit and listen for your voice. Create spaces in my life where I can sit in your peace. Amen.

September 15   God's Love Invites Joy and Laughter

For you shall go out in joy, and be led back in peace; the mountains and the hills before you shall burst into song, and all the trees of the field shall clap their hands. (Isaiah 55:12 NRSV)

God intends for us to have joy. This scripture gives us an amazing picture of nature joining in the celebration with singing and clapping. Joy and celebration are part of the healing love we experience as we rest in our relationship with God.

Howard Clinebell, a pastor who has written extensively on well-being, believes there are seven areas of well-being, one of which is *play*. Our ability to enjoy life includes our ability to bring playfulness into our daily tasks.

Joy is even connected to physical healing. Author Norman Cousins healed himself of a chronic disease by watching funny movies and reading humorous books. Being able to laugh at ourselves and *with* others is a way of maintaining good emotional and spiritual health as well.

Take a moment to read a funny story. Notice how relaxed you are when you laugh. This is the joy God intends for you.

Dear Lord, thank you for the gift of laughter. Keep our hearts and minds full of your joy; help us bring joy to others. Amen.

September 16   God's Love Offers New Gifts

See, I am doing a new thing! Now it springs up; do you not perceive it? (Isaiah 43:19 NIV)

Old things have passed away. God is doing a new thing in your life. Of course, if you're too busy to pay attention, you may miss the changes.

Have you begun a new relationship with God or made a new covenant with God to improve your spiritual, emotional, and physical well-being? One of the signs that you are developing and expanding your relationship with God is that your life is growing healthier in very basic and important ways and you're no longer looking at your purpose in life in the same way. You have a new vision for yourself and your future.

It may have been difficult to pay attention to how you treated your body before, but now you are reminded that when you care for your body, you are praising God. It may have been difficult to treat yourself as a precious gift before, but now you know that the gift of your body is a gift from God and that you are valuable. God is doing a new thing in you. Don't forget to look.

Dear God, you continue to offer new things that help me become more connected to my purpose and more in relationship with you. Thank you. Amen.

September 17   God's Love Nurtures Self

The Lord GOD has given me the tongue of a teacher, that I may know how to sustain the weary with a word. (Isaiah 50:4a NRSV)

Have you ever had just the right word for someone who was grieving or weary? It is a gift to be able to restore the spirit of someone with just the right word. Many of us are very good with just the right words to bring healing to a wounded spirit. But think about how often you don't use kind words to yourself. What is the last nice word you said to yourself?

June Jordan, African American poet and civil rights activist, once said that she must seek to love and respect herself as if her life depended on her ability to do so (1978 address to the Black Writers' Conference, Howard University, included in *Moving Towards Home: Political Essays,* 1989). Jordan was right: Your very life *does* depend on the love you show for yourself and how well you respect yourself, even when you feel you have let yourself or others down.

Think about the names God calls you: "my faithful ones" (Psalm 50:5); "daughters of kings" (Psalm 45:9); "the apple of the eye" (Psalm 17:8). Be reminded that you are God's beloved.

Think of the things you say to show your love for yourself. Take time today to speak words of love to yourself. Kind words are healing. You should save some for yourself.

Loving God, remind me of how much you love me and that I am special because you made me. Give me the "tongue" to say those words to myself. Amen.

September 18   God's Love Names Us in Love

Fear not, for I have redeemed you; I have called you by your name; You are Mine." (Isaiah 43:1b NKJV)

God tells us that we have no reason to be afraid. Not only has God paid the price for us; God has also named us. We belong to God. What a feeling of security we should have!

In some cultures a baby is named in a beautiful ceremony with the entire community present. I was asked to speak a few words at the baby-naming ceremony of some friends from Nigeria. When I arrived, there were long tables spread with food and gifts and many people gathered around. There was so much joy, celebration, and love. After the speakers spoke uplifting words and told of precious memories of the baby and family, the parents recounted the blessing of each of their children. Then they gave the baby's name and told what each part of his name meant. His African name spoke of the promise of his life, of his connection to the ancestors, and of his relationship to God. Naming is an important community ritual.

Imagine God taking the time to name each of us. Our names point us to our purpose, speak of our connection to all God's people, and, best of all, tell of our relationship to God.

O Creator God, thank you for naming me so that I know I belong to you. Amen.

September 19   God's Healing Love Sustains Us in the Flood

When you pass through the waters, I will be with you; and through the rivers, they shall not overwhelm you. (Isaiah 43:2a NRSV)

How often do we feel as if we're caught in the swirling waters of a flood? Responsibilities at work, home, church, and the community all begin to catch us up in their energy and move us along without any regard for what we want. The flood often comes at a time when we cannot resist its power. Once again we are swept along, unable to say no—just trying to keep our heads above water.

God says to us today: "Do not be afraid. The waters will not overwhelm you. All those responsibilities are not yours alone. I am with you." Take time today and sit in a comfortable position. Take a few deep breaths and allow yourself to relax. Close your eyes and imagine yourself being caught in a flood. Try to catch some of the items floating by to keep yourself above water. Imagine you see a large, dry patch of land, and suddenly you are gently moved there. The land is dry; the sun comes out. You are safe. God will not let the flood overwhelm you. You will pass through the waters. You are not alone. God is with you.

O God of presence, remind us that we will get through anything that tries to overwhelm us. Thank you for your presence in the floods of life. Amen.

September 20   God's Healing Love Opens Our Hearts

"He has blinded their eyes and deadened their hearts, so they can neither see with their eyes, nor understand with their hearts, nor turn—and I would heal them." *(John 12:40 NIV)*

So far this month we have looked at God's love in all seasons and the peace of God as found in Isaiah. Now we will end the month looking at how God's love is present in the life of Jesus.

In today's verse, Jesus was quoting the prophet Isaiah, who was lamenting the fact that the people's hardened hearts would not turn to God for healing. Jesus also was saddened that, in spite of all the healings they had seen him do, the people would not turn to him and allow him to heal their lives.

Today, God wants you to open your heart to receive healing in your life. Consider these three ways to experience healing as you allow the power of God's love in your life:

1) Let go of feelings of shame and guilt. You can be free by remembering that God loves you just as you are.

2) Encourage beliefs that make sense for who you are today. (In her book *Girlfriend to Girlfriend: Everyday Wisdom and Affirmations from the Sister Circle,* Julia Boyd says, "We think about what we 'should have,' 'could have,' or 'would have' done differently, but there's no way to recapture the past" [E. P. Dutton, 1995, p. 45].)

3) Have healthy relationships with others. Remember: God created you to be in community with other people.

Dear God, I invite your healing love into my life. Give me an open heart to give and receive love. Amen.

September 21   God's Healing Love Gives Thanks for Blessings

As he entered a village, ten lepers approached him. Keeping their distance, they called out, saying, "Jesus, Master, have mercy on us!" When he saw them, he said to them, "Go and show yourselves to the priests." And as they went, they were made clean. Then one of them, when he saw that he was healed, turned back, praising God with a loud voice. (Luke 17:12-15 NRSV)

In a sermon I heard on this passage, the preacher asked, "Where were the other nine?" She suggested that we are like the other nine. There are times when God answers our prayer, "Help me, Lord. Make me well," or "O God, give me that job; that house; that husband." And we are so thrilled that we immediately begin enjoying our blessing. We never look back to say thank you.

The preacher suggested that it is never too late to say thank you. God is always present, listening to the prayers of our hearts. We can take the time to say how grateful we were to get off that bed of illness and be restored to health, or how grateful we are to have our mates. Our prayers will be heard regardless of how many years have passed.

Maybe there is someone in your life who would be delighted to hear from you after many years of silence. It may be someone who helped you in big ways, such as a former teacher or preacher. Or it may be someone who was only in your life for a brief season, but you want her to know that she is not forgotten—and neither is her kindness. Take time to say thank you. You will be blessed.

My God who is always faithful, I thank you for always answering my prayers. Remind me to let others know how grateful I am for their presence. Amen.

September 22   God's Healing Love Sees Beyond Limitations

Jesus said to him, "Go; your faith has made you well." Immediately he regained his sight and followed him on the way. (Mark 10:52 NRSV)

Jesus healed Bartimaeus of his blindness because of his faith. I am moved by this story. Bartimaeus reminds me that I am more than my limitations. He is a model for action.

Bartimaeus's blindness was not his full identity. When we define Bartimaeus solely by his physical limitations, we ignore his spiritual possibilities. He had a relationship with Jesus. He had to have been familiar with Jesus because he called out to him. He knew that his relationship with God gave him an identity larger than that of blind beggar. He did not allow himself to become discouraged by how others expected him to behave, for Bartimaeus's blindness did not keep him from being bold.

One of the saddest things we do to ourselves is allow our limitations to keep us from finding healing in God. We make a mistake by allowing tradition, fear, or community to define who we are. Value all of who you are; your limitations are God's opportunities.

O God, who sees me as whole and healed, thank you for hearing my voice and seeing beyond my limitations. Amen.

September 23   God's Love Chooses Peace Over Anger

Jesus answered and said to them, "Render to Caesar the things that are Caesar's, and to God the things that are God's." (Mark 12:17a NKJV)

In Mark 12, we read how the Pharisees were trying to trick Jesus into saying the wrong answer regarding taxes so that they could make him look bad.

Doesn't it always seem that the closer we try to get to God and the harder we try to do the right thing, the more we are surrounded by people who are trying to bring us down? But there's good news. We have the love of God who gives us the wisdom and courage to choose the more difficult and more loving action. We can turn a difficult situation into one of triumph by turning to God in prayer and trusting him.

The Pharisees and the Sadducees tried to create distress in Jesus' life, but Jesus was connected to God, the source of his power—and of ours. He chose to show them the healing love of God.

We have the ability to choose, too. We can decide to stop, relax, and allow God's peace to help us think. By choosing peace over anger, we can keep our emotional health and our spiritual well-being.

Find ways to have peace in your life today. Stop. Relax. Pray.

Dear God, in all things help me remember that you are the source of my power and peace. Let me triumph over difficult situations. Amen.

September 24   God's Love Expects Miracles

Then Jesus took the loaves, and when he had given thanks, he distributed them to those who were seated; so also the fish, as much as they wanted. (John 6:11 NRSV)

Jesus' feeding more than five thousand is one of many miracles that showed his relationship with God and his love for God's people. The Bible tells us they had as much as they wanted. No one was hungry.

Think about the miracles you have witnessed in your own life. How did you receive the miracles? Did someone else have to point out to you how awesome God had been in your life?

It is faith that allows us to receive the miracles God has for us. Faith helps us to overcome the facts we see in front of us.

Fact: A woman had been bent over and crippled for years. *Faith:* Jesus straightened out her body and gave her a new life. *Fact:* Jesus was approached by a Canaanite woman, an outsider, who wanted her daughter to be healed. *Faith:* Jesus healed her in spite of her marginal position in society.

Your faith can turn facts into miracles. Don't let your vision for your life be limited by what you can see. Walk by faith, not by fact.

Loving Jesus, allow me to see my future through faith. Remind me to expect a miracle. Amen.

September 25   God's Love Invites Us to Rest

"Come to Me, all you who labor and are heavy laden, and I will give you rest." *(Matthew 11:28 NKJV)*

The first thing women say when I tell them they need to take some time for themselves is "I don't have time." Many of us don't automatically have time for ourselves. We have families, jobs, church work, community activities, and the list goes on and on. As women, we are taught to take care of others and work hard.

In *Sisters of the Yam: Black Women and Self-Recovery,* bell hooks says, "We do not know when to quit." She goes on to say, "Knowing when to quit is linked to knowing one's value. . . . Since society rewards us most . . . when we are willing to push ourselves to the limit and beyond, we need a life-affirming practice, a counter-system of valuation in order to resist this agenda" (Boston: South End Press, 1993, p. 56).

Today's scripture gives the formula for the "counter-system": resting in Jesus. When you are asked to do one more thing, schedule an appointment with Jesus. Then find a quiet place and rest in Jesus' healing love. Enjoy the time you spend in communion with Jesus. Leave your burdens there when you go. Schedule your next appointment.

Precious Lord, thank you for inviting us to find rest in you. Amen.

September 26   God's Love Says Yes to Abundant Life

"The thief comes only to steal and kill and destroy. I came that they may have life, and have it abundantly." (John 10:10 NRSV)

There are many actions, attitudes, and beliefs that are unhealthy. These are the "thieves" that can steal our joy, kill our spirits, and destroy our well-being. And these thieves are not easy to overcome. Perhaps you face a thief of illness that can be improved through eating a proper diet. Or your thief may be a past choice that you need to put behind you. Or perhaps your thief is a harmful behavior that is robbing your life of peace and joy.

We have to say no to risky behaviors, and that is not an easy thing to do. Sometimes saying no means that we will lose relationships, but we must remind ourselves that relationships that contribute to unhealthy behaviors are not worth saving. Saying no to harmful actions means we're saying yes to the abundant life of Jesus!

We don't have to practice saying no by ourselves; the love of God will give us strength. Today, say no to harmful behaviors and say yes to the full life Jesus offers.

Loving Savior, you offer us abundant life, rather than thieves that steal our joy. Help us choose you. Amen.

September 27   God's Love Builds Community

Jesus loved Martha and her sister and Lazarus. (John 11:5 NIV)

Jesus believed in relationships. His first miracle took place at a wedding where family and friends gathered to celebrate. Later he brought together a group to walk with him and be his disciples. Even at his crucifixion he made sure that his mother was cared for by connecting her with John, his beloved disciple. Jesus recognized that our relationships sustain us during times of trouble and bring us joy during times of celebration.

This story in John tells of the loss of Mary and Martha's brother, Lazarus. Jesus arrived in their home after the death of Lazarus. Mary and Martha were grieving, and Jesus wept with them. Jesus understands our sorrows and pain, too. He weeps with us during those times just as he wept with Mary and Martha.

Jesus does not ask us to spend our lives in solitude; he believed in community. If you are spending too much time alone, find a way to be part of a special community. Connect with a church or faith community in your area. If Jesus found support in the company of others, you can expect to benefit from the company of others, too.

Lord of families, communities, and friends, guide us into trusted relationships. Amen.

September 28 God's Love Remembers Our Stories to Children

When he noticed how the guests chose the places of honor, he told them a parable. (Luke 14:7a NRSV)

Jesus told many stories to teach his lessons. We remember stories because they tell us about ourselves; they remind us of our connection to others. Stories are healing because they remind us that we are not alone.

When my daughter was a child, I read her a bedtime story every night. Story time was our way of connecting with each other and with something bigger than both of us. Sometimes the stories were about Black history, and sometimes they were just fun stories with a lesson carefully hidden in the rhymes and colorful characters. But the stories she loved most were the stories I told her about myself—funny stories of my family, stories about her father and his family, and stories about the many twists and turns I've taken in life. When she heard my stories, she felt connected to me. I loved telling them because, in some way, I was giving her the gift of myself. Both of us gained something special.

Take time to tell your story to a child. Jesus did.

Loving Lord, let me share the story of your love for us so that others and I may be healed. Amen.

September 29 God's Love Strengthens Faith

"For truly I tell you, if you have faith the size of a mustard seed, you will say to this mountain, 'Move from here to there,' and it will move; and nothing will be impossible for you." (Matthew 17:21 NRSV)

Sometimes it is easier to talk about having faith than to actually practice it. Jesus said that if our faith is only as large as a tiny grain of mustard seed, we can move mountains. Similarly, the writer of Hebrews says that faith is being sure of what we hope for and certain of what we do not see (Hebrews 11:1).

So, how do we live in faith? I offer three ways we can measure our faith:

When you have faith, you boldly ask God for what you want.
When you have faith, you are willing to wait for an answer.
When you have faith, you are willing to take action when the answer comes.

In the words of Kirk Franklin, "I can do the impossible; I can see the invisible because I got faith; because I got faith" (*Nu Nation Project,* Gospocentric, 1998, Audio CD).

Got faith?

O Loving Lord, when I seek you, my faith grows. Help me "seek God and God's strength; seek God's presence continually" (Psalm 105:4, author's paraphrase). Amen.

September 30   God's Love Leaves Us with Peace

"Peace I leave with you; my peace I give to you." (John 14: 27a NRSV)

God's healing love brings peace. Jesus gave his life that we might have joy, life, and peace. We live in a time when war is more common than peace. There are few countries that are not engaged in war somewhere in the world. How can we talk about peace when there is no peace?

Jesus tells us that the peace that endures in the face of mounting strife across the globe is the peace that he leaves with us. The peace Jesus speaks of tells us to forgive seventy times seven. Forgiving creates peace. The peace Jesus expects us to have is the peace that passes all understanding, because it comes from keeping our minds and hearts on the love Jesus has for us. It is not the peace of the world that we keep. We trust the peace that comes from faith in our God.

So, when the world says there is no peace, receive the peace that Jesus gives. It is a peace for all seasons, for all time. Go in God's peace and God's healing love.

Loving Lord, thank you for your peace. Help me hold it in my heart for every season. Amen.

OCTOBER

The Road to Repentance

Sallie Dye

October 1   **The Serpent's Question**

Now the serpent was more crafty than any of the wild animals the LORD God had made. He said to the woman, "Did God really say, 'You must not eat from any tree in the garden'?" (Genesis 3:1 NIV)

*S*in. You won't find it on the top-ten list of popular conversation topics, but it's the number one topic, or theme, of the Bible. And if we want to know God intimately and grow in our relationship with him, it's a topic we must address—not once, not occasionally, but *daily*.

Why daily? Because the temptation to sin comes quickly and subtly, with a thought. In Eve's case, that thought originated from Satan strategically questioning the word of God to "get her off track" in her thinking.

How often do we "get off track" in our own thinking? How easy it is to listen to the world's subtle questioning of our faith, opening ourselves up for deception and lies to take root in our minds. The only hope of stopping wayward thoughts is focusing on the truth. We must spend time daily in God's Word and prayer if our thoughts are to remain grounded in what is true and right.

This month we will travel with Adam and Eve along their road to temptation, sin, and repentance. Then we will journey with David as he finds joy in his own repentance. I encourage you to spend time in reflection and prayer after reading each day's brief devotion. Ask the Lord to use these devotions to reveal areas of sin in your own life that need his attention and your release. Though the journey may be uncomfortable or difficult at times, the destination is well worth it!

Dear God, help me get back on track so that I may know your truth and abide in that knowledge. Allow the Holy Spirit to speak to areas of sin in my own life and guide me on the road to repentance. Amen.

October 2   Eve's Answer

The woman said to the serpent, "We may eat fruit from the trees in the garden, but God did say, 'You must not eat fruit from the tree that is in the middle of the garden, and you must not touch it, or you will die.'" (Genesis 3:2 NIV)

Eve's answer to the serpent's question showed that either she exaggerated God's word, or she hadn't listened to God's word. God had said that *eating* the fruit would cause death, not merely *touching* it (Genesis 2:17). Regardless of the reason for Eve's blunder, she did not have the complete truth of God's word in her heart; and Satan seized the opportunity.

If we journey through life without a thorough knowledge of God's Word, we also open ourselves up to be deceived. We can be Christians and fall again and again into various sins because we don't have the truth of the Scriptures stamped in our hearts. We must be careful not to "rearrange" or reinterpret God's truth to suit our own desires. Instead, we should ask God to give us the desire to live out his truth however difficult or unpopular it may be.

Almighty God, give me a hunger to grow in knowledge and wisdom, and please show me the scripture that you want me to hide in my heart today. Amen.

October 3   Satan's Lie

"You will not surely die," the serpent said to the woman. (Genesis 3:4 NIV)

Satan, through the serpent, lied to Eve. He took advantage of her weakness, her lack of focus on God's truth, and he told her she would not die.

Never doubt that Satan will tell a lie at every opportunity given to him. Whenever God's truth is absent or "watered down," Satan will step in to fill the void. He is a deceiver, yet he has a will for our life just as God does. The difference is that Satan's will leads us to shame and devastation.

God, however, does not lie (see Psalm 119:160; 1 John 5:20). God has a wonderful plan for each one of us (see Jeremiah 29:11-14). Though we may face difficult or uncomfortable seasons in our life, God has a wonderful plan for each of us and promises to fulfill it if we will trust in him.

Today, let us praise God and ask of him, as David did in Psalm 25:5, "Guide me in your truth and teach me" (NIV).

Dear Lord, show me the lies I have believed, and teach me to depend on your truth. I praise you, Lord, and ask that you help transform me into the image of Jesus Christ. Amen.

October 4   It's Going to Be Great!

"For God knows that when you eat of it your eyes will be opened, and you will be like God, knowing good and evil." (Genesis 3:5 NIV)

Eve was given a picture of how wonderful the consequence of eating the forbidden fruit—her sin—would be. After lying to her, Satan began to give her an expectation of counterfeit joy.

It's not easy to take steps backward after we have listened to Satan's lies. After he distorts God's truth, he quickly appeals to our desires and dreams. We must pray that God will expose the lies and prevent us from going any further. God will always provide a way out of temptation, but we must call on his name and be obedient to his every word.

Satan led Eve to believe she would be better than she was. In what areas of your life do you feel insignificant, unloved, unappreciated, or overlooked? Ask God right now to fill those weak areas with his presence.

Dear heavenly Father, let my hungers seek satisfaction in you alone. Take my vulnerabilities and use them for your glory. Amen.

October 5   Eve's Choice

When the woman saw that the fruit of the tree was good for food and pleasing to the eye, and also desirable for gaining wisdom, she took some and ate it. (Genesis 3:6a NIV)

Rather than believing God, Eve chose to believe Satan. She ate the fruit because it was good and pleasing, and because she might attain more wisdom.

Temptations rarely look bad. Satan wants us to believe the sin is good for us. Eve chose an action that seemed good, rather than believe the excellent word of God.

How often do we choose to do something that we know is wrong but that seems so good for us? How often do we forgo blessings from God because of our refusal to make the right decision, the excellent decision, the decision backed by the truth of the Scriptures?

Believe God today.

Dear Lord, I want to believe that what you say is best for me. Increase my belief. Amen.

October 6   Inviting Another to Sin

She also gave some to her husband, who was with her, and he ate it. (Genesis 3:6b NIV)

Choosing to sin rarely affects only ourselves. As women, God has given us something very powerful: the gift of influence. If we are not careful, our words and actions can very easily cause others to follow us in sin. Mothers probably have more impact on our society than anyone else. Are you a mother who builds up your family rather than tearing them down? As a wife, do you influence your husband in a godly way or in a selfish way? As a single woman, do others see evidence of Christ in you at work or in your relationships? Choose today to be a person of godly influence.

Dear God, help me use my influence to move others toward Christ, not away from him. Amen.

October 7   Covering Up Shame

Then the eyes of both of them were opened, and they realized they were naked; so they sewed fig leaves together and made coverings for themselves. (Genesis 3:7 NIV)

Adam and Eve felt the very first consequence of sin: shame. Realizing their nakedness and vulnerability because of their refusal to stay under the providence of God's word, they tried to cover up their shame with their own handmade solution.

Our own ideas for covering ourselves don't work. In our shame, after falling into sin, do we try to "redecorate" and hope the sin will go unnoticed? The problem with this action is that God is interested in our hearts, and no amount of covering up will heal a heart that has been tainted by sin.

Ask God to replace any shame in your heart with a desire for renewed holiness.

Dear heavenly Father, I want to appear blameless before you. Take my guilt and shame and replace it with your holiness. Amen.

October 8   Broken Fellowship

Then the man and his wife heard the sound of the LORD God as he was walking in the garden in the cool of the day, and they hid from the LORD God among the trees of the garden. (Genesis 3:8 NIV)

Adam and Eve were suffering the worst consequence of sin: broken fellowship with God. How they must have longed to walk through that garden with God; but, instead, they had to hide among the trees.

When fellowship with God is broken because of our sin, it is then that we realize the sin wasn't worth it after all. How many times in our past have we missed the blessing of walking closely with God because of choosing to bring sin into our lives and holding on to an unrepentant heart? Ask God today to forgive you for whatever sin you hold dear to your heart, so that you may walk closely with God through the garden of life.

Dear God, please forgive me for my distance. Teach me that I should treasure nothing more than walking with you in the garden of life. Amen.

October 9   God Questions Adam

But the LORD God called to the man, "Where are you?" (Genesis 3:9 NIV)

God called to Adam, asking a question. God, being sovereign, did not ask the question to get information; he asked the question to make Adam reveal his separation from God.

God never forces us to confess. Instead, he specifically asks us, as he did Adam, "Where are you now in your life?" He causes us to consider our relationship with him. In that probing question from Almighty God, Adam could not help seeing his own shame very clearly. God knows that in order for us to learn and grow through our mistakes, we must learn to reach out to him. We must learn to take the first step toward reconciliation, and he'll gladly meet us there with corrective yet loving arms.

Dear Abba, teach me to trust you and lean upon your strength so that I may move away from my own foolish ways. Allow me to learn from your wonderful, perfect, fatherly love. Amen.

October 10   Admitting the Shame

He answered, "I heard you in the garden, and I was afraid because I was naked; so I hid." (Genesis 3:10 NIV)

Adam confessed not the actual sin committed, but the feeling caused by the sin. He admitted to God that he felt shameful.

Sometimes we can have feelings of shame, fear, guilt, or perhaps bitterness, yet we do not confess the actual sin that caused the feeling. We may not know. If we want true joy and peace in our relationship with God, then we may need to dive deeper into our negative emotions. We should ask God for insight as to why we behave or feel a certain way. Sometimes it may be necessary to seek counseling.

Jesus Christ, the Great Healer, is waiting to help us be holy and blameless by allowing us to confess those sins that have created havoc in our lives for so long. Let go of the shame and grab on to his name!

Dear Great Healer, heal me today from any wickedness that lurks under the surface of my soul. Give me a feeling of release and joy as I give myself completely to you. Amen.

October 11   The Truth from God

And he said, "Who told you that you were naked? Have you eaten from the tree that I commanded you not to eat from?" (Genesis 3:11 NIV)

God reveals through his questions to Adam the disobedience of Adam's action. Adam heard the convicting truth from the word of God.

We have a tendency today to shrink sin and say that it is not really "as big a deal" as it was in the Bible. God and his word are the same yesterday, today, and tomorrow. God loves the sinner but hates sin. He can't be near it. And we can't be close to God when sin is in us. It was so important for God to make Adam see that his commands were the key to life. Adam needed to know that he had disobeyed God's word.

We, too, need to know when we disobey God. If a particular scripture seems to keep "popping up" around you, consider the possibility that God may be reminding you to check your obedience to that part of scripture. Remember, it is the truth that will set us free!

Dear Lord, give me a desire to want to follow your commandments. I love you so much and know that the safest place for me is to be nearest you. Amen.

October 12   Standing Up for What Is Right

The man said, "The woman you put here with me—she gave me some fruit from the tree, and I ate it." (Genesis 3:12 NIV)

Adam had been given the truth, but he allowed Eve to influence and persuade him to sin. In our modern language, Adam might have said, "OK, honey, whatever you say!" When answering God, he didn't try to pass the blame on to Eve or cover for her; his answer was honest. He allowed her to lead him into sin. He could have said, "No, I will not do this wicked thing," but, instead, he fell right along with her.

Are we brave enough to stand up for what is right? In our families or workplaces, do we have the strength to say no when everyone around us is diving in and saying yes? That strength comes only from knowing God and keeping his commandments by the power of the Holy Spirit dwelling within us. Be an influence for what is good and right. Don't choose to be a follower of the deceived; be a leader for Jesus Christ!

Dear Jesus, thank you for your difficult obedience at the cross that led to my salvation. The least I can do to repay you is risk looking a little foolish for your name's sake. Amen.

October 13

God Questions Eve

Then the LORD God said to the woman, "What is this you have done?" (Genesis 3:13a NIV)

Finally, God confronted Eve. Again God asked a question: "What have you done?" He put before her a question to set the stage for her confession. In order for her to gain back her peace, she had to confess in a specific way.

God always wants us to get specific in our confessions. Through our realization of our own mistakes, we are humbled and realize our human frailty. Somehow thinking specifically about our sin—about what it was and what it did—makes us see our need for God.

Don't ever think that God doesn't use confessed sin for his glory. What we learn from our mistakes gives us strength to combat future temptations.

Dear heavenly Father, strengthen me each time I humble myself and admit my mistakes. Always pursue me until I realize that I must constantly pursue you in prayer and meditation on your Word. Amen.

October 14

Eve's Confession

The woman said, "The serpent deceived me, and I ate." (Genesis 3:13b NIV)

After being questioned by God, Eve confessed her sin, admitting that Satan had deceived her and that she had *chosen* to follow him. She gave a complete confession.

So many times we confess incompletely. We blame only Satan or negative influences around us for our own actions; or we confess and say, "It was my own fault," while being oblivious to Satan's influence in our choice to sin. We have to completely confess. We must acknowledge that Satan has the power to deceive us, but we also must acknowledge that we have the power of Jesus Christ in us to combat Satan and his evil ways.

Praise God today for that awesome power that is inside you, and use it!

Dear God, thank you for your goodness and mercy to save me from Satan's wicked ways. From this day forward, help me trust you and see my sin from your perspective. Holiness is impossible without you. Amen.

October 15   David's Plea for Mercy

Have mercy on me, O God, according to your unfailing love; according to your great compassion blot out my transgressions. Wash away all my iniquity and cleanse me from my sin. (Psalm 51:1-2 NIV)

We have left Eve and her final confession and now journey with David through his own steps of repentance and restoration with God.

David, after committing adultery with Bathsheba and murdering her husband, suffered a long period of broken fellowship with God. He asked God for mercy and stated what he knew about God: that he is a God of unfailing love and compassion. David desired fellowship with God and wanted the burden of sin washed away. He knew that only God has that power.

How wonderful it is that we have a merciful, loving, and compassionate God! He loves us no matter what. If we want the fullness of that love, then we have the responsibility of confessing our sins. It is up to us to reach out to God; and, through Jesus Christ, our sin has already been paid for on the cross. Why would we want to pay for it again and again by harboring it, unconfessed, in our hearts?

Dear Lord, you are a God of love and compassion. Thank you for loving me today wherever I am in my life. Of all the wonderful things you created in this universe, thank you for cherishing me, a sinner. Amen.

October 16   Tripping Over Sin

For I know my transgressions, and my sin is always before me. (Psalm 51:3 NIV)

David recognized that he could not get away from his unconfessed sins. They were always there to block the vision ahead.

Try as you might to move forward in life, you will trip over unconfessed sin every time. Just when you think you have gotten away with hiding something, there comes a similar temptation or negative feeling. The question is, will you continue tripping over sin while trying to patch the wounds yourself, or will you keep your feet on solid ground and call out to the Great Wound Healer?

Call on God, confess your sins, and your vision will become clearer. You still may fall from time to time, but you will know by experience how to get up again. Begin today to investigate patterns of sin in your life and ask God for help.

Dear God, I want to see my walk with you clearly. I want sin to be removed from my way. Only you can do that. I know I should seek your face instead of hiding my own. Transform my vision! Amen.

October 17   Pleasing God

Against you, you only, have I sinned and done what is evil in your sight. (Psalm 51:4a NIV)

David came to realize a most important perspective concerning his sins. In his steps toward repentance, he came to see that his offense was against God Almighty. As we read in Isaiah 63:10, our sin grieves the Holy Spirit. David, no doubt, saw the hurt his sins had caused other people, but how keen he was to see the grief his sins had caused God.

In our own lives, our sin may hurt others deeply, or sometimes others may be unaffected by our sin. In either case, our sin must be placed in one category: an offense to God. If we keep this perspective, we will remain grounded in pleasing God, not grieving God.

Do you want to please God? Are there thoughts or actions in your life that may be sinful but don't appear to hurt others? Place those things before God and ask him to give you a desire to please only him.

Dear Lord, I am so sorry I have sinned against you by _____. Please forgive me for seeking to please myself rather than you. You are a great and awesome God, and I have only a small, pitiful idea of your magnificent holiness. I treasure your love for me. Amen.

October 18   Natural-born Sinners

Surely I was sinful at birth, sinful from the time my mother conceived me. (Psalm 51:5 NIV)

David realized something we have a hard time accepting: We are natural sinners. We are born thinking of ourselves and of our needs, and we struggle with this selfishness our whole lives. Because we are natural sinners, we desperately need God, our Savior. Yet we have a hard time accepting this as well. We want to be independent, self-sufficient.

We can be good and do many nice things, but unless we accept Jesus Christ as our Savior and Lord, it's all done in vain. Pride is such a subtle sin. It makes us think we don't need God. It makes us think we are good enough without God. Yet the key to true goodness is admitting our inability to be good!

When we discover our pride and see the damage it does to ourselves and to others, then we can surrender to God and let him replace the void with humility. Humbled people are a breeding ground for true goodness.

Dear God, I know I wrestle with pride in so many areas in my life. Make these areas known to me. I want to let go of pride and taste true humility. Amen.

October 19   The Inmost Place

Surely you desire truth in the inner parts; you teach me wisdom in the inmost place. (Psalm 51:6 NIV)

David desired what God desired for him. He wanted God's truth and wisdom to fill him. The best way to be filled with God's truth and wisdom is to read and internalize the Bible. Psalm 1:2 says of the blessed, "[Their] delight is in the law of the LORD, and on his law [they] meditate day and night" (NRSV).

Do you meditate on God's Word day and night? Do you delight in the Bible? Do you memorize scripture? Do you simply read and forget, or are you a "doer" of the Word (James 1:23)? Do others say of you, "She seems so blessed because she has the peace of God's truth inside her"?

These are convicting questions for each of us. If you answered no to any, ask God today for the same desire that King David had—a longing to be filled with God's truth.

Dear heavenly Father, please fill me with your truth. Give me a hunger to gain knowledge and wisdom. I want to have an impact for your kingdom and bless others through my example. Amen.

October 20   Being Washed

Cleanse me with hyssop, and I will be clean; wash me, and I will be whiter than snow. (Psalm 51:7 NIV)

David was so weary of feeling unclean. He knew that God alone was capable of cleansing him, purifying him, and making him holy again.

Have you ever had to go for an extended period of time without a bath, perhaps because of illness or a wilderness camping trip? Do you remember how refreshed you felt after finally taking a bath? God offers us a good bath after we have confessed and repented of our sins. Why would we want to stay weary and dirty when we have the chance to be cleaned up thoroughly by Jesus Christ? There is such relief after repenting of a season of impurity in our souls. God has blessed us by allowing us to feel many positive emotions. My favorite one is relief.

Dear Jesus, no attempt to hide or cover up my sin will cleanse my soul. Only you are capable of that cleansing. Please take my sin and replace it with blessed relief! Amen.

October 21   Rejoicing Despite Crushed Bones

Let me hear joy and gladness; let the bones you have crushed rejoice. (Psalm 51:8 NIV)

David, no doubt, is referring to God "crushing him" by announcing through Nathan the prophet that his son would die (2 Samuel 12:14). Yet David desired joy and gladness in the Lord even though he was experiencing sadness.

Just because we do the right thing by confessing our sin does not mean we don't suffer consequences for the sin committed. David knew that God was his loving Father, and sometimes it is a father's job to allow consequences to fall where they will and not shelter a child from pain. David did not ask God not to crush his bones; he asked God for a heart to rejoice through his suffering. Through his grief, he wanted God's presence and the joy it brings.

You may be dealing with suffering in your life right now that you feel might be linked to previous sin. Perhaps God has allowed this suffering for growth or humility in your life. Let go of blaming God and ask him to replace your bitterness with joy, gladness, and rejoicing.

Dear Lord, I want you near when I struggle with pain and sorrow. I want a heart that rejoices in you even when I am hurting so. Deliver me from the oppression of my enemy, and let me shout praises to you, my loving Father. Amen.

October 22   A Fresh Start

Hide your face from my sins and blot out all my iniquity. Create in me a pure heart, O God, and renew a steadfast spirit within me. (Psalm 51:9-10 NIV)

David wanted a fresh start. He asked God to forgive his sins, give him a pure heart, and provide a steadfast spirit to be renewed in him. David was wise to ask for a pure heart. His heart had led him astray before. He had shut God out, and his own selfishness had taken precedence in his heart. His heart had lost its purity.

Take a look at your own heart. Are you at a place in your life where you need a fresh start, or have you ever been in that place? God loves to give fresh starts. Testimonies of faith are based on these wonderful heart changes in our lives. Surrender to God today, or reflect on a past surrender, and share your testimony with someone today. Sharing the love of Christ will renew a steadfast spirit in you.

Dear God, your mercy is an incredible thing to experience. I want my words to express the purity of my heart instead of the shame of my sin. Make me a new person, full of your mercy and love, and send me a person today with whom I may share this mercy and love. Amen.

October 23   The Fullness of the Holy Spirit

Do not cast me from your presence or take your Holy Spirit from me. (Psalm 51:11 NIV)

God chose specific servants in the Old Testament to experience the presence of the Holy Spirit. David was one of these. He relished the presence of God and knew when he had quenched the Spirit, or had gone too long without the fullness of the Spirit.

First Thessalonians 5:19 speaks of not putting out the Spirit's fire. David put out the Spirit's fire by throwing the "water" of sin upon it. When have you, like David, experienced a "quenching" of the Holy Spirit? Have you experienced a season of sin when you could not sense God's presence or direction in your life? Was your sensitivity dulled, causing you to long for that presence and fullness? God certainly doesn't leave us without the Holy Spirit, but we can decrease the fullness that the Spirit brings to our lives by our own turning away. Where do you stand today? Could you use more filling up? Turn toward God and step back into the fullness of his presence.

Dear heavenly Father, thank you for the blessing of having your Holy Spirit living inside me. Today, may I not quench your Holy Spirit but, instead, ignite your power in my life. Reveal and stop those thoughts or actions that would turn me away from your presence. Amen.

October 24   Joy

Restore to me the joy of your salvation and grant me a willing spirit, to sustain me. (Psalm 51:12 NIV)

David needed joy in his life again, and he knew that the greatest joy resulted from a realization of his salvation from God.

God doesn't remember our past sins, but there are times when it is beneficial for us to do that very thing. Obviously, it is good to remember our past sins so that we do not repeat them, but a more important reason is so that we are overwhelmed with joy at the way God has saved us and brought us to a peaceful place.

Are you at a peaceful place, full of joy, or are you sensing something is not quite right? Reflect on past sins in your life. Relive the forgiveness and mercy that God has shown you. Search for ways God has blessed you, even though you didn't deserve those blessings. Meditate and ask God to restore the joy of his salvation.

God is so good! Thank him today for whatever goodness is in your life, and be joyful! Trade any present burden of sin you have for the wonderful peace and joy his forgiveness brings.

Dear Lord Jesus, thank you for your gift of salvation and the joy this gift brings. Thank you for your mercy and forgiveness. May I, in turn, be merciful and forgiving of others. Amen.

October 25   Leading Others

Then I will teach transgressors your ways, and sinners will turn back to you. (Psalm 51:13 NIV)

David was king, yet he knew he had not been in a right position to lead and help his people during his long period of unconfessed sins. He knew that repentance and a "pure heart" were necessary for effective leadership. In this verse of David's prayer of repentance, we see that he had a servant's heart and wanted to be effective in leading others to God.

Like David, we cannot be effective leaders unless we keep ourselves in check, confessing and repenting of our sins. If you are a leader in your church, workplace, or family, how is the state of your heart? Do you have the joy of salvation within you? Do you desire to teach others about God? Do you long for persons around you to turn from their sin and accept Christ as their Savior?

God wants to use you, even if you aren't a recognized leader, to have an impact on many people. Pray today for God to send some searching souls your way.

Dear God, use me wherever I am today, either knowingly or unknowingly, to steer others to the cross. I pray for my own heart to remain true to your Word and ready to reveal you in my life to others. Amen.

October 26   Desiring Righteousness

Save me from bloodguilt, O God, the God who saves me, and my tongue will sing of your righteousness. (Psalm 51:14 NIV)

In this psalm, David may have been asking God to keep him from being put to death for his own murder of Uriah (2 Samuel 12:9). David was promising God that he would use his tongue to sing of God's righteousness.

God indeed rescued David—not only from death, but also from his burden of sin. David must have felt that he had a renewed mission on earth, and that his purpose was not yet complete. We know from his other writings that he certainly had a deep gratitude for God's forgiveness and mercy. No doubt, part of his renewed mission must have been to sing of God's righteousness, as he had promised.

God had shown David the path of righteousness, and David could not be quiet. He couldn't be quiet any more than the people could be quiet about Jesus, for as Jesus said, "I tell you ... if they keep quiet, the stones will cry out" (Luke 19:40 NIV).

Have you ever been so full of gratitude for God's mercy and love that you couldn't hold it in—you had to share it? Don't hold back. Share and sing of God's righteousness. Infect others' lives immediately with that joy. It's very contagious!

Dear Lord, I am overjoyed in my salvation! I want to spread the truth and love that you have offered me to many other people, for you are a righteous God! Amen.

October 27   Words of Praise

O Lord, open my lips, and my mouth will declare your praise. (Psalm 51:15 NIV)

David asked God to open his lips so that he could praise him.

Other than prayer, there is nothing like praise to chase away the enemy. How easy it is to get in the habit of speaking negatively. How many opportunities for sharing God's love and healing power do we miss because of our negative words? Even when we don't necessarily speak negatively, we may miss opportunities for praise by not giving God the credit for the good things he has done in our lives.

When something goes well in our lives, do we tell others of God's goodness and blessing, or do we fail to mention God at all? David knew that God had to open his lips for praise. If he did not call upon the Lord, then his fleshly nature would have gladly taken control of his lips.

Today as you converse with others, ask God to open your lips for his praise.

Dear Lord, I speak so many words in a day, yet how many are to your glory? Show me how I can turn a hopeless, negative remark into a transforming word full of promise and praise. Amen.

October 28   Obedience, Not Sacrifice

You do not delight in sacrifice, or I would bring it; you do not take pleasure in burnt offerings. (Psalm 51:16 NIV)

David knew that God would rather have obedience to his word than sacrificial acts.

When giving to church and others, what is your motivation? Consider that deeply. Have you ever given with an attitude other than the pure joy of giving to the Lord? Every penny you give and every service you involve yourself in should be done because you find joy in doing it for God. That does not mean that it will not be difficult at times; but if you feel any bitterness or resentment in giving, then you are no longer abiding in God's love.

One key is not to focus on what will happen to your money or to others during or after your service is complete. Those results are for God alone to know. You are his vessel, and you should find contentment in your relationship with him.

Let us be obedient lovers of God, not resentful givers of sacrifices.

Dear Sovereign Lord, I serve you alone, and it is not my business to know the effects my giving has on others unless you wish for me to know. Help me abide in you and not abide in sacrifice without you. It is the walk with you that brings me joy. Amen.

October 29   A Humbled Heart

The sacrifices of God are a broken spirit; a broken and contrite heart, O God, you will not despise. (Psalm 51:17 NIV)

David once had a broken heart that turned into a humbled heart. God both listened and came to him in that state of brokenheartedness.

Though it may sound strange, God seems to do his best work in us when we are broken and weak. God doesn't desire us to be sad and empty. His desire is what will be the outcome of that emptiness: a humble, repentant heart ready to listen to him.

Have you ever been overwhelmed with problems, change, or grief? At those times you are a perfect candidate for God's power to come into your life. When you are at the end of your rope, God wants you to seek him for help. By admitting that we can't, God can step in and say, "I CAN!" Allow him to do that today. Offer something to God that you can't do, and watch him work!

Dear heavenly Father, take my emptiness and make me whole. Do that difficult task for me. Reach out to that person who is unlovable. It feels so good sometimes to say, "I can't, but you can!" Amen.

October 30   A Good Example

In your good pleasure make Zion prosper; build up the walls of Jerusalem. (Psalm 51:18 NIV)

Perhaps David wanted God to keep David's own bad example from infecting his kingdom. After his repentance, he asked God to make Zion, or Jerusalem, prosper and to build up the walls of protection around the city. David, the people's leader, had allowed temptations to become sins. As long as he remained unrepentant, he no doubt had a negative effect on his people and his kingdom, for he had lowered the "walls of protection" by choosing to sin and not seek restoration immediately.

As women who "set the tone" of our homes, it is important for us to be diligent in our walk with God. If we are hiding sins, we may be surprised to discover that much of the stress we and our families feel is related to our refusal to be transparent and humble with God. Unconfessed sins make our families easy targets for Satan. We must strive to walk closely with God by confessing all our sins and repenting of them. As we do this, we provide protection to those we lead, especially children. Many lives will be safer because of our excellent example!

Dear God, how precious you are to me, and how precious are those I love. Teach me to extend your love to others. Be my "everything" so that those you've entrusted me to lead will have peace. Amen.

October 31   A Hopeful Future

Then there will be righteous sacrifices, whole burnt offerings to delight you; then bulls will be offered on your altar. (Psalm 51:19 NIV)

David was stating his enthusiastic optimism for the future. He was predicting that when God's righteousness was at work through him as king, and perhaps as father, many blessings would be returned to God. David was hopeful for his people.

How incredible it is to consider the impact each one of us has on the future. Many family trees have had one bad apple after another until, finally, one apple decides not to fall, but to cling to the tree of life. When that one person lives differently than the ones that came before, her or his choice affects the family tree from that point on. Wow, what an awesome power God gives us if we choose obedience!

Today, meditate on how special and important the Son of David, Jesus Christ, thinks you are, and prayerfully consider how you might make a positive impact on future generations. It is important to understand how we are tempted, how we fall, and how we get back up again. True repentance brings such joy and fullness to our lives, leaving a wonderful spiritual legacy for those who follow.

I have enjoyed our journey together this month. May you continue on your walk with the Son of David, allowing him to lead you down the road to repentance and righteousness.

Dear Father God, I will never completely understand why I am so special to you. I only know how special you make me feel. Thank you for the wonderful future I have—growing closer to you each day while on earth, and, ultimately, seeing you up close and personal in heaven. I can't wait! Amen.

NOVEMBER

Be Empowered!

Monica Johnson

November 1   **It's Time to Get Intimate**

I have hidden your word in my heart that I might not sin against you. (Psalm 119:11 NIV)

I received salvation at age thirteen. However, because I was not taught the principles of discipleship, I strayed away from the church as a teen. Then, at age twenty-one, spiritually broken and crying out to God for help, I rededicated my life to Christ. I joined a Bible-believing and Spirit-filled church and began studying the Word of God through Bible study and weekly Sunday worship. The Word was precious to me and became my source of strength. It was in my heart and very near in my time of need.

The rewards for studying the Word paid off. While lying in shock trauma after a terrible car accident, I heard dark voices trying to convince me that I would die. Meanwhile, the Word of God rose from my heart, and I began to encourage myself. I did not have access to a Bible, but I was able to freely confess God's Word. I was able to say to the mountain of death, "I will not die but live" (Psalm 118:17 NIV) and "No weapon formed against [me] shall prosper" (Isaiah 54:17a NKJV). Intimate time with God had empowered me for warfare.

Are you spending time studying the Word and praying? If not, it's time to get intimate! This month we will consider what happens when we eat the Word daily as spiritual food, just as we feed ourselves naturally throughout the day. We will consider what it means to believe what God's Word says, know him intimately, and *be empowered*!

225

Dear God, I believe your Word has power to deliver me from the fears of this world. I rebuke every distraction that hinders me from being empowered by your Word. Amen.

November 2   "I'm Not Going to Take It Anymore!"

Behold, I give unto you power to tread on serpents and scorpions, and over all the power of the enemy; and nothing shall by any means hurt you. (Luke 10:18 KJV)

"I'm not going take it anymore!" Those were the words I declared when I realized I didn't have to live with sickness, depression, loneliness, gluttony, resentment, or unforgiveness. I was determined to study every scripture that promised me victory over sin. Wherever there was sin in my life—whether inward or outward, sins of omission or commission—it always resulted in death. I no longer wanted to hold my head down in low self-esteem. I no longer wanted to suffer with an illness I thought was from God. I no longer wanted to live in lack and defeat.

I became empowered as I learned about the promises God has for his children. I am the righteousness of Christ (Romans 5:17, 18). I am more than a conqueror (Romans 8:37). God's Spirit is great within me (1 John 4:4). I became empowered!

What are you being robbed of because you have not tapped into the mighty Word of God?

Dear God, I receive your resurrecting power to conquer every sin in my life. I have been empowered to help build the kingdom of the Lord. Amen.

November 3   Can They Tell?

When Moses came down from Mount Sinai with the two tablets of the Testimony in his hands, he was not aware that his face was radiant because he had spoken with the LORD. (Exodus 34:29 NIV)

As I've mentioned, several years ago I experienced a horrific car accident. I lay helplessly in shock trauma, kept alive on a life-support machine. My family has shared the miraculous stories of how I communicated with them during this comatose state.

At one point of my illness, the doctors threw in the towel because the life-support machine no longer breathed for me. I was in need of lung transplants but too critically ill to endure the surgery. The prognosis was death. Although the doctors said that I was dead, my sister was convinced that I was with Jesus. The glow on my face was so bright that she said she experienced Jesus while in my presence. I desire to still reflect Christ by the indwelling of his Spirit.

Moses' look expressed the light and life that dwelt within him after being in the presence of Jesus. Others were able to witness God's glory.

The Bible tells us to draw nigh to God and he will draw nigh to us. Can others tell that you've been with Jesus?

Glorious Father, let your light shine on me. I desire to bring you glory through my living. Amen.

November 4   More Like Jesus

Do not lie to each other, since you have taken off your old self with its practices and have put on the new self, which is being renewed in knowledge in the image of its Creator. (Colossians 3:9-10 NIV)

One day the Spirit of the Lord instructed me to ask the parents of some kids I had been ministering to this question: "If the only Jesus your kids witnessed was in you, what would they say Jesus is like? Would they describe Jesus as immoral, unfaithful, dishonest, hateful, and unforgiving; or would they say that the Jesus they know is loving, merciful, kind, gentle, patient, humble, and unconditionally loving?"

Then I turned the question around on myself. It allowed me to see what areas in my life I needed to change in order to become more like Jesus.

God is the same yesterday, today, and forever; and we are created in God's image. Can our family and friends count on us to be the same, or do they wonder if we're going to be forgiving and loving today?

Since God is love, and we are made in God's image, we should act in his nature. Instead of reading 1 Corinthians 13 as "Love is —," insert your name, saying "[Your name] is ——." Ask yourself if your life exemplifies God's love.

Father, please teach me your ways, and help me become more like you. I desire for others to know you through me. Amen.

November 5   It's a Heart Issue

Above all else, guard your heart, for it is the wellspring of life. (Proverbs 4:23 NIV)

The Bible says we are to guard our hearts, to secure the truth in our heart. We must be careful not to allow the enemy to enter our hearts and rob us of life.

I had a specific situation that challenged my ability to love. I wanted to become bitter and respond in anger. A friend attempted to encourage me with scriptures. I told her I didn't need another scripture. I felt so angry that my heart began to fail, so I cried out to the Lord. I knew that if I was to resist the enemy and overcome this horrific ordeal, God had to show up.

And so it was! In my desperate cry, the Spirit miraculously touched my aching heart and healed my hurt. I was able to meditate on the words of life, and I overcame the temptation to hate and run.

Have you ever been in a situation that, no matter what others said to help you, the pain wouldn't stop and you needed a miracle to change the outcome? Are there areas of doubt within your heart that have caused you to live in bitterness, lack, hate, or fear? No longer meditate on the negative things that the enemy has spoken to your heart. Hear what the Lord is saying. Then, with childlike faith, hold fast to those promises. Hide them in your heart.

Above all else, guard those things so that you may have life—*abundant* life.

Dear Lord, teach me how to guard my heart so that I may experience life in abundance. Amen.

November 6   A Fasted Lifestyle

So I say, live by the Spirit, and you will not gratify the desires of the sinful nature. (Galatians 5:16 NIV)

I was a baby in Christ when I began to seek God for understanding about fasting. After studying the Bible and reading books about fasting, I began to put the teaching into practice. The results were phenomenal. As I stripped my flesh of its desires, I became victorious in the things of the Spirit.

One day as I was about to order fast food, I heard the Spirit command me to order light. I later realized that if I had overindulged, I would have been so full that I would have needed to sleep immediately after and, therefore, would have missed being used by God later that day. It was then that I realized God was calling me to a fasted lifestyle.

There are pleasures of the flesh that become our god and eventually consume us. Fasting allows us to be more attentive to the things of the Spirit. Jesus apparently lived a fasted lifestyle. What if we lived a lifestyle of denying our flesh all the things that prevent us from hearing the voice of the Lord? What if we heard the Lord daily in every area of our lives? Let us pray and ask God to show us the ways we should "fast."

Heavenly Father, I desire to hear you daily. Give me the strength to walk in the Spirit and live a fasted lifestyle, not fulfilling the lust of my flesh. Amen.

November 7   It's Gonna Make Me Holy

"And anyone who does not take his cross and follow me is not worthy of me." (Matthew 10:38 NIV)

Early in my walk with God, I was bitter and hateful. It was often a challenge not to operate in the works of the flesh (Galatians 5:19-21). I was ignorant of life in the Spirit. It wasn't long before I was asking God for help and understanding.

Jesus, who walked the earth, was tempted to sin in every point but sinned not. He paved the way for me. As a believer, I, too, had the power to overcome the works of the flesh. In order for me to walk in the Spirit (Galatians 5:22-23), I had to nail my flesh to the cross and rise in the Spirit, letting go of the desires of the old nature. Crossbearing is a daily walk; therefore, each relationship I enter is ultimately making me holy.

What relationships challenge you to deny your flesh? What are some situations in which you've prayed for change but things have remained the same? What situation could God be using to make you holy? What if your situation never changes? Could it be that God is calling you to deny yourself of a last word, an immoral act, or an unforgiving heart?

Gracious Father, show me! Then empower me so that I may bear my cross in victory. Amen.

November 8   Claim Your Inheritance

"Do you think I cannot call on my Father, and he will at once put at my disposal more than twelve legions of angels?" (Matthew 26:53 NIV)

Judas had betrayed Jesus prior to his arrest. In haste and defense on Jesus' behalf, one of the disciples, Peter, struck a temple guard with his sword, cutting off his ear. Jesus replied with the powerful scripture above.

I used to react in the flesh to challenging situations just as Peter did. I was not aware that my warfare was not against flesh and blood (Ephesians 6:12). So, it was easy for me to raise my hand to a fight, use filthy language to tear a person down, or use other manipulative actions to win a quarrel.

Once I received Jesus as my Savior and Lord, I gained understanding in how to be victorious in challenging situations. I learned that I was an heir and co-heir to the Lord Jesus (Romans 8:17), which privileged me to have access, through Jesus, to the very angels that Jesus could have called upon to save him from the impending crucifixion.

Have you felt defeated, alone, or unprotected because you were not aware of your inheritance as a believer? Claim your inheritance and call upon the Lord!

Dear God, I ask you to dispatch your holy angels around me to protect and guide me. I ask you to remind me to call upon you in my time of need. Amen.

November 9   How Can I Wait?

I waited patiently for the LORD; he turned to me and heard my cry. (Psalm 40:1 NIV)

The psalmist David said that he was in a horrible situation (slimy pit), singing a song that probably sounded like "Nobody knows the trouble I've seen." Still, the psalm doesn't end in sadness. David said that the Lord "put a new song in [his] mouth, a song of praise to our God. Many will see and fear, and put their trust in the LORD" (Psalm 40:3 NRSV). Most likely, David's victory was a result of his attitude while he waited—patiently!

Several years ago, I had to wait on a healing to manifest in my paralyzed arm. I believed God for my healing, but it did not happen immediately. Though I initially waited without complaining, I became weary and acted in an ungodly nature.

Waiting patiently requires a mind-set of long-suffering, which allows us to be tolerant while serving God and others. While waiting, I realized I was no longer singing the song I had sung in the past: "Things never go right for me; I'll never be healed." In time, God put a new song in my mouth even before my healing manifested. I sang praises to God. He heard my cry and restored mobility to my arm. Others witnessed the miracle of my patient waiting (not just the miraculous healing), and put *their* trust in the Lord.

Sometimes physical healing does not manifest in our lives while we're living here on earth. Still, how many people have put their trust in the Lord because they've witnessed you waiting patiently for God to deliver, heal, or bless you?

Father, forgive me for not waiting patiently. I believe you for my miracle, and I will serve you joyfully until the miracle is manifested. Amen.

November 10   I Want the Gain

For to me, to live is Christ and to die is gain. (Philippians 1:21 NIV)

Sometimes the death of a loved one or the trials of life can make us feel like we want to die. However, Paul gives us understanding of why we are to remain. Paul was confident that his destiny was heaven, and that if he died, he would receive eternal glory. Still, he did not want to see others perish. Paul endured great hardships and sincerely desired to depart and be with Christ, yet he knew it was necessary for others for him to remain. He knew he had to touch more lives.

In order for us to gain it all, we must first secure our place in heaven. We must be born again. Then, as we endure, we must continue to do the work of the Lord so that others may come into the knowledge of the Lord also.

God knows how much we can bear. Allow the Holy Spirit to help you overcome the trials that come to rob us of our faith. Then boldly confess that you will joyfully remain for the progress of others—that through you, their joy in Christ will overflow (Philippians 1:25-26).

Be empowered to know that to live in Christ is the way to gain it all. Any other way will forfeit your reward.

Father, thank you for giving me only what I can bear. Thank you for my eternal destiny. Amen.

November 11   Clean Up Your House

"When an evil spirit comes out of a man, it goes through arid places seeking rest and does not find it. Then it says, 'I will return to the house I left.' When it arrives, it finds the house unoccupied, swept clean and put in order. Then it goes and takes with it seven other spirits more wicked than itself, and they go in and live there. And the final condition of that man is worse than the first." (Matthew 12:43-45b NIV)

A believer's body houses the Holy Spirit. To maintain a clean house, we must continually pray, walk in faith, and be vigilant. All the unclean spirits (for example, adultery, addiction, malice) leave the cleaned house in search of a place to reside. Yet if we continue in the same ways and are not empowered through prayer and studying the Word, they return to our cleaned house. The very things that we were delivered from return seven times stronger.

An empty house is a house that's idle. The affections are no longer concerned with the things of God but now are attentive to the vanities of the world. An empty house has been swept of the fruit of the Spirit and is furnished with foolishness and worldliness. The evil habits that have multiplied are now more fatal.

Have you ever experienced the return of bad habits? Have you wondered why it was so difficult to give up that destructive habit the second time around? Sweeping your temple without adding "godly furniture" leads to a stronger stronghold. Be empowered by 1 Peter 5:8: "Be sober, be vigilant; because your adversary the devil walks about like a roaring lion, seeking whom he may devour" (NKJV).

Dear Lord, help me renounce the things that do not concern you. Please renew a clean heart and a right spirit within me. Amen.

November 12   No Confidence in the Flesh

For we ... have no confidence in the flesh. (Philippians 3:3 NKJV)

Just when I thought I had it all together, it seemed as if I had failed again. My hair was fixed just right, my clothes were of the finest designer and tailored to fit, my makeup was perfect, and my confidence was at its peak; but somehow the message I went to preach was not effective. Looking back, there was one thing I forgot to do: I forgot to put God first.

Have you ever tried to do something within the church or on your job and it ended in financial, physical, or mental disaster? As you looked back, you couldn't figure out what went wrong; and still today you question the negative results. Just maybe, God did not allow it to prosper because your confidence was in your ability (your flesh) and not in God.

The apostle Paul said that if anyone had a right to put confidence in the flesh, he did. He was circumcised (Jewish), of Israel (chosen nation), from the tribe of Benjamin, a Pharisee (knowledgeable of the law), to name a few reasons. Yet Paul said we are to put no confidence in the flesh.

Father, I repent for putting confidence in my flesh. I yield to you so that I may walk victoriously in the Spirit. Amen.

November 13   Thy Kingdom Come

For the kingdom of God is not a matter of eating and drinking, but of righteousness, peace, and joy in the Holy Spirit. (Romans 14:17 NIV)

Have you ever wondered why Matthew 6:33 tells us to seek first God's kingdom? Oftentimes when we hear of the Kingdom, we think about heaven. But the scripture says that the Kingdom is more than a matter of eating and drinking. The kingdom is righteousness (holiness of the heart and life), peace (harmonizing heart), and joy (solid spiritual happiness). The kingdom is contentment while weathering a storm. It is what keeps us at peace when affliction hits.

Whenever I become focused on the issues in my life, I quickly lose my state of peacefulness. I begin to worry about those things that the Bible says will be given to me "Therefore I tell you, do not worry about your life.... For the pagans run after all these things, and your heavenly Father knows that you need them. But seek first his kingdom and his righteousness, and *all* these things *will be given* to you as well" (Matthew 6:25-33 NIV, *emphasis added*). Seeking worldly things prevents us from experiencing God's kingdom here on earth.

Lord God, please help me maintain a state of peace, joy, and righteousness so that I may receive all the things I have need of today. Amen.

November 14   It Is Written

Jesus answered, "It is written: 'Man does not live on bread alone, but on every word that comes from the mouth of God.'" (Matthew 4:4 NIV)

In this passage, Jesus is in the wilderness, being tempted by Satan. Satan comes when Jesus is hungry. Hunger naturally diminishes the strength of the body, distorts thinking, and makes one easily irritated. Hunger can cause one to become unbalanced and lack vigilance. As a result, the lack of balance and prayer produce impatience. With Jesus in this state, Satan has a decided advantage. When Satan comes to tempt Jesus, he is actually telling him to distrust God's divine providence and use illicit means for his necessities. He does the same with us.

It can become dangerously easy to accept the illicit provisions of the tempter when we are not being sustained by the Word of God. God's Word is provision; it is appointed and promised. Yet, if we do not study the Word of God, we are unable to tell the tempter, "It is written..."

In what areas are you being tempted, causing you to feel defeated? Today, find scriptures pertaining to your specific situation and tell Satan, "It is written...!"

Jesus said that we can't live by bread alone. We must live on the Word and promises of God!

In the name of Jesus, I declare that I will not be defeated by temptation but will be empowered by the Word of God. Amen.

November 15   I Almost Slipped

"I made a covenant with my eyes not to look lustfully at a girl." (Job 31:1 NIV)

Job's story is told time and time again. Job avoided committing the sin of adultery by first setting his mind not to look at a woman lustfully. Although Job was talking about adultery in the physical sense, Job was also innocent spiritually.

When we enter into covenant with God, we enter into a spiritual marriage with him. If we begin to lust for the things of the world and partake in the spiritual food of the enemy (strife, jealousy, and so forth), we are committing spiritual adultery.

The psalmist Asaph said in Psalm 73 that after witnessing the goodness of God, he almost slipped. Asaph almost lost his anchor in God because he allowed his eyes to focus on the wicked.

What is causing you to "almost slip"? Allow the Word of God to empower you to enter into covenant relationship with God; only then may you avoid the outward and inward sins that result in spiritual adultery.

God, forgive me for the things I have looked upon that have caused me to sin, and help me be faithful to you. Amen.

November 16   Seek Solitude

Very early in the morning, while it was still dark, Jesus got up, left the house and went off to a solitary place, where he prayed. (Mark 1:35 NIV)

Seeking solitude was a priority for Jesus. With his busy life and ongoing call to ministry, Jesus made time to be alone with the Father. Spending time with the Father in prayer nurtures our relationship with him and equips us to meet life's challenges and struggles. If you notice in the Gospels, before Jesus performed miracles and cast out demons, he first spent time with the Father. (See Matthew 14:22-23; John 14:13; and John 11:41, to name a few.)

Jesus was our example. He even dealt with the death of his cousin John alone in prayer. However, he did not dwell on it. He returned to the ministry that he was sent to do.

What is keeping you from being empowered to do ministry? Seek solitude to hear the Father's instruction as well as to be empowered spiritually.

Precious and Holy Father, I will seek you early. I will be empowered by my time alone with you to complete the ministry you have assigned to my hands. Amen.

November 17   A High Price

I have been crucified with Christ and I no longer live, but Christ lives in me. The life I live in the body, I live by faith in the Son of God, who loved me and gave himself for me. (Galatians 2:20-21 NIV)

When I became a born-again believer, my outlook on life changed drastically. I initially based success on status. Now, my desire for riches took a backseat to the anointing of God. I desired intimacy with Christ. I watched a woman in my church as she praised God with her hands, body, and mouth. I stood in awe when she danced in the Spirit. It was as if the man of her dreams was romancing her. I soon realized she was dancing with the Holy Spirit, who was the most important romance in her life. I asked God for some of what she had. He told me it was "a high price" to pay. She lived a disciplined lifestyle. She sought God early, trained to know his voice, and sacrificed the lusts of her flesh to walk in great power and victory over sin.

Often single women want God to give them a holy, spirit-filled husband, yet they are in no condition for God to present them to that mate. Often they want God to send them forth in ministry, but he can't present them to the world if they live compromising lifestyles. They want the anointing, but they don't want to forgive. It's a high price!

It's a high price to pay, but it's not unattainable. Our ultimate goal is to die to self so that we can say, "I no longer live, but Christ lives in me."

Dear God, I no longer want to live a mediocre life. Help me die to my earthly desires so that I can receive your anointing and the promises ahead. Amen.

November 18   Lucky or Blessed?

A righteous man may have many troubles, but the LORD delivers him from them all. (Psalm 34:19 NIV)

One day while teaching a group of students, I shared the events that led me to become a sign-language teacher. In those events, I included the afflictions that changed the course of my life from medicine to teaching. Some of those afflictions included a car accident that resulted in multiple life-threatening injuries. Then I was led to share testimonies about the many trials my family had endured. As I spoke, the room was silent. Then, one of the young ladies said, "Your family sure is cursed!"

With a smile on my face I explained that I have now been restored completely from all the injuries of the car accident. I explained the victory of each testimony. Then she said, "Oh, you all are lucky!" I said, "No, we are blessed!"

Afflictions are not a sign of God's love, but deliverance is! Deliverance may not always manifest in the physical. The greatest deliverance is in the spirit—when a person is able to continue living in peace and victory even if deliverance does not manifest physically.

Dear God, you are my protector. I believe you, Father, to deliver me out of my afflictions. Amen.

He who dwells in the shelter of the Most High will rest in the shadow of the Almighty. I will say of the LORD, "He is my refuge and my fortress, my God, in whom I trust." (Psalm 91:1-2 NIV)

Once I drove straight into a dangerous thunderstorm. The rain was dreadful as it hammered mercilessly on my windshield. I was driving the pace of a turtle. I literally could not see the road in front of me. I was frightened. I contemplated pulling over to the side, but it was impossible to see even a foot in front of me. Then I contemplated taking an exit to get a hotel because I didn't know how long the storm would last. Unable to see the exit, I cautiously continued.

I prayed for God to calm my fears and direct my path. Then, I prayed for protection. Shortly, the rain began to taper off. I realized I had driven through the storm. Then I saw the most magnificent view ever. As the mist fell, ahead was a soft pink sky. It was gentle and inviting.

As I sighed, I heard the Lord say, "When weathering the storms of life, stay focused, don't pull over, don't sit on the side of the road, and don't detour!"

When the storms come, we must call on God to direct us instead of giving up or taking a route that God did not pave for us. It is when visibility is gone and faith is our path that we please God.

Dear God, you are my strength and guide. I will trust in you in the storms. Amen.

For if the firstfruit be holy, the lump is also holy: and if the root be holy, so are the branches. (Romans 11:16 KJV)

The word *holy* in this verse refers to being consecrated and set apart for sacred use. The reference is to Abraham, Isaac, and Jacob. As they practiced holiness and devotion to God, they were received into God's covenant agreement. Their descendasnts (the branches) inherited the same covenant blessings.

A few years ago I began dedicating the first thirty-six days of the year to the Lord as my firstfruit. Thirty-six days is a tenth of a year. During this time

I fast from the things that my flesh enjoys most—the television, leisure phone time, and sweets, to name a few. I deny myself these things so that I will rise in the Spirit and hear God's voice more clearly. Then I intentionally pray concerning the upcoming year and what the Lord wills for my life. I believe that by consecrating myself and my time to the Lord, I will have a blessed and productive year. Likewise, others will be blessed through my sacrifice, my hearing God, and my walk of obedience.

What would it mean for you to consecrate yourself to God? In this season of thanksgiving, what firstfruit can you offer to God? How might others be set free by your example or help?

Heavenly Father, please teach me how to give you the firstfruit in every area of my life. Then, as I (the root) remain holy, so will others (the branches) be holy. Amen.

November 21   Can God Trust You?

But the angel said to her, "Do not be afraid, Mary, you have found favor with God."
(Luke 1:30 NIV)

Mary was an ordinary young woman, yet she was chosen by God to give birth to the Messiah. Though ordinary, she was given extraordinary work to do. Have you ever wondered why God chose Mary?

What was it about Mary that allowed the angel of the Lord to call her "highly favored" and "blessed ... among women" (Luke 1:28 NKJV)? Was it because of her astonishing appearance, her boldness, or her stature? Surely not! The Bible tells us nothing about her physical attributes. When God called Mary, she was willing to believe and obey at any cost. God chose Mary because he knew he could trust her, even through suffering.

It's easy to trust God when blessings are flowing and prosperity is at hand. Yet how many of us remain loyal during tribulation? Do we quit believing when suffering is unbearable? Do we curse God? Seek our own will?

Can God trust you to be faithful in the work he has given you—no matter what? Can you be trusted with the extraordinary work of the Lord?

Father, may my relationship with you be based on the fact that you can trust me for the destiny you have for my life. Amen.

November 22   Confidence, Not Curse

In the land of Uz there lived a man whose name was Job. This man was blameless and upright; he feared God and shunned evil. (Job 1:1-2 NIV)

Job, a man of wealth, loved God. Yet God granted Satan permission to destroy Job's possessions, family, and health. Job's loss was no fault of his own. He trusted God even when his friends blamed the disasters on hidden sin. By the end of Job's story, one thing is certain: Job's test was due to God's confidence in Job.

As the result of my car accident, I lost my apartment, my car, my savings, and my health. Although I had lived a holy, consecrated life, friends still attributed the accident to hidden sin. Through Job's story, I realized that my car accident was not God's judgment against me but God's confidence in me. We serve a merciful God, not a harsh, cruel God. Surely we reap what we sow; however, God showed me that he was entrusting me for extraordinary work.

I'm so thankful that God restored my health, cancelled my debt, and blessed me with material provisions. I married a holy man of God and am blessed with three beautiful children.

Maybe your challenging situation is not a curse but, instead, a sign of God's confidence in you.

Lord, I give you permission to put your confidence in me. I will remain faithful to you and your principles even when the going gets rough. Amen.

November 23   But Now My Eyes Have Seen You

"My ears had heard of you but now my eyes have seen you." (Job 42:5 NIV)

I cautiously drove the incline of the bridge. As I approached the top, I gazed into the rearview mirror. All was behind me. The very bridge where my car had torn into another car, leaving my lifeless body for death, was behind me now. The pain of the trauma to my body, the needles, the tubes, the life-support machine, and the rehabilitation were all behind me now. I had been restored to health. I had defeated the prognosis of death, and I was victorious. I had conquered my last fear, the fear of driving, and now it was all behind me.

I had heard about the things of God, but now I had seen him for myself. I would never be the same. I saw God as my comforter, my protector, my healer, my friend, my provider, my miracle worker.

Have you been questioning if God is real? Maybe God is near but you've missed him because of your complaining or worrying. Don't wait for others to tell you about God; use your storm as an opportunity to experience him. Then you will say just as Job said, "My ears had heard of you but now my eyes have seen you."

Dear God, open my eyes that I may see you. Amen.

November 24   Start Boasting!

Some boast in chariots, and some in horses; But we will boast in the name of the LORD, our God. (Psalm 20:7 NASB)

In Old Testament days, chariots and horses were a means of protection and escape. Today our "chariots and horses" have become whatever we run to as an escape. They are tangible and visible means of protection or escape. Yet, are these really a secured source of protection? Of course not! Proverbs 21:31 says, "The horse is prepared against the day of battle: but safety is of the Lord" (KJV).

In days of trouble or need, we are to run to our God and put our trust in him only. That is why the Lord says, "Call upon me in day of trouble: I will deliver thee, and thou shalt glorify me" (Psalm 50:15 KJV).

So, why don't we run to the arms of our all-sufficient God? Why do we collapse when troubled and tested? Why don't we take an aggressive stand in the face of fear? Because, for the most part, we don't boast in the name of our God. What does it mean to boast in the name of God? In the Hebrew language, the phrase "to boast" means to have confidence in God's name.

Will you boast in the name of the Lord? It's time to lay claim to God as your protector, deliverer, and Lord.

God, teach me your names so that I may run to you for help in time of need. I desire to know you as the only true God (John 17:3). Amen.

November 25   Why Are You Running?

But one thing I do: Forgetting what is behind and straining toward what is ahead, I press on toward the goal to win the prize for which God has called me heavenward in Christ Jesus. (Philippians 3:13b-14 NIV)

Have you known people who profess to be Christians, yet they have not become kinder, more forgiving, or more loving than the day you met them? Instead, they are more negative, prideful, faultfinding, and bitter as the years pass. Consider asking them this question: "Why are you running the Christian race?"

Some people are running under the false pretense that it will secure them a place in heaven. Others are running for recognition, prestige, or some other misplaced, sinful motive. If we're running the race for any reason other than becoming more like Christ, we should consider getting out of the race! The apostle Paul said that, as believers, we are to forget those things that are behind us—let go of yesterday's failures, past hurts, unforgiveness—and press, or run, toward the goal that is ahead. The goal is to become like Christ Jesus.

If we're going to run the race, then we must allow the teaching and preaching of the Word of God to change us. If we're going to run the race, then something should be different about us. We should be constantly changing into the image of Christ.

Why are *you* running?

Lord, as I run this Christian race, help me become more like Christ each day. Help me run this race as if my life depended on it, for it does. Amen.

November 26   Fix Your Eyes

Surely God is good to Israel, to those who are pure in heart. But as for me, my feet had almost slipped; I had nearly lost my foothold. For I envied the arrogant when I saw the prosperity of the wicked. (Psalm 73:1-3 NIV)

The psalmist Asaph begins this scripture certain of God's faithfulness to those who live holy lives. He had seen the miracles of God and witnessed God's faithfulness to bless his people. However, in the second verse, Asaph loses his focus and begins to doubt and fear God's ability to reward him for his pure heart. Asaph's spiritual vision is blurred because his eyes have become fixed on things.

Our spiritual vision is our ability to clearly see what God wants us to do. Spiritual vision also means to see the world from God's perspective. This kind of vision can easily get clouded. Self-serving desires, interests, and goals as well as family and job situations can block that vision.

Serving God, getting into his presence through prayer, and fellowshipping with other victorious sisters and brothers in Christ can quickly restore spiritual vision. Hebrews 12:2 tells us to "fix our eyes on Jesus, the author and perfecter of our faith" (NIV). Asaph's "eyes" were looking in the wrong direction. We must remember to "let [our] eyes look straight ahead, fix [our] gaze directly before [us]" (Proverbs 4:25 NIV).

Father, help me remain pure, both inwardly and outwardly, as I keep my eyes fixed on you. Amen.

November 27   Are You of One Mind?

Submit yourselves, then, to God. Resist the devil, and he will flee from you. Come near to God and he will come near to you. Wash your hands, you sinners, and purify your hearts, you double-minded. (James 4:7-8 NIV)

For years I had heard people say, "Resist the devil and he will flee." For years I tried to resist the temptations of the devil but was defeated. To resist means to oppose, to refuse to go along with, or to refuse to accept. Even though I was resisting, it seemed as if my efforts always resulted in sin. I would fall by speaking a harsh word or by being doubtful or negative. These sinful mishaps would stop my victory. It seemed the devil would never flee.

I did not become empowered until I received the fullness of today's scripture. The key to resisting is "submitting" first to God! I had to present myself to God and allow him to clothe me with his tenderness and love. Then I had to be of one mind, wanting what he wanted for me. I could not be double-minded by wanting to please God yet wanting to win an argument, fulfill the lust of my flesh, or doubt God's ability to be God. Only then was I empowered to resist the devil and watch him flee!

In the name of Jesus, I present myself—spirit, soul, and body—to my heavenly Father. I have the mind of Christ, and I am empowered for greatness. Amen.

November 28   Hold Fast!

So shall my word be that goeth forth out of my mouth: it shall not return unto me void, but it shall accomplish that which I please, and it shall prosper in the thing whereto I sent it. (Isaiah 55:11 KJV)

Have you ever mailed a card to brighten someone's day only to find out a few days later that the person never received the card? Instead, it was returned because there was not enough postage or the person was no longer at the address. I imagine you were quite disappointed because the intent of your card was not fulfilled.

I was in desperate need of a healing. I studied the scriptures and believed God's Word to heal me; however, after a few months, I wondered if the healing would ever manifest in my body. I was disappointed that God's Word did not do as it said.

As I cried out to the Lord, I was empowered by Isaiah 55:11, which says that it is impossible for God's word to be void. If God sends forth a word, it *will prosper* in our lives—not always in the way we expect, but in the way God intends. Hebrews 10:23 says we must "hold fast the profession of our faith [what we are believing] without wavering; for he is faithful that promised" (KJV). When we hold fast to our faith, God is able to fulfill his promises in ways that work for our good.

God has a word that will bring peace, healing, and deliverance for your specific situation. God has enough postage to deliver; will you receive it?

Dear God, I declare that I will hold fast to my confession of faith until your deliverance is complete. Amen.

November 29   Experience the Kingdom

"But if I drive out demons by the Spirit of God, then the kingdom of God has come upon you." (Matthew 12:28 NIV)

Why would the scripture say that driving out demons will cause the kingdom of God to come upon you? What is the Kingdom? Romans 14:17 says, "For the kingdom of God is not food and drink but righteousness and peace and joy in the Holy Spirit" (NRSV). Until we drive out the demonic forces in our lives—rebellion, hatred, discontentment, jealously, turmoil, and so forth—we will always live in discontentment. Christ came that we might live life in abundance. He gives us a peace unlike the temporal peace the world offers. Yet, we forfeit our peace when we allow demonic forces to reign in our minds and hearts.

Are you using your authority through Christ to drive out the strongholds that the enemy has placed in your home, job, church, and self? Now is the time to command every wicked spirit to leave you so that you may experience the

Kingdom—righteousness without sin, joy without mental agony or distressing fear, and peace without inward disturbance. Remember, "the kingdom of God is within you" (Luke 17:21 NIV).

Father, I thank you for giving me the power over every demonic force through your Son. I am empowered to walk in your righteousness, peace, and joy in the Holy Spirit. Amen.

November 30   Live a Life Worthy of Your Call

As a prisoner for the Lord, then, I urge you to live a life worthy of the calling you have received. Be completely humble and gentle; be patient, bearing with one another in love. (Ephesians 4:1-2 NIV)

The call to live a life worthy of our calling is to everyone who has accepted Christ as Savior. What has God called us to? As believers, we have already accepted the "call to salvation." Let's live a life worthy of it! God also calls us to practice holiness (1 Peter 1:15; 1 Thessalonians 4:7); to share in Christ's kingdom (1 Thessalonians 2:12); to be changed into Christ (Romans 8:29-30); to come out of darkness (1 Peter 2:9); and to belong to Christ, to be saints (Romans 1:6-7). Let's live a life that is worthy!

Maybe God has called you from your comfort zone, from your kindred, from tradition, or from an unhealthy relationship. Maybe God is calling you to begin to operate in your gift. Whatever the call, live worthy of it!

Those of us who are married, let's live a life worthy of the call to be godly wives. As Paul urges, let us be completely humble, gentle, and patient, bearing with one another in love. Those who are single, live a life worthy of the call to purity. Psalm 119:9 says, "How can a young [woman] keep [her] way pure? By living according to [God's] word."

According to Ephesians 4:11-13, God has given us preachers and teachers to equip (empower) us to be mature Christians. Be empowered to live a simplistic, victorious life in Christ Jesus!

Father, I realize the call of/to _____ that is on my life. I repent of my sins and declare that, with your help, I will live a life worthy of it. Amen.

244

DECEMBER

Women of Confidence

Ellen Mohney

December 1   **God's Call**

Now faith is being sure of what we hope for and certain of what we do not see.
(Hebrews 11:1 NIV)

Think about the basic statements of faith you have believed—statements such as God is good; God loves me unconditionally; God is in control; because of Jesus, I am made worthy; and so forth. My bet is that if we really believed these things, we would live our lives in a radically different way.

As it is, many of us are full of insecurity, worry, and fear of the future, which are evidences that we do not truly believe what God's Word says. God's Word is absolute Truth, and it is unshakable. Our souls, not to mention our emotional, mental, and physical well-beings, will greatly benefit if we will derive our confidence from God's Truth instead of from the fickle things of this world such as our relationships, jobs, achievements, and looks.

God's call to each of us is to live a life of faith, and I believe that today God is calling us to radical, unshakable faith as never before. If, by his grace, we rid ourselves of the unbelief that so burdens our lives, we will walk boldly as women of confidence.

Dear Jesus, transform my faith from mere lip service to true belief.
Amen.

December 2   Confidence, Not Insecurity

We have come to share in Christ if we hold firmly till the end the confidence we had at first. (Hebrews 3:14 NIV)

As Christian women, we can be the most confident and peace-filled women in the world. We have a God who loves us unconditionally and says we are his beloved. Because of Jesus, we are new creations; the bride of Christ; the righteousness of God; a royal priesthood; co-heirs with Christ; freed captives; sanctified, holy, and blameless daughters of God—and the list goes on. With such an identity, why are so many Christian women insecure instead of confident?

This month we are going to look at faith and belief and how the two, through the grace of Christ, free us to live a life of confidence that naturally comes when we really believe what we say we believe. Before we begin our journey, consider your faith. When you read scripture, especially about God's character and your own identity, is it easy for you to believe what it says, or do you find yourself in doubt? Do you say you believe God's Word yet still derive your confidence (and insecurities) from things of this world instead of from Christ?

Lord Jesus, as I embark on this journey, I pray you will increase my faith as I rest in your grace. Amen.

December 3   Believe in Greek

Abram believed the LORD, and he credited it to him as righteousness. (Genesis 15:6 NIV)

For many of us, the words "I believe" have lost the weight they should rightly carry. In our pluralistic society, it seems everyone professes belief in something, whether it be yoga, the five-step plan to losing weight, seven great ways to rid yourself of stress, or the gods of pop culture. But what does it really mean to believe?

In the original Greek, the verb "to believe" means to be persuaded of, to place confidence in, to trust, to have reliance upon. To believe is more than simply thinking that something "works" or is good. It implies that our whole being relies on it. Picture us leaning against a wall. If the wall crumbles, then we fall.

So it is with God. To believe him is to bank our entire lives on him to the point that if his Truth falters, we fall on our faces. The good news is that we know the end of the story: God's Truth does not falter. He is the only One worthy of our trust. Since we know that we can rely on him for everything, the question then becomes, *Why don't we?*

Lord, it is so easy for words to make sense in my head, but I pray that by your grace the meaning of belief will make sense in my heart. Amen.

December 4   Faith Is Not a Feeling

But when he asks, he must believe and not doubt, because he who doubts is like a wave of the sea, blown and tossed by the wind. That man should not think he will receive anything from the Lord; he is a double-minded man, unstable in all he does. (James 1:6-8 NIV)

Before we can live a life of faith, we must understand that faith is not a feeling. We all know this in our heads, but do we know it in our hearts?

Picture an overdramatic preteen girl who cries every night because she thinks her boyfriend is going to break up with her, despite his calling her, holding her hand, and doing everything else he can to show her that he likes her. Sadly, we often act the same way with the Lord! Even though he gave us the ultimate sacrifice of his Son to show us how much he loves us, we still wallow in self-pity and despair when we don't *feel* his closeness or love. That is even more ridiculous than the preteen!

Faith is not a feeling. If it were, it would not be faith but merely an emotion. As we journey on, we must understand that mature faith does not waver, even when God seems distant.

Lord Jesus, forgive me for the times I have doubted your presence and love, and help me believe you regardless of what my emotions tell me. Amen.

December 5   Lessons Learned at the Mall

Anyone who listens to the word and does not do what it says is like a man who looks at his face in the mirror and, after looking at himself, goes away and immediately forgets what he looks like. But the man who looks intently into the perfect law that gives freedom, and continues to do this, not forgetting what he has heard, but doing it—he will be blessed in what he does. (James 1:23-25 NIV)

247

Have you ever walked into the mall feeling fairly confident of who you are, how your life is going, and how you look, only to walk out feeling depressed, defeated, and "not good enough"? Perhaps you even started the day by reading Proverbs 31:30, which says, "Charm is deceptive, and beauty is fleeting; but a woman who fears the LORD is to be praised," and you really believed it! But when you walked into the mall and were faced with the unnaturally skinny models, the high fashions, and the subliminal message that you can't be happy if you don't look like this, it was as if you had never read God's Word.

We may "believe" Christ for a few fleeting moments, but when we are faced with situations that tell us otherwise and our faith is challenged, we often falter and lose the confidence we once had. The good news is that we do not have to continue living such precarious lives, if only we will believe.

Lord, be my confidence, the One in whom I can believe all day long. Amen.

December 6   Don't Be Caught Off Guard

Fight the good fight of the faith. (1 Timothy 6:12a NIV)

Paul was onto something when he encouraged young Timothy to "fight the good fight of the faith." Indeed, these words could not have come from a more reliable source, because Paul literally had to fight for his faith. He was beaten, shipwrecked, stoned, and left for dead more times than we can imagine.

If we want to become women of faith, we cannot expect the road to be easy. Persecution will come, doubts will come, and friends and family may not understand us at times. So, why can't we just passively resist these threats to our faith and quietly go about our business? Because faith is worth fighting for and *must* be fought for. The enemy is forever looking for opportunities to deceive us, and it's when we aren't consciously "fighting for our faith" (such as seeking God's opinion first, remaining in the Word even when we don't feel like it, and standing up for what we believe no matter what the cost) that our defenses are down and we are more susceptible to the evil one. May we never be caught off guard.

Jesus, give me the courage to fight for my faith every moment of every day while I trust in your grace, which covers my life. Amen.

December 7   Carrying Us to Completion

Being confident of this, that he who began a good work in you will carry it on to completion until the day of Christ Jesus. (Philippians 1:6 NIV)

Have there ever been circumstances in your life that have made you wonder why something turned out the way it did? It's in times like those that I find myself asking, "Lord, how in the world are you using this for good?"

The scripture the Lord always brings me back to is Philippians 1:6, which is the promise that at all times, in every situation, God is carrying me to completion. Do you trust that, even now, he who began a good work in you will not stop until Jesus comes back?

Wherever you are in your walk with the Lord, you can trust that even as you read this he is molding you into the woman of God he intended you to be from the beginning. May our confidence rest on his promise!

Merciful God, thanks for never giving up on me and, in all things at all times, molding me to be more like your Son. Amen.

December 8   Prayers of the Righteous

The prayer of the righteous is powerful and effective. (James 5:16b NRSV)

It's easy to read this verse and think that it is reserved for the truly "righteous," such as pastors or missionaries or the "spiritual giants" we know, but not for ourselves. I, like you, know myself; and if there is one thing I'm sure of, it's that I am *not* righteous.

Though it's true that we possess nothing righteous in and of ourselves, we are made righteous through the renewing blood of Jesus. That's what Paul meant in 2 Corinthians 5:21 when he said, "God made him who had no sin to be sin for us, so that in him we might become the righteousness of God" (NIV).

Do you believe that your prayers to the Father are powerful? Do you believe they are effective in bringing about his will? If God's Word is Truth, then our prayers really do make a difference. Indeed, they are imperative. Let us come before the Father with strong conviction and expectancy, praying in the confidence that he not only hears us but also, by the means of our prayers, accomplishes his ends.

Lord, you are calling me to pray with more authority and conviction than I feel comfortable with. Help me overcome my unbelief and know that as I pray, I do so covered by your grace. Amen.

December 9   Our Worthiness

For all have sinned and fall short of the glory of God, and are justified freely by his grace through the redemption that came by Christ Jesus. (Romans 3:23-24 NIV)

There comes a time when we ask ourselves, "Does my life really matter? What have I done to prove my worth?" I have asked myself these questions before and have come up with lists of things that, in my opinion, make me "worthy"—of affirmation, friendship, a good education, and so forth. As I have grown in my relationship with the Lord, though, my sin and unworthiness have become all the more apparent. I have learned that no matter what I do or how virtuous I am, I can do nothing to merit worth with God.

We are not worthy of God's love, nor are we worthy of heaven. But this does not mean that we are without hope! Though we are unworthy of God's affections, we are justified and made worthy through our belief in Christ.

As women of faith, our confidence must rest in the truth that we are worthy, not because of anything we have done but because of the grace of Christ.

Christ Jesus, thank you for your grace. Thank you for making me worthy so that I may stand before the throne of God with confidence. Amen.

December 10   Worrying About the Future

"For I know the plans I have for you," declares the LORD, "plans to prosper you and not to harm you, plans to give you hope and a future." (Jeremiah 29:11 NIV)

"So, what do you want to do with your life?" Since I am graduating college next year, I get asked this question a lot. When I face the fact that I don't know exactly where I'm going to be or what I'm going to be doing, it's easy for me to be consumed with worry. When I reflect on my life, though, I realize that many times I had no idea where I was going to be until the last minute, and it ended up being perfect. Why do I worry about my future when the Lord already knows exactly where I'll be and exactly how I'll get there? It's because I don't *really* trust him.

We women tend to worry a lot—about where we'll be, whom we'll be with, what we'll be doing, and whether we'll feel secure. If we would just believe Christ and trust his Word, our lives would be so much more peaceful. Trusting Christ doesn't mean that we don't plan or organize, but it does mean that we *believe* him when he says, "Seek first his kingdom and his righteousness, and all these things will be given to you as well" (Matthew 6:33 NIV).

Father, thank you for your sovereignty. I pray that, by your grace, I will trust you when the future seems foggy. Amen.

December 11   No Miracles

And he did not do many miracles there because of their lack of faith. (Matthew 13:58 NIV)

When Jesus went to his hometown, people had a hard time believing he was really the Son of God because they had known him growing up as a mere carpenter's son. Though Jesus performed some miracles while he was there, he did not perform many because of their lack of faith.

I believe God is showing us in this verse that, although his workings do not depend solely on our faith, where faith abounds, so do his miracles. Had the people in Nazareth believed Jesus was more than a carpenter's son, it is implied that he would have performed more miracles and the power of God would have been proclaimed throughout the land. Instead, however, the people of Nazareth missed the blessings of God.

May we never be found without faith and, therefore, miss the miracles God wants to work in our lives.

Dear Jesus, I pray that as your eyes search the land, I will be found to be a woman of faith who believes that you work miracles even today. Amen.

December 12   The Grass Is Always Greener

Be joyful always; pray continually; give thanks in all circumstances, for this is God's will for you in Christ Jesus. (1 Thessalonians 5:16-18 NIV)

Does anyone else have the "grass is always greener on the other side" mind-set? I know I do. It seems that no matter what is going on in my life, I can always imagine something else that would be even better.

God has taught me again and again that this is unbelief! Those of us who have this mind-set are basically saying to the Lord, "I don't really believe you are sovereign or good; and since I know what's best for me, I'm going to orchestrate my life to fit my needs."

That may sound a bit blatant, but when we have this kind of mind-set, that is essentially what we are saying to God. In doing so, we miss out on the wonderful blessings he has for us in our own situations, if only we would trust him with our whole lives.

Lord, you are good. Thank you for where you have me right now, and help me truly believe that only you know what's best for me. Amen.

December 13   Jesus Is Enough

And such confidence we have through Christ toward God. Not that we are adequate in ourselves to consider anything as coming from ourselves, but our adequacy is from God. (2 Corinthians 3:4-5 NASB)

Take a moment to consider all your accomplishments, your joys, your loves—all the things that have given you some sense of security. Now imagine that none of those things ever happened. Imagine that you were never recognized for doing good, that you never achieved a particular goal or accomplishment, that you never experienced the joy of loving relationships. If all you had to validate yourself was Jesus, would he be enough? Would you feel as secure now about who you are if the only title you could claim was "Child of God"?

I am not saying that all the extra securities in life are bad; indeed, they are wonderful blessings from God. But when it comes down to it, none of these things validates us or brings us true security. The question is, amidst our blessings and worldly securities, do we believe Jesus is all we really need? If all other things were to fall away, would we feel as secure as we do right now?

Lord, forgive my unbelief. Help me today to walk in grace, believing with every ounce of my being that you are more than enough for me. Amen.

December 14   Superspiritual People

If the whole body were an eye, where would the sense of hearing be? If the whole body were an ear, where would the sense of smell be? But in fact God has arranged the parts in the body, every one of them, just as he wanted them to be. If they were all one part, where would the body be? (1 Corinthians 12:17-19 NIV)

Have you ever been around someone who seems to be so much more "spiritual" than you could ever dream of becoming? Maybe she speaks unceasingly about the Lord or is forever living her life for others. Or perhaps she is able to interpret and understand scripture in a way that seems impossible to you.

When we're around these superspiritual people, it's easy to feel inadequate and "beat ourselves up" because we're not like them. Then we begin to judge our spiritual condition based on how closely our lives line up with theirs. Friends, the good news is we are not supposed to be like them! The only person whose life we are to imitate is that of Jesus Christ.

God created each of us with different personalities and gifts. Some people were made with more outgoing personalities or outwardly evident gifts, while others were made with more introverted personalities or less public gifts. Whoever you are, you are an indispensable part of the Body of Christ. Throw off your preconceived notion that some people are more valuable to Christ than others, for such belief only serves to discourage you, and believe that God created you perfectly to bring him glory and to serve the Body of Christ with the gifts you have been given.

Holy Lord, thank you for the gifts you have given me, and grant me wisdom to know the best ways to use them to further your kingdom. Amen.

December 15   Resisting God's Grace

Let us then approach the throne of grace with confidence, so that we may receive mercy and find grace to help us in our time of need. (Hebrews 4:16 NIV)

How many times I've returned to the Father ashamed of my unfaithfulness, embarrassed of how I have let my heart wander yet again. Other times I've come to him having committed the same old sins, even though I know better. It's in times like these that I wish God would just be angry with me—that would at least make me feel better, like I got what I deserved.

What I've learned is that when we resist God's grace, Satan uses that as a stronghold to make us believe we really don't deserve to be restored to a right relationship with the Lord. But God is faithful in spite of our unfaithfulness. It is for this very reason that we may walk in the confidence that "nothing can separate us from the love of Christ" (Romans 8:39). Do we really claim God's grace over our sin, or do we live in bondage, thinking we must deserve God's grace before he will offer it? If grace were deserved, it would not be grace!

Heavenly Father, help me live in the freedom of Christ, trusting in your grace to cover my life. Amen.

December 16   Wisdom for All

If any of you lacks wisdom, he should ask God, who gives generously to all without finding fault, and it will be given to him. But when he asks, he must believe and not doubt. (James 1:5-6a NIV)

There's something about the presence of a white-headed, elderly woman who is still in love with the Lord that commands quiet respect. So much experience, so much wisdom lies behind her gentle eyes, if only there was a way to somehow tap in to it. Wisdom can only come with age, though, for wisdom requires experience. Or does it?

I think what James is trying to get us to understand in this passage is that, though wisdom does come with age, it also comes with prayer, for our God is the source of all wisdom. God's promise is that he will give wisdom generously to *all,* not just to the more experienced or more righteous. What is the condition for such freely given wisdom? It is a heart that believes and does not doubt. Let us begin to pray for wisdom, believing in faith that the Lord keeps his promises. When we do, we will receive what we ask according to his good will.

God of infinite wisdom and grace, grant me wisdom to handle the everyday situations of life in a manner that is pleasing to you. Amen.

December 17   Evangelism

However, I consider my life worth nothing to me, if only I may finish the race and complete the task the Lord Jesus has given me—the task of testifying to the gospel of God's grace. (Acts 20:24 NIV)

Evangelism. It's one of those Christian duties that give most of us a knot in our stomach because sharing our faith with an unbeliever requires that we step way out of our comfort zone. Insecurities fill our minds with questions, such as wondering, *How will they react? What if they reject me? What if they think I'm a freak?* But if our evangelism is weak, what does that say about how convinced we are of the transforming power of the gospel? Do we believe that the gospel is worth sharing, that it truly is a matter of life or death?

The gospel is *life,* and every time we choose not to share it, we are telling Christ that his life really isn't worth risking our reputations. Though we can't hear it audibly, the souls of the lost are crying out to be found, if only someone would show them the way. When we believe in the transforming power of the gospel, we may participate with Christ in spreading his saving message to the ends of the earth.

Lord, put a sense of urgency in my heart to share your gospel, having patience as I trust in your sovereignty. Amen.

December 18   No Confidence in the Flesh

For it is we who are the circumcision, we who worship by the Spirit of God, who glory in Christ Jesus, and who put no confidence in the flesh—though I myself have reasons for such confidence. (Philippians 3:3-4 NIV)

What does it mean to put "no confidence in the flesh"? John Calvin defined *flesh* as anything that comes between yourself and Christ. It's easy for us to understand how dangerous it is to put any sort of confidence in the flesh, such as our careers, our social status, or our looks. What is important to realize, though, is that *flesh* can even refer to our own righteousness. I think that is exactly what Paul was alluding to in this chapter of Philippians, because it was his own piousness that put a wall between himself and Christ.

God has called us to trust *him* with all of our hearts, not to trust in our knowledge of him. He has called us to base all our confidence in *him,* not in the fact that we read our Bibles every day. He has called us to love *him* with all our hearts, not to love the fact that we have an intimate relationship with him. Everything apart from Christ, even our own righteousness, is a hindrance. Do you really believe that Christ can be the one and only basis of your confidence?

Heavenly Father, forgive me for trusting in my own faith. Cover me with your grace and help me throw off everything that hinders me from you. Amen.

December 19   Repentance Leads to Freedom

For we know that our old self was crucified with him so that the body of sin might be done away with, that we should no longer be slaves to sin—because anyone who has died has been freed from sin.... For sin shall not be your master, because you are not under law, but under grace. (Romans 6:6-7, 14 NIV)

Of all God's promises, I think the ones about forgiveness and grace are hardest to accept. If you're like me, when you sin you ask the Lord for forgiveness and say that you repent of it, but in your mind you still condemn yourself for committing the sin. Instead of walking in God's grace, you tell yourself that you don't deserve to live in such freedom and try somehow to punish yourself. At least that makes you feel like you got what you deserved. Does this sound familiar?

And we wonder why we feel like we live in bondage! Ladies, repentance is not a suggestion, it is a command; and like all of God's commands, it leads to freedom. If you find yourself stuck in self-condemnation or living in bondage to sin, then you don't really *believe* the power of the cross.

Have you been robbed of freedom in Christ because of this kind of unbelief? Do not let sin be your master any longer; walk in grace! Know that sin is not acceptable, but through Christ's blood, we may repent, receive forgiveness, and walk in the confidence that, no matter what, we are beloved by the King!

Lord, it truly is your kindness that leads us to repentance. Forgive our unbelieving hearts and help us walk in the freedom you intend for us. Amen.

December 20   The Reality of God

So we fix our eyes not on what is seen, but on what is unseen. For what is seen is temporary, but what is unseen is eternal. (2 Corinthians 4:18 NIV)

Sometimes at the end of the day, I find myself feeling unfulfilled and discontented. Usually when I reflect on what happened that day, I realize that most of my conversations centered on the petty things of this world, or that my work was done with a "this-worldly" mind-set. I get so disgusted when I live like this because I know I have been living in unbelief and have missed out on communing with the Lord. Do you ever find this to be true in your life?

Right now, what seems more real to you: the pages of this book or the Holy Spirit's presence in your life? If the pages seem more real than the Spirit's presence, then I encourage you to consider your *belief* in the reality of God. The good news is that the spiritual, unseen realm of God is more real than anything we can see! The things of this world are temporary and will pass away as if they never were, but God is eternal. He is the only true reality. Do you *really believe*?

Lord, I praise you that not only are you real, but also you are my loving Father. May your presence become more of a reality to me than the skin on my body. Amen.

December 21   Citizenship in Heaven

But our citizenship is in heaven. And we eagerly await a Savior from there, the Lord Jesus Christ. (Philippians 3:20 NIV)

Even though I live my day-to-day life in Birmingham, where I go to school, my home is in Chattanooga, where I grew up; and after being away at school for a while, going home is a huge relief.

Sometimes I wonder if heaven will feel like that. If we truly believe that this world is not our home—if we long for heaven, knowing we are strangers in this land—then death will be a relief. But for most of us, we live as if this earth were our true home. We make sure we are as comfortable here as possible. We've fallen so "in love with life that we have lost our thirst for the waters of Life," as John Eldredge puts it in *Journey of Desire*. Eldredge says that we get more excited about a European vacation than we do about going to heaven (Nashville: Thomas Nelson, 2000).

If this is true of you, then this is an area of unbelief in your life. This world is not our home. We have to stop living as if it were and, instead, turn our hearts toward heaven as we "eagerly await a Savior from there."

Lord God, it's so easy to forget this is not my true home. Lift my eyes from this place and put a longing in my heart for the day I will truly go home. Amen.

December 22   Touching His Cloak

Just then a woman who had been subject to bleeding for twelve years came up behind him and touched the edge of his cloak. She said to herself, "If I only touch his cloak, I will be healed." Jesus turned and saw her. "Take heart, daughter," he said, "your faith has healed you." And the woman was healed from that moment. (Matthew 9:20-22 NIV)

The story of the woman with the hemorrhage is beautiful. She believed Jesus was so powerful that even a touch of his cloak would heal her. That, in itself, is a challenge for us.

How many times, when we are in great need, do we feel that we must invest hours in prayer to God—and ask others to do the same—in order to receive aid? Do we really think Jesus' healing touch is "far away"? Do we think we must somehow prove to God that we are prayer warriors in order to merit his healing touch?

What we learn from the woman with the hemorrhage is this: All we need to do is extend our hand to Jesus, acknowledging our need and believing that this small gesture of faith is enough. He will see us and will intervene in our lives.

God of heaven, thank you for being closer to me than my breath. Increase my faith as I trust in your grace and love, which cover my life. Amen.

December 23   I Believe, Help My Unbelief

"But if you can do anything, take pity on us and help us." "If you can?" said Jesus. "Everything is possible for him who believes." Immediately the boy's father exclaimed, "I do believe; help me overcome my unbelief!" (Mark 9:22b-24 NIV)

This man's life of faith is a lot like my own. I remember the first time I read this story, I thought the father must have been so immature in his faith to actually look Jesus in the eye and say, "*If* you can do anything." Can you imagine standing before Almighty God and questioning his power? I couldn't at first, until I realized that I identify with this man more than I want to admit. Now when I read this story, I just grin because that man is me! The moment I say "I believe" is the moment doubt starts to creep in and I have to ask for God's grace to help me in my unbelief.

Oh, how I long to believe and not doubt! What we can learn from this father is that the best way to sustain our faith is to be honest with God about our unbelief. Instead of trying to put up a front that we never doubt, let's be honest with him when we do. Only in doing so is our faith authenticated.

Lord, I want to believe; help my unbelief! Amen.

December 24   Mary's Grace of Acceptance

"Blessed is she who has believed that what the Lord has said to her will be accomplished!" (Luke 1:45 NIV)

Can you imagine what it must have been like for Mary when the angel told her that she was going to give birth to the Son of God? What stands out to me is the quiet grace with which she accepted God's word. Mary asked only one question, and after the angel Gabriel answered her, Mary said, "May it be to me as you have said."

Oh, what blessed lives we would live if we would simply take God at his word as Mary did. To read his Scripture, receive it as Truth, and then continue to walk in grace and confidence, placing all our trust in him—what a rich life we would live! And it seems that it should be so easy. Yet, if you're like me, taking God at his word is like a foreign concept because you think first you must answer all your questions, analyze all different points of view, and get at least three other people's opinions on the subject before you will decide what you believe. While thorough study of God's Word is important, it's my prayer that we may become like Mary, simply taking God at his word and being blessed in the process.

Lord, make my faith simple yet grounded in your Word. Amen.

December 25   Unto Us a *Child* Is Born

But made himself nothing, taking the very nature of a servant, being made in human likeness. And being found in appearance as a man, he humbled himself. (Philippians 2:7-8a NIV)

Christianity is full of seeming paradoxes—ideas such as the first will be last; when we are weak, then God is strong; those who mourn will be comforted; the greatest must become the servant of all; and the meek will inherit the earth. All are concepts that are hard to believe at first. Perhaps the greatest paradox of all, however, is that which we celebrate today: The all-powerful and omniscient God of the universe "made himself nothing" and became a tiny baby, the most vulnerable life stage of all. Yet, in Jesus, all the fullness of God dwelt. What a beautiful paradox!

May we stand in awe today as we celebrate by faith the birth of Christ Jesus, who came to pay a debt he did not owe so that we could have eternal life.

Sweet Jesus, you are awesome in power and majestic in holiness. Thank you for humbling yourself so that I might live. Amen.

December 26 — Believe God

"We went into the land to which you sent us, and it does flow with milk and honey! Here is its fruit. But the people who live there are powerful, and the cities are fortified and very large.... We can't attack those people; they are stronger than we are." Then Caleb silenced the people before Moses and said, "We should go up and take possession of the land, for we can certainly do it." (Numbers 13:27-28, 31, 30 NIV)

When the Israelites lost all hope in God providing the promised land, Caleb took a stand and chose to believe God's promise rather than the voices of unbelief in the crowd. His unwavering faith exemplifies a quote by Anselm: "For I do not seek to understand that I may believe, but I believe in order to understand." Caleb believed God. Period. He may not have known how God was going to give them the promised land, but he didn't have to. His faith was based on God's promise rather than on common sense or certainty. More than being a man of great faith, Caleb knew he was a man of a great God.

We serve the same great God. Though we may not consider ourselves to be women of great faith, we can all testify that we have a great and faithful God. May our faith be like Caleb's—one that is not based on our own capacity for faith, but on God's promise to be faithful, for when "we are faithless, he will remain faithful" (2 Timothy 2:13 NIV).

Father, your faithfulness stretches to the skies. Help me base my faith on that promise instead of on my own ability to trust you. Amen.

December 27   In God's Perfect Time

For in this hope we are saved. But hope that is seen is no hope at all. Who hopes for what he already has? But if we hope for what we do not yet have, we wait for it patiently. (Romans 8:24-25 NIV)

One of the greatest testimonies of faith I have witnessed is that of a woman named Harriet. Harriet has lived in a Jamaican infirmary ever since a bus hit her more than fifteen years ago. Having little medical attention, her broken legs healed intertwined, causing her to be bedridden. When I visited Harriet, she told me how she had kept her faith in Jesus through it all by praying every day for her legs to straighten once again. Then she said, "And look what the Lord has done!" Full of determination and intensity, Harriet slowly straightened her legs! Though she could only keep them straight for a few seconds, I will remember those seconds forever.

When I think of Harriet's long-suffering faith, I'm embarrassed by the way I expect to see immediate results from the Lord, losing heart if he doesn't answer right away. Though our culture feeds our desire for instant gratification, we must remember that the Lord works in his own perfect time. Let us, like Harriet, hold firm to the promise of God to be faithful even when it seems he does not hear us.

Lord, thank you for Harriet and her faith. Help me believe in your faithfulness even when I don't see results. Amen.

December 28   Faith for Our Friends

Some men brought to him a paralytic, lying on a mat. When Jesus saw their faith, he said to the paralytic, "Take heart, son; your sins are forgiven." ...Then he said to the paralytic, "Get up, take your mat and go home." And the man got up and went home. (Matthew 9:2, 6b-7 NIV)

Isn't it interesting that in this passage Jesus does not heal the paralytic because of his faith alone, but also because of his friends' faith? This story has always challenged me in regard to my unbelieving friends, or even those who have simply strayed from the faith and confidence they once had in Christ. Though I try to encourage them in the faith and pray for them, most of the time I feel inadequate to make any sort of positive difference in their lives.

In these situations, what we forget is that we can have faith for them.

What I mean is that we can believe God *will* intervene in their lives, even when they don't think he will. Just because they lack faith does not mean we should as well.

Think of those you want to come to faith yet struggle to understand the reason for the hope that you have. Our challenge is to have the kind of faith the paralytic's friends had; we are to bring our friends to Jesus' feet in prayer, expecting, through faith, Christ to intervene.

Heavenly Father, thank you for imparting to us the blessing of faith. Broaden my understanding of what living a life of faith really means. Amen.

December 29   The Bridegroom Will Come

Let us rejoice and be glad and give him glory! For the wedding of the Lamb has come, and his bride has made herself ready. (Revelation 19:7 NIV)

Oh, what a glorious day it will be when Jesus comes back and we finally get to feast at the banquet table after our union with him! But what are we to do in the time between now and then? What does God expect of us, his bride? John tells us in Revelation that we are to make ourselves ready. Though this entails a lot of different things, one thing it does not entail is sitting idly by. Every day is a new opportunity to prepare ourselves for our true wedding day and our one Bridegroom.

Just as we believe that Christ is coming back, so also may we believe that we are called to be diligent in making ourselves ready for our Groom. In other words, let us each be a bride who deepens her relationships with her Groom every day, who lives by faith and not by sight, and who trusts in his unfailing love. Our wedding day is coming soon!

Come, Lord Jesus. We eagerly await your appearance and pray that you will help us prepare ourselves every day for our glorious union with you. Amen.

December 30   Jump!

They feast on the abundance of your house; you give them drink from your river of delights. For with you is the fountain of life; in your light we see light. (Psalm 36:8-9 NIV)

This month we have looked at faith in action and what it means to truly believe what we say we believe. For some of you, this is nothing new; for others, living this kind of life seems foreign, unattainable, and maybe a bit scary. Wherever you are in your journey, though, remember that faith isn't faith until you "jump in." Right now you have a decision to make. Will you go to the shallow end and slowly ease yourself into the water, missing out on the spiritual adventure God has in store for you, or will you take the plunge and jump in? I guarantee that God is in the water waiting to catch you!

Lord, I want to jump in! Please give me faith to trust that you will catch me. Amen.

December 31 God Offers Freedom
and Confidence

"Yet not what I will, but what you will." (Mark 14:36b NIV)

As we come to the end of our journey, I hope you have been encouraged to have faith that is more than lip service—faith that is genuine and that truly believes God's promises. I do have a word of caution, however.

It's easy to fall into the trap of thinking that when we become women of authentic faith, God is somehow obliged to answer our prayers in our way and in our time. We have to remember that our faith, no matter how strong, will never merit favor with the Lord or somehow automatically cause everything in our lives to work out the way we think it should. God's ways are not our own, and while he calls us to live faithful lives, we cannot believe that such a life will put God at our beck and call.

With that said, let us continue our journey into the new year as women of faith in a great God who keeps his promises and offers a life of freedom and confidence to all who would believe him.

Lord Jesus, you have nurtured us and ministered to our hearts, and for that we give you thanks. Help us walk in grace as we seek to live holy and perfect lives before you. Amen.